Autodata

Car Repair Manual

MINOR

Compiled and Written by
SIMON COWEN

Morris Minor

1956-1971

| Morris Minor | Minor 1000 (1098 cc) | Minor Van |
| Minor 1000 (948 cc) | Minor Traveller | Minor Pick-Up |

The Editor would like to acknowledge the help from the following companies in the preparation of this repair manual:

British Leyland UK Ltd
Champion Sparking Plug Co. Ltd
Radiomobile Ltd
Sound Service (Oxford) Ltd
Lucas Electrical Ltd
K L Automotive Products Ltd

Autodata Car Repair Manual for the Minor 1000

Compiled and Edited by Simon Cowen
Layout and paste-up: Mandy Way
Composing: Sajan Neal and Simer Bharji

Published by Autodata Limited
St. Peter's Road, Maidenhead, Berkshire, SL6 7QU. England

ACRM 271

ISBN 0-85666-046-9

Printed in England by Page Bros (Norwich) Ltd

Introduction

You are reading one of the best accessories that you could purchase for your car. Whether you are a keen do-it-yourself enthusiast or just eager to cut the cost of motoring, this repair manual will guide you through all the stages of various mechanical repairs - from a simple oil and filter change; fitting new brake shoes; checking the hydraulics; tuning the engine; dealing with the electrics; or even removing and overhauling the engine - all the knowledge and information you are likely to need are here!

The easy-reference contents page and individual chapter headings will guide you to the appropriate section dealing with the part of your car to be checked or repaired. The clear line-drawings will show you what fits where giving you all the confidence to tackle a job for the first time. Each chapter contains easy-to-follow repair sequences with a comprehensive Technical Data section included at the end. If problems occur that can't be solved easily then turn to the special Trouble-shooting chart to be found at the end of the appropriate section.

A large proportion of this manual is devoted to routine and preventative maintenance with a complete chapter covering the servicing of your car - indeed, a money saver in itself!

Tools are of obvious importance to the do-it-yourself car owner and, like this repair manual, can be termed as a good investment. Purchase wisely, not over-spending but just purchasing good quality tools needed for a certain job and building up your equipment as you go. Tools required for general servicing aren't that many but it will be the wise do-it-yourself motorist who invests in a good jack and axle stands or wheel ramps. Some of the operations shown in this book require special tools and, in many cases, they can be hired locally. If specialist knowledge is required then we state as much. If it is possible to manage without special aids then we tell you how. Sometimes a little ingenuity can save a lot of time and money.

Now you can be the expert and the cost of this repair manual will be easily recovered the first time that you use it.

Jack Hay

Editor

Brief History

AUGUST 1948

The Morris Minor made its debut in the form of the MM series. This model was powered with a 918 cc side valve engine. Apart from small alteration, the Minor looked very similar until it was phased out of production 23 years later. At that time, the car was produced by Morris Motors Ltd.

DECEMBER 1952

Soon after Morris Motors Ltd was taken over by BMC - the British Motor Corporation — an updated version of the Minor, the Series II, was introduced. The only major difference between the MM and the Series II was the engine, the new version being powered with an 803 cc overhead valve unit.

SEPTEMBER 1956

The first of the Minor 1000 cars were produced. Again, the only major change from the previous model - the Series II - was a different engine. This time it was a 948 cc overhead valve unit which powered the car.

AUGUST 1962

Various design changes and safety features were introduced in the basically unchanged Minor 1000. Among them was the change from a split-type windscreen to a one piece toughened screen. At the same time, yet another engine change, the last, was made. This time, the 948 cc unit was discarded in favour of the 1098 cc overhead valve engine.

JUNE 1968

The British Motor Corporation was taken over by British Motor Holding, merged with Leyland Motor Corporation and became British Leyland Motor Corporation Ltd. Production of the Minor 1000 continued with the new company.

AUGUST 1971

Production of the Minor 1000 ceased. Over a million had been made and the car had been Britain's longest production running car.

Quick Reference Data

GENERAL DIMENSIONS

Overall length
    Saloon . . . . 148 in (3759 mm)
    Traveller . . . . 149 in (3785 mm)
Overall width . . . . 61 in (1549 mm)
Overall height
    Saloon . . . . 60 in (1524 mm)
    Traveller . . . . 60.5 in (1537 mm)
Wheelbase . . . . 86 in (2184 mm)
Turning circle . . . . 33 ft (10.1 m)
Ground clearance . . . . 6.75 in (171 mm)
Dry weight
    Two door saloon . . . . 1686 lbs (764 kg)
    Four door saloon . . . . 1733 lbs (786 kg)
    Convertible . . . . 1688 lbs (766 kg)
    Traveller . . . . 1821 lbs (826 kg)

ENGINE

Firing order . . . . 1 - 3 - 4 - 2
Spark plug
    Type . . . . Champion N5
    Gap . . . . 0.024-0.026 in (0.61-0.66 mm)
Distributor
    Type . . . . Lucas 25D4
    Points gap . . . . 0.014-0.016 in (0.36-0.40 mm)
Dwell angle . . . . $60^{\circ} \pm 3^{\circ}$
Timing marks . . . . Pointers on timing cover,
    notch on crankshaft pulley
Ignition timing
    948 cc HC . . . . 5° BTDC
    948 cc LC . . . . 4° BTDC
    1098 cc . . . . 3° BTDC

CAPACITIES

Steering rack . . . . 0.5 pint
Engine oil (incl. filter) . . . . 6.5 pints
Gearbox . . . . 2.25 pints
Rear axle . . . . 1.5 pints
Fuel tank . . . . 6.5 gallons
Cooling system
    998 cc without heater . . . . 9.75 pints
    998 cc with heater . . . . 10.75 pints
    1098 cc without heater . . . . 8.75 pints
    1098 cc with heater . . . . 9.75 pints

TYRE PRESSURES - lb/in^2 (kg/cm^2)

	Normal		Fully Laden	
	Front	Rear	Front	Rear
All models				
5.00 x 14 crossply . . .	22 (1.6)	22 (1.6)	22 (1.6)	24 (1.7)

Contents

Pass the MoT

Once a year, the MoT test falls due for vehicles, three years old or more (UK only). The test fee paid to the garage covers the cost of carrying out the inspection whether the vehicle passes the test or fails, so it makes sense to ensure that you get the maximum value out of the inspection by carrying out your own pre-test check beforehand.

In this way, you can possibly save yourself the cost of a failure certificate by putting right any likely reasons for failure. Bear in mind that an 'official' tester will more than likely follow a different criterion when examining the same component as the DIY owner, but, by just being aware of what checks the tester will make could avoid a needless failure certificate. Even a simple item like a brake light or one of the screen washers not working could 'fail' the test.

All the items that will come under the tester's scrutiny are included in this repair manual in one way or another although it is obviously not compiled specifically for passing the test. However, if you work your way through the check list below, and turn to the appropriate page number referred to, you will have the information required either to check or to service the relevant components.

LIGHTING EQUIPMENT, STOP LIGHTS, REFLECTORS, INDICATORS . . . . **Pages 18, 110**
All external lights must be in working order - including the headlamp main and dipped beams - and visible from a reasonable distance. Light lenses must not be damaged or missing. The indicators must flash at the correct rate - between one and two flashes per second - and the panel warning lights must also be functioning. Headlamps must be correctly aligned.

STEERING . . . . **Pages 16, 93**
Check for excessive play in all the steering components from the road wheels to the steering wheel. Check the tightness of all nuts and clamp bolts. Check for any unusual stiffness in the steering operation. Examine the steering rack for oil leaks.

FRONT WHEEL BEARINGS . . . . **Page 96**
Raise and support the front of the vehicle and check for bearing roughness by rotating the front wheels. A worn bearing will either be heard or felt at the tyre as the wheel turns. Check for excessive or insufficient bearing clearance.

SUSPENSION. . . . . **Pages 16, 84, 87**
The vehicle will have to be raised and supported to check the suspension. Using a suitable long lever or screwdriver to give leverage, check for excessive play in all the suspension joints. Check the condition of all shock absorber units - looking for fluid leakage and the security of the upper and lower mountings. Check the damping operation of the shock absorbers with the car on the road, by bouncing it at all four corners.

BRAKES . . . . **Pages 14, 101**
Check the operation of the brakes and the handbrake. Check for brakes pulling to one side and ascertain the cause. Check the condition of the flexible brake hoses looking for signs of cracking and for corrosion on the rigid metal pipes - especially around the rear axle. Check that the brake servo - if fitted, is working properly. Remember that the testing station now uses a 'roller brake tester' to check the efficiency of each wheel.

WHEELS AND TYRES . . . . **Page 16**
Check the condition of the tyres - the tread depth, the side walls, both inner as well as outer, and that they are inflated to the correct pressure (the latter may affect the brake test). Check the tyre 'mix' - radial tyres to the rear and cross-plies on the front wheels. Check the condition of the wheel rims for damage or distortion.

SEAT BELTS . . . . **Page 20**
Check the seat belts, if fitted, for security and the fabric for chafing or obvious damage.

GENERAL - WIPERS, WASHERS, HORN, EXHAUST. . . . . **Page 20, 114, 116**
Both the windscreen wipers and washers should be working efficiently. The horn should also operate clearly. Check that the exhaust system does not leak or make an excessive amount of noise. The best way to check for a leaking exhaust is to place a gloved hand over the end of the tailpipe with the engine idling and listen for the 'hiss' of any leakage.

CORROSION . . . . **Page 130**
Check the body panels for any damage or corrosion on the vehicle likely to render it unsafe.

NOTE: The above check list is only a guide so that the keen DIY owner can check his or her Minor before submitting it for the MoT test. Although it is based on the official MoT check list at the time of publication, it is only a guide and should be treated as such.

Service Schedule

WEEKLY OR BEFORE A LONG JOURNEY

- Top up engine oil
- Check and top up battery as necessary
- Check and top up screen washer bottle - if fitted
- Check drive belt tension
- Check tyre pressures
- Check operation of all lights

EVERY 3,000 MILES (5,000 KM) OR THREE MONTHS, WHICHEVER IS SOONER

- Check drive belt; adjust or renew as necessary
- Clean and adjust sparking plugs
- Top up battery electrolyte as necessary
- Adjust clutch free play
- Check and top up rear axle oil level
- Lubricate steering swivels
- Lubricate suspension pivots
- Oil handbrake linkage
- Lubricate propshaft universal joint
- Check and top up the brake master cylinder
- Check and adjust brake linings
- Check condition of tyres
- Change engine oil
- Check and top up the cooling system

EVERY 6,000 MILES (10,000 KM) OR SIX MONTHS, WHICHEVER IS SOONER
as for 3,000 miles (5,000 km) service, plus items shown below

- Check condition of steering linkage and seals
- Check and tighten the steering rack mountings
- Check and top up the shock absorbers
- Check and adjust handbrake
- Check and tighten wheel nuts
- Check and repack wheel bearings with grease
- Check security of exhaust system and mountings
- Lubricate the dynamo
- Lubricate the throttle linkage
- Check condition of the fan belt
- Check and adjust valve clearances
- Renew the distributor contact breaker
- Check distributor advance retard mechanism
- Clean fuel pump filter
- Clean air filter (oil type), or replace (dry type)
- Top up carburettor damper
- Check radiator hoses
- Clean and smear battery terminals with grease
- Lubricate all door locks and hinges and check operation
- Check and adjust front wheel alignment
- Lubricate clutch pedal shaft
- Check ignition timing
- Check for any leaks from engine

EVERY 12,000 MILES (20,000 KM) OR TWELVE MONTHS, WHICHEVER IS SOONER
as for 6,000 miles (10,000 KM) service, plug items listed below

- Drain and refill gearbox oil
- Clean brake drums
- Renew brake linings
- Renew sparking plugs
- Clean distributor cap
- Clean and secure HT leads
- Check security of inlet and exhaust manifolds
- Check and adjust balance of road wheels
- Check and adjust headlamp alignment

EVERY 18,000 MILES (30,000 KM) OR 18 MONTHS, WHICHEVER IS SOONER
as for 6,000 miles (10,000 km) service, plus items listed below

- Change brake fluid
- Check flexible hoses
- Fit all new hydraulic seals

Routine Maintenance

INTRODUCTION . . . . [1]

There is little doubt that the more knowledge you have about your car, the more equipped you will be to put things right if and when they go wrong. Certainly tackling the servicing or routine maintenance yourself will give you the opportunity of getting to know your car, at the same time saving yourself a lot of money.

The aim of this particular section is to guide the owner through the maze of service items to be found in the major service. You will see that on a previous page we have a Service Schedule which lists all the relevant checks at the appropriate intervals. This schedule does not necessarily list the items in the order that they should be tackled or checked. To save yourself time it would be better to divide the larger service into three or four sections. For example, all the under-bonnet operations could be tackled first - from topping up the various fluid levels to tuning the engine (covered in the next chapter). Then, perhaps, the brakes can be checked along with other items to be checked under the car. Finally, you might end up with tackling the lubrication side of the service, finishing up with light lubrication of the door locks and hinges.

It is worthwhile first reading the Routine Maintenance and Tune-up chapter thoroughly before actually starting to service your car so that you are aware of the work entailed and the tools and parts that you are likely to require beforehand. You can refer to the Service Data at the end of this chapter for details of all the lubricants that will be needed.

Apart from carrying out specific service operations, a certain amount of inspection and checking will be required. Remember that a fault, such as an oil leak, spotted now could save you a major, costly overhaul or replacement at a later date.

If you wish just to refer to one particular service item, then simply check the headings at the top of this page and turn to the appropriate check or operation.

ENGINE OIL & FILTER . . . . [2]

Oil Level

The oil level should be checked at least once a week and always before a long run. Ensure that the car is standing on level ground when checking the oil.

The dipstick is located on the right-hand side of the engine. The oil level should be maintained at the 'MAX' or 'FULL' mark on the dipstick and should never be allowed to fall below the 'MIN' mark, if indicated (Fig. A:1).

The oil filler cap is located on the rocker cover and oil should be added through the filler neck as necessary to bring the level up to the 'MAX' or 'FULL' mark.

Oil and Filter Change

The engine oil and the oil filter should be changed at the recommended intervals, or more frequently under severe operating conditions.

The most severe type of operation, and that which gives rise to sludge formation, is light engine loading, slow speeds and short journeys. High speeds over long distance are generally kinder to the engine. Modern engine oils contain additives which go a long way towards preventing sludge formation, but even they have certain limitations.

The dipstick can provide some guide as to the condition of the engine oil. An additive type of oil keeps the carbon particles in suspension, and even a small amount of carbon causes the oil to darken rapidly. However, if the dipstick is found to be heavily coated with sludge, then obviously the oil should be changed. The presence of beads of moisture on the valve rockers, as seen through the oil filler neck, indicates adverse running conditions. When such is the case, more frequent draining and renewal of the oil is highly desirable.

Drain the oil when the engine is warm. Allow at least 10 minutes for draining before refitting the sump plug

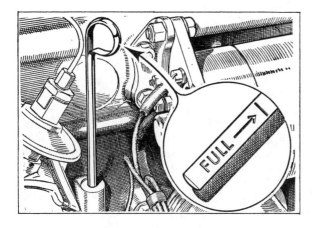

Fig. A:1 Dipstick for checking the oil level

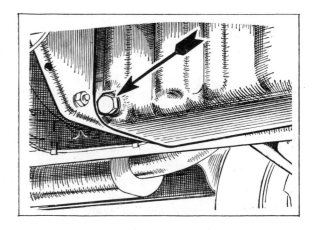

Fig. A:2 Engine oil drain plug

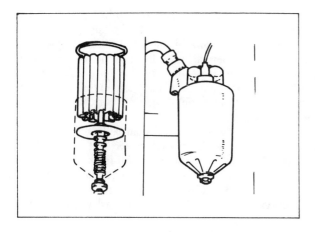

Fig. A:3 Oil filter assembly

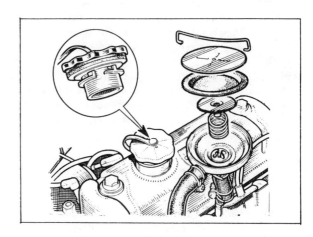

Fig. A:4 Crankcase breather control valve

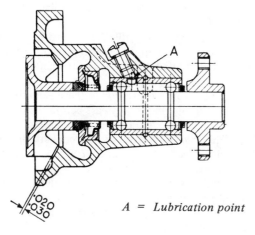

A = Lubrication point

Fig. A:5 Cross-section of water pump assembly

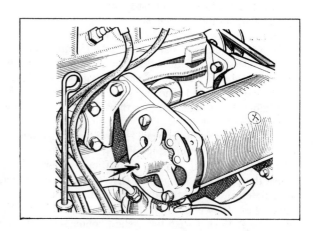

Fig. A:6 Dynamo lubrication point

©BLUK

(Fig. A:2). Clean the drain plug and refit it, using a new copper sealing ring if necessary. Tighten the plug securely but do not overtighten.

On all Minor 1000 models, the oil filter is of the replaceable element type, and is located on the right-hand side of the cylinder block (Fig. A:3). The filter is released by undoing the centre-bolt securing the filter bowl to the filter head. Place a container under the filter to catch the oil which will be released as soon as the bolt is unscrewed. Wash out the bowl with petrol before fitting the new element. Check that the small felt or rubber washer fitted between the element pressure plate and the metal washer above the pressure spring inside the filter bowl, if fitted, is correctly positioned and in good condition. It is essential for correct oil filtration that this washer is a snug fit on the centre-bolt. Also check that the external sealing ring at the centre-bolt head is in satisfactory condition.

Extract the large sealing ring from its groove in the filter head and discard it. Fit a new sealing ring in the groove, ensuring that it is correctly seated.

Refit the assembly to the filter head, rotating the bowl while tightening to ensure that it is correctly located on the sealing ring. Do NOT over-tighten the centre-bolt, otherwise the sealing ring may be damaged.

Once the filter has been replaced, refill the engine with the fresh oil. Start the engine and check the filter for leaks - stop the engine immediately if any are present as this indicates that the filter bowl is not sealing correctly. If all is well, stop the engine and recheck the oil level after waiting a few minutes.

CRANKCASE BREATHER SYSTEM . . . . [3]

The air intake filter for the engine ventilation system is incorporated in the oil filler cap on the rocker cover and must be renewed together with the cap as a complete assembly (Fig. A:4).

Replacement of the system filter at the recommended intervals is quite important as otherwise a pressure build-up in the crankcase can occur, causing subsequent oil leaks with an increase in oil consumption.

The operation of the system control valve can be tested by removing the oil filler cap from the rocker cover with the engine at normal operating temperature and running at idle speed. If the valve is functioning correctly the engine speed will increase by approximately 200 rev/min. as the cap is removed. The change in speed will be audibly noticeable. If no change occurs, the valve must be serviced as described below.

Release the spring clip and remove the components of the valve from the housing (Fig. A:4). Clean all metal parts with petrol. If deposits are difficult to remove, immerse the parts in boiling water first. Clean the diaphragm with detergent or methylated spirits. Examine the components carefully and renew any which show signs of wear or damage. Ensure that the system connecting hoses are clear before reassembling the valve. Reassemble the components as shown in the illustration, making sure that the spigot on the metering valve engages in the cruciform guides and the diaphragm is seated correctly.

COOLING SYSTEM . . . . [4]

Coolant Level

The engine coolant level should be checked at least weekly and topped up as necessary. The level must be checked only when the system is cold.

Examine the coolant level in the radiator to see whether it is within half an inch of the filler cap. If topping up is necessary, remove the pressure cap from the radiator and add water as required. Do NOT attempt to remove the cap if the system is hot - allow it to cool down first. Even then, muffle the cap with a thick cloth to protect the hands against escaping steam and turn the cap slowly so as to release the pressure gradually. At this point, if the coolant temperature is high enough, hot vapour will be heard to escape. Only when this ceases should the cap be turned past the final stop and removed.

Anti-freeze

Because of the properties of anti-freeze in lowering the freezing point and raising the boiling point of the coolant, it is recommended that an 'All-Season' type anti-freeze be used permanently in the cooling system to afford maximum protection against both freezing and overheating. The presence of a corrosion inhibitor in most anti-freezes will also help prevent corrosion and the formation of scale in the system.

During the winter months an anti-freeze mixture MUST be used in the system to protect against frost damage. The concentration of the anti-freeze solution will depend on the degree of protection required, and dilution should be carried out in accordance with manufacturer's instructions. A 25% anti-freeze solution will give protection down to approximately -13°C (9°F).

Before filling the system with anti-freeze solution, inspect all hoses, hose connections and cooling system joints. Tighten or renew as necessary. After filling the system with anti-freeze, run the engine up to normal operating temperature and check for leaks.

A label should be attached to the radiator to record the date of filling.

If, once the system is filled with anti-freeze, it becomes necessary to top up the coolant level, use only anti-freeze solution diluted to the correct strength for this purpose.

The anti-freeze concentration in the system should be checked periodically and in any case before the beginning of the winter season and before travelling to a colder climate. The specific gravity of the coolant should be checked using a suitable hydrometer and brought up to the required strength as necessary.

The cooling system should be completely drained, flushed and refilled with a fresh mixture of anti-freeze and water at least every two years or as recommended by the anti-freeze manufacturer.

Water Pump Lubrication (Fig. A:5)

The water pump should be lubricated periodically.

Remove the screwed plug from the pump casing and add a small quantity of grease through the hole. Lubricate sparingly, otherwise grease will seep past the bearings on to the face of the carbon sealing ring and impair its efficiency. Do NOT pressure lubricate the pump, or the seal may be damaged.

BATTERY . . . .[5]

Electrolyte Level

The level of the battery electrolyte should be checked frequently and distilled (de-ionised) water added if the level in any cell is below the separators, or the bottom of the filling tubes on a trough-fill type battery. In some cases the battery case is translucent to allow the level to be checked without the need for lifting the vent cover. Do not overfill the battery.

It is good practice to run the car immediately after topping up the battery, especially in cold weather, to ensure thorough mixing of the acid and the water and so prevent freezing.

If the battery is found to need frequent topping up, steps should be taken to find out the reason. For example, the battery may be receiving an excessive charge, in which case the charging system charge rate should be checked.

If any cell in particular needs topping up more than the others, check the condition of the battery case. If there are signs of an electrolyte leak, the source should be traced and corrective action taken.

Specific Gravity

The specific gravity of the battery electrolyte is a good indication of the state of charge of the battery. Take hydrometer readings from each cell.

If the electrolyte level is low, top up with distilled water and recharge the battery for at least 40 minutes.

The following table relates the specific gravity to the battery condition. The figures are corrected to an electrolyte temperature of 16°C (60°F) and readings obtained must also be correct to suit the temperature of the electrolyte. For every 3°C (5°F) above 16°C add 0.002 s.g., and vice-versa.

Battery specific gravity	Climate below 27°C (80°F)	Climate above 27°C (80°F)
Cell fully charged	1.270 - 1.290	1.210 - 1.230
Cell half charged	1.190 - 1.210	1.130 - 1.150
Cell discharged	1.110 - 1.130	1.050 - 1.070

All cells should give approximately the same readings, indicating that the battery is healthy, although uniformly low reading will indicate that charging is required.

If one cell is about 0.030 lower than the rest it is probably failing, although an extended charge may revive it.

If the readings are irregular, with one or more cells 0.050 lower than the rest, the battery is not fit for further use and should be replaced.

Battery Connections

The external condition of the battery and the cable connections should be checked periodically. If the top of the battery is contaminated by acid film and dirt between the battery terminals, wash it with a dilute ammonia or soda solution to neutralise the acid present, then flush with clean water. Care must be taken to ensure that the vent plugs or cover are firmly in position so that the neutralising solution does not enter the cells and cause any damage.

To ensure good contact, the battery cables should be tight on the battery posts. If the battery posts or cable terminals are corroded, the cables should be disconnected and the terminals and posts cleaned with a soda solution and a wire brush. When reconnecting the cables to the battery posts, a thin coating of petroleum jelly should be applied.

The battery earth strap and the engine earth strap should also be checked for proper connection and condition.

DYNAMO BEARING . . . .[6]

On vehicles fitted with a dynamo the dynamo rear bearing should be lubricated periodically. Add two or three drops of engine oil to the bearing through the central hole in the rear end bearing plate (Fig. A:6). Do NOT over-oil the bearing, otherwise the commutator may become contaminated.

DYNAMO/ALTERNATOR DRIVE BELT . . .[7]

Adjustment

Correct tensioning of the drive belt is important to ensure efficient operation of the cooling and charging systems. Excessive strain will cause rapid wear of the belt and place undue strain on the water pump and dynamo bearings.

When correctly tensioned, a total deflection of 0.5 in (13 mm), or 0.75 in (20 mm) if an alternator is fitted, under moderate hand pressure should be possible at the midway point of the longest belt run between the two pulleys.

If adjustment is required, slacken the three securing bolts and move the dynamo or alternator to the required position, using only hand pressure. Avoid over-tensioning the belt. Tighten the securing bolts then recheck the tension (Figs. A:7 and A:9).

The condition of the drive belt should be checked periodically. If nicked, cut, excessively worn, or otherwise damaged, the belt should be renewed. If the belt is noisy in operation, check for misalignment of the pulleys.

Replacement

To replace the belt, proceed as for adjusting, but press the dynamo fully towards the engine and detach the belt from the pulleys. Fit the new belt, ensuring that it is not twisted, and adjust the tension as described above. Do NOT attempt to lever a new belt on to the pulleys as this can easily cause damage to the belt or pulleys.

NOTE: The tension of a new belt should be rechecked after approximately 100 miles (160 km) use.

CLUTCH...........................[8]

The clutch mechanism on Morris 1000 models is mechanical. The only point on this system which should be checked regularly is the clutch pedal free play. On the Minor 1000 fitted with the 1098 cc engine, the free play shown should be between 1.37 and 1.50 ins (35 - 38 mm). The free play on models fitted with the 948 cc engine should be 0.75 in (20.0 mm). To adjust, proceed as follows:-

Slacken the locknut on the clutch operating rod (Fig. A:8), and rotate the adjusting nut - hexagonal or spherical - in the appropriate direction. With the correct free movement at the pedal, tighten the locknut and recheck the movement.

BRAKING SYSTEM...................[9]

Brake Fluid Level

The brake master cylinder is located under the floorpan on the driver's side of the car. To gain access, remove the front carpet and mats and remove the bolts holding the small cover plate in position (Fig. A:10).

The level in the cylinder reservoir should be checked periodically and topped up if required. The reservoir filler plug should be wiped clean before unscrewing the cap to prevent the possibility of dirt entering the system. The fluid level must be maintained at approximately 0.5 in (12 mm) below the bottom of the filler neck. Use only the specified type of hydraulic fluid for topping up - see Service Data.

Before replacing the filler cap, check that the vent hole in the cap is clear of obstruction.

Brake Pedal Free Play

The brake pedal free play should not normally need adjustment, since it would have been accurately set during vehicle manufacture. However, if the pedal has to be depressed more or less than 0.75 in (19 mm) before resistance is felt, adjustment will have to be carried out. This involves removing the master cylinder (Brakes chapter) and moving the adjusting bolt on the end of the cylinder pushrod until the free play is correct (Fig. A:11).

BRAKE ADJUSTMENT................[10]

When lining wear has reached a point where the pedal travels to within 1 in (25 mm) of the floorboards when the brakes are applied heavily it is necessary to adjust the brake-shoes.

Jack up the wheel which is to be adjusted, placing suitable blocks beneath the wheels remaining in contact with the ground. Release the handbrake.

Front Brakes (Fig. A:12)

Remove the front hub cap and rubber plug from the access hole in the wheel disc, then rotate the brake-drum until both adjustment screws are visible through the holes provided in the face of the brake-drum. With a screwdriver turn the screws as far as they will go in a clockwise direction until the drum is locked solid, then turn them anti-clockwise one notch only. The brake-drum should then be free to rotate without the shoes rubbing, and the adjustment on this wheel is complete. The brake-shoes on the other front wheel must be adjusted by the same method.

Rear Brakes

The procedure is similar to that detailed for the front brakes except that there is only one adjuster, and this controls both shoes.

Handbrake (Fig. A:13)

Under normal circumstances, adjustment of the rear brakes should also automatically adjust the handbrake mechanism. If, however, there is still excessive movement at the handbrake lever or the handbrake lacks holding power, then the handbrake cable can be adjusted as follows.

The rear brakes must be adjusted as described previously before attempting to adjust the handbrake.

Chock both front wheels and jack up the rear of the car. Apply the handbrake until the pawl engages with the third notch on the ratchet, and adjust the nuts at the handbrake lever until it is just possible to rotate the wheel by hand under heavy pressure. It is important that the road wheels offer equal resistance in order to get full braking power.

Return the lever to the off position and check that both wheels are perfectly free. If they are not, remove the brake-drum of the brake that tends to bind and check that the brake-shoe pull-off springs are correctly fitted and that the wheel cylinder has not seized. Remove any stiffness present, readjust, and check.

Linings

The road wheels and brake drums must be removed to allow inspection of the brake shoes.

Release the handbrake and slacken off the brake adjuster fully by inserting a screwdriver through the aperture in the wheel. Remove the two countersunk locating screws and withdraw the brake drum.

Clean all dust from the brake shoes, backplate and brake drum, using a soft brush. Wash out any accumulated dust with methylated spirits and allow to dry.

Inspect the shoe linings for wear. If the lining material has worn down to the minimum permissible thickness of

Fig. A:7 Dynamo securing bolts

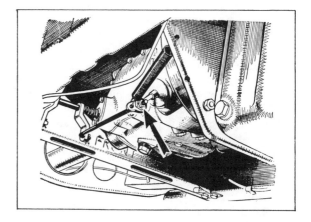

Fig. A:8 Clutch adjustment point

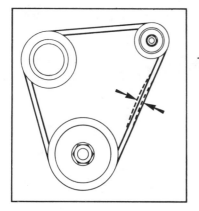

Fig. A:9 Alternator belt adjustment

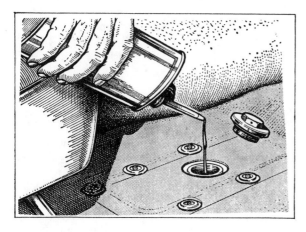

Fig. A:10 Topping up the master cylinder

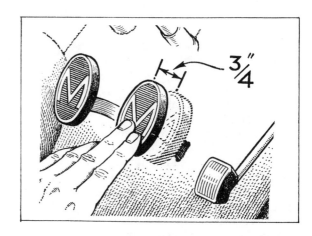

Fig. A:11 Checking the brake pedal free play

0.0625 in (1.5 mm) on bonded-type shoes, or close to the rivets, or will have done so before the next check is called for, the brake shoes must be renewed (Fig. A:14).

Inspect the wheel cylinders for signs of leakage, turning the dust boot back if necessary. If any signs of leakage are present, the cylinder seals should be renewed or the cylinder replaced as an assembly immediately.

Examine the brake drum for signs of cracking or scoring. Light scoring is permissible, but serious scoring will increase lining wear, and in this case the drum should be machined true or replaced - preferably the latter. If the wear pattern on the brake linings is uneven across its width, inspect the drums for "belling" and the backplate for distortion.

The procedure for replacing the brake shoes is fully covered in the Brakes chapter, and reference should be made to it for details.

After refitting the drum and road wheel, the brake shoes must be adjusted as detailed previously.

STEERING . . . . [11]

Steering Gear Lubrication

A lubrication nipple (Fig. A:15) is provided on the left-hand side of the rack housing (right-hand side on left-hand drive cars) for steering gear lubrication.

The lubrication nipple is accessible from inside the car by removing the carpet from the front passenger's side and removing the rubber plug from the floorpan. Give a maximum of 10 strokes with an oil gun filled with SAE 90 EP Hypoid Gear Oil.

Apply a grease gun, filled with multi-purpose grease to the nipple on each tie-rod ball joint from underneath the car (Fig. A:16).

FRONT SUSPENSION . . . . [12]

Checking for Wear

The pivot points on the front suspension are probably the parts most prone to wear on the whole car, and in most instances this is due purely to lack of regular lubrication.

The worst point of wear is normally the vertical swivel pin and bushes on which the swivel axle assembly pivots. This is followed by the threaded fulcrum pin which attaches the lower end of the swivel pin to the suspension lower link. This has a habit of turning in its eye in spite of being secured by a cotter pin.

To check these points, jack up the front of the car so that the wheel is clear of the ground. Grasp the wheel at the top and bottom and rock it to and fro. If movement is present it will be necessary to get a second person to observe exactly where the point of movement is to determine the cause.

Other points to check for wear are the damper spindle, damper arm to swivel pin upper trunnion bushes (rubber), suspension lower link inner mounting bushes (rubber) and wheel bearings.

GEARBOX . . . . [13]

Oil Level

The gearbox filler level plug is located on the left-hand side of the gearbox casing and access is gained by lifting the floor covering on the gearbox cover and removing the rubber plug (Fig. A:17). The oil level should be maintained at the bottom of the filler plug aperture threads. Top up if necessary with SAE 20W 50 engine oil. The gearbox can be drained by removing the plug shown in Fig. A:18.

REAR AXLE . . . . [14]

Oil Level

The rear axle filler level plug is located in the front of the axle casing. Ensure that the car is standing level when checking. The oil should be level with the bottom of the plug aperture. Add SAE 90 EP Gear Oil, if necessary, by reaching the filler through the opening in the rear seat pan (Fig. A:19).

WHEELS & TYRES . . . . [15]

Tyre Pressures

The tyre pressures should be checked at least once a week and adjusted to the recommended pressures where necessary - see 'Service Data' for pressures. Check the pressure when the tyres are cold as tyre pressures may increase by as much as 6 lb/in^2 (0.4 kg/cm^2) when hot.

Incorrect inflation pressures will cause abnormal tyre wear and may result in premature failure. There is an average loss of 13% tread mileage for every 10% reduction in inflation pressure below the recommended figure.

When checking the pressures, ensure that the dust caps are refitted to the valves, as apart from keeping out dirt they also provide a second seal to the valve.

The tightness of the road wheel nuts should be checked at the same time as the tyre pressures, but take care not to over-tighten - see 'Tightening Torques'. It should be noted that the wheel nuts must be fitted with their TAPERED side towards the wheel.

Tyre Inspection

The tyres should be checked periodically for wear and damage. Check the tread depth, preferably with a proper tread depth gauge. In the UK, the minimum permissible tread depth is 1 mm, but tyres should be replaced before this level is reached as road holding and resistance to punctures will have been affected long before this point.

Check the tyre casing visually for cuts in the casing fabric, exposure of ply or cords, or the presence of lumps or bulges. If any of these conditions are present, the tyre should be discarded.

Abnormal tyre wear may be caused by improper in-

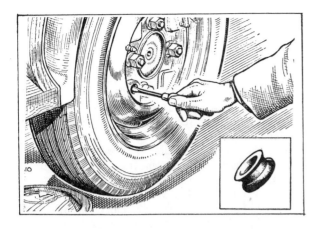

Fig. A:12 Adjusting the brake shoes

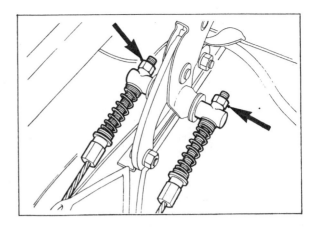

Fig. A:13 Adjusting the handbrake cables

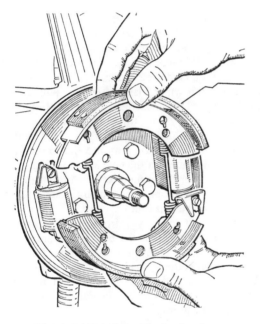

Fig. A:14 Removing the brake shoes

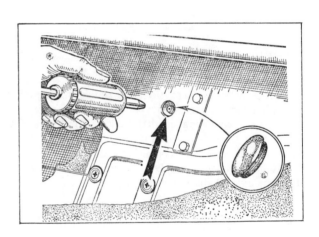

Fig. A:15 Lubricating the steering box

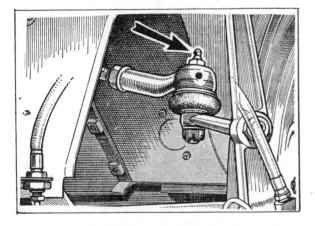

Fig. A:16 Location of the steering tie-rod grease nipple

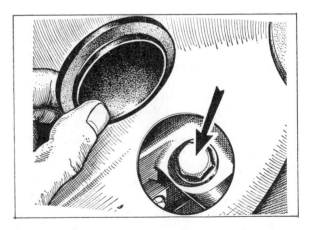

Fig. A:17 Location of the gearbox oil filler aperture

©BLUK

Routine Maintenance
17

flation pressures, wheel imbalance, misalignment of the front or rear suspension, or mechanical irregularities. When rapid or uneven tyre wear becomes apparent, the cause should be sought and rectified.

Fins or feathers on the tread surface are an indication of severe wheel misalignment. This condition takes the form of a sharp 'fin' on the edge of each pattern rib, and the position of this indicates the direction of misalignment. Fins on the outboard edges are caused by excessive toe-out, whereas fins on the inboard edges of the pattern ribs are caused by excessive toe-in. Finning on the nearside front tyre only may be due to severe road camber conditions and this cannot be eliminated by mechanical adjustment. In this event, frequent interchanging of the affected wheel to even out tyre wear is the only solution.

Some mechanical defects which could be a cause of abnormal tyre wear are:- loose wheel bearings, uneven brake adjustment, distorted brake discs, excessive looseness or damage in the suspension, loose steering connections, or bent steering arms.

Tyre Replacement

Crossply tyres were fitted as standard equipment, but either radial or crossply types can be fitted as replacements. It is recommended that they be fitted as a complete set of the same type. It is dangerous to use a vehicle fitted with an unsuitable combination of tyres.

Radial ply and crossply tyres must NOT be used on the same axle. Radial ply tyres must NOT be fitted to the front wheels when crossply tyres are fitted to the rear. Radial ply tyres may be fitted to the rear wheels only, but this is not recommended. It is far safer to fit radial or crossply tyres in complete sets of four. The spare tyre should also be of the same type.

GREASE POINTS.....................[16]

There are several grease points around the car, mainly on the front suspension, which must be lubricated periodically to ensure efficient operation and minimise wear.

Wipe the grease nipples clean before use. Give each nipple three or four strokes with a grease gun filled with suitable multi-purpose grease, preferably of the Lithium based type (e.g. Castrol LM Grease). Wipe off any excess grease when finished.

Grease nipples are located at the following points, and should receive attention at the specified intervals (see 'Service Schedule').
1. Steering knuckles (four nipples), three or four strokes.
2. Steering tie-rod ball ends (two nipples), three or four strokes.
3. Propeller shaft universal joints (two nipples), three or four strokes (Fig. A:20).
4. Fan spindle (one nipple), two strokes.

WINDSCREEN WIPERS & WASHERS.....[17]

Windscreen Washers

The windscreen washer reservoir, if fitted, should be checked frequently, especially during the winter months, and topped up as necessary. The addition of a proprietary brand of screen wash solvent is recommended as this will help to remove oil film and insect smears from the screen. In winter, the further addition of approximately 25% methylated spirits will help prevent freezing of the solvent solution. Do NOT use radiator anti-freeze.

To check the operation of the screen washer, press the control knob and note the position of the spray on the screen. If the delivery is incorrect, turn the jet assembly using a small screwdriver to adjust the height of the spray.

The condition of the wiper blade rubbers should be examined periodically and the blade assemblies renewed if these are perished or defective. If the spring in the wiper arm is weak, it will exert insufficient pressure on the screen in use, and in this case the arm should also be renewed. Springs can be replaced separately.

To ensure efficient wiping, it is recommended that the wiper blades be renewed annually.

To renew the wiper blade assembly, pull the wiper arm away from the windscreen, hold the fastener and spring retainer away from the arm retaining spring clip and withdraw the blade assembly from the arm (Fig. A:21). Insert the end of the arm into the spring fastener of the new blade and push the new blade into engagement with the arm. Lower the arm on to the windscreen.

If the wiper blade operating arc on the screen is incorrect, it can be adjusted as follows:-

Lift the wiper arm away from the windscreen and find the small spring clip at the base of the arm. The clip engages in a retaining groove on the spindle. The arm can be withdrawn when the spring is held clear of the retaining groove (Fig. A:22). Refit the arm in the required position and push it down hard on to the spindle until the retaining clip engages in the groove.

A further item of wiper maintenance is occasionally to lubricate the rubber grommet or washer around the wheelbox spindles with a few drops of glycerine. This will prevent the spindles seizing or causing excessive drag on the motor and linkage.

HEADLAMP ALIGNMENT ....[18]

Two adjusting screws are provided on each headlamp for beam setting (Fig. A:23). The screw at the top of the lamp controls the adjustment in the vertical plane, and the screw at the side of the lamp controls the horizontal adjustment.

It should be noted that the beam setting is affected by the load on the car, and therefore the beam should always be set with the normal load on the car.

The beams should be set so that the main beams are straight ahead and parallel with the road surface and with

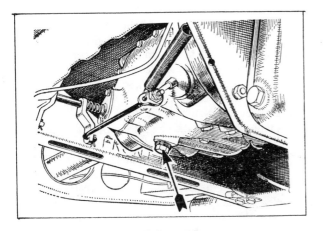

Fig. A:18 Location of the gearbox drain plug
(arrowed)

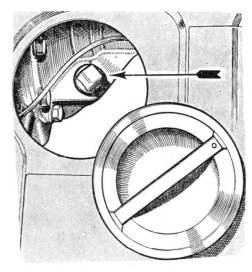

Fig. A:19 Location of the rear axle oil filler

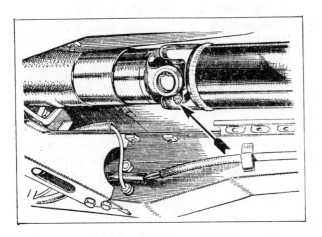

Fig. A:20 Grease nipple for the propshaft
universal joint

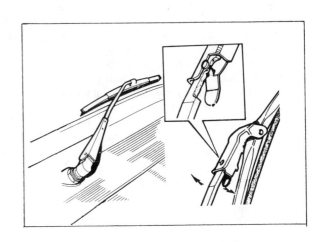

Fig. A:21 Wiper blade replacement

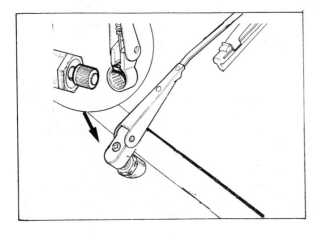

Fig. A:22 Wiper arm removal

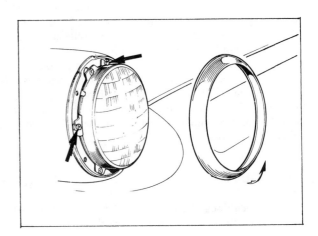

Fig. A:23 Headlamp adjustment screws

each other, or in accordance with the current local regulations.

It is recommended that the checking and resetting be entrusted to an Authorised Dealer who will have the specialist equipment necessary to carry out this work.

JACKING PROCEDURE . . . . [19]

Jacking Points

Use only the proper support locations beneath the body. It is important that only these positions are used when raising the car, otherwise damage could result.

When raising the complete vehicle, always lift the rear end first. When jacking the rear of the car on the differential housing, a wooden block should be made up to prevent the jack head touching the component.

When using axle stands to support the car at the sill jacking points, use only square head type stands with wooden cushion pads on top. Only use three legged stands, making sure one of the legs points outwards from the car. Take care when fitting a stand that the pad does not foul anything.

Always raise the rear of the car by lifting it under the differential and always raise the front of the car by placing the jack so that its pad lifts the underframe support member in front of the engine.

When working underneath the car, always fit stands. Never rely on a jack alone, except when wheel changing.

DISTRIBUTOR. . . . . [20]

Lubrication

Lubrication of the distributor should be carried out at the same time as the engine oil change.

Unclip and remove the distributor cap and pull off the rotor arm from the central spindle.

Apply one or two drops of clean engine oil to the felt wick in the end of the cam spindle.

Lightly smear the spindle cam with high melting point grease. Use a screwdriver or similar instrument to distribute the lubricant uniformly around the cam surface. When the cam is rotated a small fillet of lubricant should be built up on the back of the points rubbing block.

Avoid over lubricating. Carefully wipe away any surplus lubricant and check that the contact breaker points are perfectly clean and dry. Refit the rotor arm and distributor cap. See Tune-up chapter for details on contact breaker inspection and replacement.

SEAT BELTS . . . . [21]

Although seat belts are fitted to a car this doesn't necessarily mean that they are working efficiently or,

indeed, that they are capable of doing their job when they are actually needed. This is why the condition of the seat belts is now included in the annual MoT test. There are some simple checks to be made on a regular basis to see that they are in working order. They are as follows:-

1. Pull each seat belt against its anchorage to see that it is properly secured to the vehicle structure.
2. Examine carefully the condition of the webbing looking for cuts or obvious signs of deterioration.
3. Fasten each seat belt locking mechanism and then try to pull the locked sections apart. Operate the mechanism, whilst pulling on the belt to determine that the mechanism releases when required.
4. Check the condition of the attachment fittings and adjusting fitting on each belt for distortion or fracture.
5. As far as practicable check the condition of the vehicle structure around the seat belt anchorages - this will be best carried out from below the vehicle.
6. If the seat belt is of the retracting type, pull a section of the webbing from the reel unit and then release it to see that the webbing automatically winds back. Bear in mind that some inertia reel belts require some manual assistance before retraction takes place.

EXHAUST SYSTEM. . . . . [22]

Checking

The exhaust system should be checked periodically for leaks and security. It is a good practice to spend a few minutes checking the system whenever work is being carried out under the car.

Check the alignment of the system to ensure that none of the suspension points is strained.

Inspect the exhaust pipes and silencer box for damage, corrosion or signs of blowing. The latter is best checked with the engine running at a fast idle and a gloved hand placed over the tailpipe to pressurise the system. Badly rusted components can be detected by tapping the pipes and boxes with a screwdriver handle or similar light tool. Take care not to strike the system with a heavy tool as this may damage the system.

Check the rubber mountings for splits and ensure they are adequately supporting the system.

LOCKS, HINGES, ETC. . . . . [23]

All locks, hinges and door check straps should be lubricated periodically to prevent them seizing. Also lightly oil the bonnet catch and the boot or rear door catch.

The lock cylinders in the doors and boot lid should be lubricated with oil, or preferably graphite powder, by dipping the key in the lubricant then inserting it into the lock and turning it a few times.

Service Data

SPECIFIED LUBRICANTS

Engine Oil . . . . 20W/50 oil
Gearbox . . . . 20W/50 oil
Rear axle . . . . Hypoid 90 oil
Steering rack . . . . Hypoid 90 oil
Water pump . . . . Multi-purpose grease
Shock absorbers . . . . 20W/20 oil
General greasing . . . . Multi-purpose grease
Brake fluid . . . . Lockhead super heavy duty, or
any conforming to SAE 70 R3

CAPACITIES

Engine oil (incl. filter) . . . . 6.5 pints (3.7 litres)
Gearbox . . . . 2.25 pints (1.3 litres)
Rear axle . . . . 1.5 pints (0.85 litres)
Cooling system
    1098 cc without heater. . . . . 8.75 pints (5 litres)
    1098 cc with heater . . . . 9.75 pints (5.5 litres)
    948 cc without heater . . . . 9.75 pints (5.5 litres)
    948 cc with heater. . . . . 10.75 pints (6 litres)
Fuel tank. . . . . 6.5 gallons (30 litres)
Steering rack . . . . 0.5 pints (0.28 litres)

CHASSIS

Generator drive belt tension (dynamo) . . . . .0.5 in (1.27 cm)
Alternator drive belt tension . . . . .0.75 in (1.91 cm)
Front wheel alignment . . . . 0.0938 in (2.38 mm) toe-in

TYRE PRESSURES - lb/in^2 (kg/cm^2)

| | Normal | | Fully Laden | |
	Front	Rear	Front	Rear
All models				
5.00 x 14 crossply	22 (1.6)	22 (1.6)	22 (1.6)	24 (1.7)

Tune-Up

INTRODUCTION . . . .[1]

Poor performance, excessive fuel consumption and bad starting can be some of the problems that can be associated with an engine that is badly worn or out of tune. This is why at every major service the engine components should be checked and tuned according to the manufacturer's Service Schedule (see page 9). We have deliberately not covered the engine tune-up in the previous Routine Maintenance so that if your car is in between services and is misbehaving then you can tackle the engine separately. It is possible that there is only one component or part that is at fault and consequently you do not wish to tune the complete engine. However, it is only by gradual elimination that usually the culprit component(s) can be traced. If your car will not start at all then we have included a comprehensive trouble-tracing chart at the end of this section.

The following checks and adjustments have been compiled into a logical sequence and, if checking and tuning the engine, we would advise that you follow the order set out. However, if you just wish to tackle the sparking plugs or, perhaps, the contact breaker points then simply refer to that particular heading. This way just one component can be tackled, or, if desired, all of them.

COMPRESSION CHECK. . . . .[2]

You can waste your time trying to tune an engine that is badly worn. So, depending on the mileage covered by your vehicle, it is always worthwhile checking the cylinder compression pressures first. To carry out this operation you will obviously need a compression tester (Fig. B:1) which can be purchased quite cheaply or even hired. Before starting, check what the compression readings should be - these are listed at the end of this section. The procedure is as follows:
1. Remove the HT leads by grasping each end firmly and pulling off the spark plug.

2. Using a sparking plug socket or box spanner, remove all the spark plugs (refer to **SPARK PLUGS** later in this section).
3. Screw or push the compression tester into the first plug hole and, with the throttle wide open, turn the engine over with the starter motor. If the compression tester has to be held in position by hand then hold it firmly, ensuring that there is no leakage of compression. Make a note of the reading.
4. Pass on to the next spark plug hole and carry out the same test and make a note of the reading.
5. Carry out the same procedure on each cylinder.
6. Compare the readings.

Provided all the readings are high and within 5-10 lb/in^2 (3-7 kg/cm^2) of each other then the engine should be considered in order, provided that the readings are close to the manufacturer's recommendations.

If one or two cylinders are lower than the others, then it is likely that a cylinder head valve or piston and bore is worn. Either can be confirmed by carrying out another compression test on the suspect cylinder, only this time adding a small amount of oil to the cylinder beforehand. This is called a 'wet' test as opposed to the previous 'dry' test. If the 'wet' test causes the compression reading to rise, then it is likely that there is a fault with either the bore, piston or rings. If the reading remains the same, then it is likely that there is a faulty valve in the cylinder head, or perhaps the cylinder head gasket is faulty.

If this is the case, then refer to the Engine section, which will describe how these faults can be put right.

EXHAUST SYSTEM. . . . .[3]

The exhaust system has an important bearing on engine performance. The complete system should therefore be checked periodically for leaks and security. It is good practice to spend a few minutes checking the system whenever work is being carried out under the car.

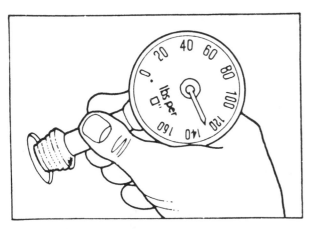

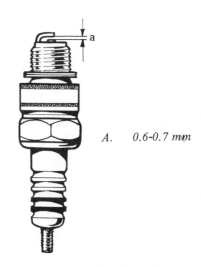

A.   0.6-0.7 mm

Fig. B:1 Checking the cylinder compressions

Fig. B:2 Checking spark plug electrode gap

1. NORMAL – Core nose will be lightly coated with grey-brown deposits. Replace after 10,000 miles.

2. HEAVY DEPOSITS – Condition could be due to worn valve guides. Plug can be used again after servicing.

3. CARBON FOULING – Caused by rich mixture through faulty carburettor, choke or a clogged air cleaner.

4. OIL FOULING – Cuased by worn valve guides, bores or piston rings. Hotter plug may cure.

5. OVERHEATING – Reasons could be over-advanced ignition timing, a worn distributor or weak fuel mixture.

6. PRE-IGNITION – This problem is caused through serious overheating. This could result in engine damage.

Fig. B:3 Typical spark plug conditions

Inspect the exhaust pipe and the silencer box for damage, corrosion or signs of blowing. The latter will be better checked with the engine running at fast idle.

Check the alignment of the system to ensure that none of the suspension points is unduly strained. Check the suspension points to ensure they are adequately supporting the system.

VALVE CLEARANCES . . . . [4]

The procedure for checking and adjusting the valve rocker clearances is fully covered in the Engine section and reference should be made to it for details.

SPARK PLUGS . . . . [5]

The spark plugs should be removed and examined periodically (Fig. B:2).

When disconnecting the leads from the spark plugs, grasp the moulded cap of the lead, then twist and pull the cap off the plug. Do NOT pull on the lead, otherwise the connection inside the cap may become separated.

Brush or blow any dirt away from around the plug hole before removing the spark plug.

Inspect the condition of the insulator tip and the electrodes. Typical examples of spark plug conditions are shown in Fig. B:3 and should be interpreted as follows:-

Normal (Fig. B:3.1)

Ideally the plugs should look like the condition shown in this photograph. The colour of the electrodes should appear greyish-brown or tan-coloured. White to yellow deposits usually mean that the car has been used for long periods at high, constant speeds. Provided that the sparking plugs have not covered a large mileage they can be cleaned, re-set and refitted.

Heavy Deposits (Fig. B:3.2)

The sparking plug in this condition will probably look worse than it is. Heavy deposits could mean worn valve guides. When deposits have been cleaned off, the sparking plug should be okay to use again providing it is not worn.

Carbon Fouled (Fig. B:3.3)

This is identified by dry, fluffy deposits which result from incomplete combustion. Too rich an air/fuel mixture

or faulty action of the choke can cause incomplete burning. The mixture being too rich can often be traced to a dirty or blocked air cleaner.

Defective or dirty high tension cables can reduce voltage supplied to the sparking plug and cause misfiring. If fouling is evident in only one or two cylinders, sticking valves may be the problem. Excessive idling, slow speeds or stop/start driving can also keep plug temperatures so low that normal combustion deposits are not burned off.

Oil Fouled (Fig. B:3.4)

This is identified by black wet sludge deposits and is traceable to oil entering the combustion chamber either past the pistons and bores or through the valve guides. Hotter sparking plugs may cure the problem temporarily, but in severe cases an engine overhaul is called for.

Overheated (Fig. B:3.5)

Overheated sparking plugs are usually identified by a white or blistered insulator nose and badly eroded electrodes. The engine overheating or improper ignition timing could be responsible for this problem. If only a couple of sparking plugs are affected the cause may be uneven distribution of the coolant. Abnormal fast driving for sustained periods can also cause high temperatures in the combustion chambers and, in these circumstances, colder sparking plugs should be used.

Spark plugs which are in good condition and with low mileage can be cleaned, preferably with a sand-blast cleaner. Clean the electrode surfaces and file them flat with a points file.

Check the electrode gap with a gap setting gauge or feeler gauge. The gap should be 0.025 in (0.64 mm). If necessary, adjust the gap by bending the outer electrode; NEVER attempt to bend the inner electrode, otherwise the central insulator may be cracked or broken. When fitting new spark plugs, the electrode gap should be checked before installing them in the engine.

Tighten the spark plugs to their correct torque - 20 lb.ft (2.8 kg m) when refitting them in the cylinder head. If a torque wrench is not available, fit the spark plugs finger-tight then tighten them a further quarter turn. Do NOT over-tighten them.

DISTRIBUTOR . . . . [6]

Lubrication (Fig. B:4)

To lubricate the distributor, the distributor cap and rotor arm must first be removed.

Very lightly smear the breaker cam and breaker arm pivot post with grease or petroleum jelly (Fig. B:4).

Apply a few drops of oil through the gap between the contact plate and cam spindle to lubricate the centrifugal weights.

Apply a few drops of oil to the top of the cam spindle. It is not necessary to remove the screw from the centre of the cam spindle as clearance is provided for oil to pass.

Carefully wipe away any surplus lubricant and check that the contact breaker points are perfectly clean and dry. Refit the rotor arm and distributor cap.

Points Inspection

The contact breaker points should be inspected carefully before attempting to adjust them. If the points are worn or burned, or if excessive metal transfer has occurred, they should be renewed. Metal transfer is considered excessive when the pip on one of the contacts equals or exceeds the recommended gap setting.

Burnt or oxidised points may be caused by oil or grease contamination on the contact surfaces, a defective condenser, or a loose connection in the low tension circuit. Check for these conditions when burnt contacts are encountered.

Points which are in satisfactory condition, but have become dirty or contaminated with oil or grease, should be cleaned with a stiff brush and methylated spirit.

As the contact set is a relatively inexpensive item which has great bearing on good engine performance, it is recommended that it be replaced if any doubt exists as to the condition of the contacts.

The contact points can be dressed using a fine-cut contact file, but replacement is preferable.

Points Adjustment (Fig. B:5)

The contact points can be set either by measuring the gap with a feeler gauge, or by measuring the dwell angle with a meter. The latter is preferable as it is a more accurate method of checking the setting, especially in the case of used points where metal transfer has taken place.

To check the contact points using a feeler gauge, turn the crankshaft until the contacts are fully open, i.e. until the breaker arm rubbing block is resting on the highest point of the cam lobe. This can be achieved by engaging third or top gear and pushing the car backwards, however it may be necessary to remove the spark plugs.

Check the contact gap by inserting a CLEAN 0.015 in (0.38 mm) feeler gauge between the contact points; the gauge should be a neat sliding fit in the gap.

NOTE: When measuring used contact points where a pip has formed on the face of one contact, the gap measurement should be made outside the formation to achieve a correct reading.

If adjustment is required, slacken the contact plate securing screw and adjust the position of the plate to alter the gap (Fig. B:5). This is achieved by inserting a screwdriver in the notched hole at the end of the contact plate. Turn the screwdriver clockwise to decrease the gap, or anti-clockwise to increase it. When the gap is correct, tighten the plate securing screw and recheck the gap.

To check the points setting with a dwell meter, connect the meter in accordance with the equipment manufacturer's instructions. Crank the engine at starter speed and note the reading indicated on the meter. The dwell angle should be 60°, with a tolerance of 3° either side.

If the reading is outside these limits, adjustment should be carried out as described above for setting the contact gap with a feeler gauge. If the dwell angle is greater than the upper limit, the points gap is too small and requires opening up, and if below the lower limit the gap should be decreased.

Points Replacement

Unscrew the nut from the terminal post and detach the flanged nylon bush together with the two electrical leads. Remove the contact plate securing screw with its spring and plain washers and lift the contact set from the breaker plate.

Before fitting the new contact set wipe the points clean with methylated spirits.

Apply a film of grease or petroleum jelly to the breaker cam. Check that the lower half of the nylon insulating bush is correctly positioned below the spring loop on the terminal post, then position the contact set on the breaker plate and lightly tighten the securing screw. Locate the two leads on the upper half of the insulating bush and fit the bush over the terminal post and into the spring loop. Fit the nut on the terminal post and tighten securely.

Lightly smear the pivot post with grease or petroleum jelly, but do not over-lubricate.

Set the points gap as described above. However, in this case the contact gap should be set to 0.016 in (0.40 mm) - or even 0.018 in (0.45 mm) - to allow for bedding-in of the breaker arm rubbing block.

Distributor Cap, HT Leads, etc.

Thoroughly clean the distributor cap inside and out with a clean cloth, paying particular attention to the space between the metal electrodes. Check that the electrodes are not excessively eroded (Fig. B:6) and that there are no signs of tracking (hairline tracks between contacts). Ensure that the small carbon brush in the centre of the cap is undamaged and moves freely in its holder.

Similarly, clean the rotor arm and check for damage or excessive erosion of the electrode. Also check that the arm is a neat fit on the distributor spindle without excessive play.

Clean the outside surface of the coil tower and check for signs of damage or tracking.

Wipe all grease and dirt from the HT leads and check all leads for signs of cracking, chafing, etc. Ensure that all connections at the spark plugs, ignition coil and distributor cap are secure and the moisture seals at each end of the HT leads are firmly in place.

IGNITION TIMING . . . . [7]

The contact breaker points gap must be correctly set before attempting to check or adjust the ignition timing. Conversely, the ignition timing should be checked after cleaning, resetting or renewing the contact set.

Checking (Figs. B:12 & B:13)

The ignition timing mark or scale is located on the engine front cover and is visible from the front of the engine. Clean the timing pointer(s) and the timing notch on the crankshaft pulley and mark the notch on the pulley with white paint to enable it to be seen more easily.

Remove the distributor cap. Rotate the crankshaft in its normal direction of rotation until the rotor arm is pointing approximately between the No. 2 and No. 1 segments in the distributor cap. The rotor arm rotation is anti-clockwise, viewed from above.

The crankshaft can be rotated by applying a suitable socket to the crankshaft pulley nut. As an alternative, this can be achieved by engaging top gear and pushing the car forwards.

The point at which the contact points open can be determined by observing the spark at the contacts, but a simple electrical test circuit will ensure greater accuracy. Connect a 12 volt test lamp between the distributor low tension terminal, or the corresponding terminal on the ignition coil, and a good earth. This is connected in parallel with the existing wiring.

With the ignition switched on, the test lamp should now be lit. Rotate the crankshaft slowly until the test lamp just goes out. The rotor arm should be pressed gently in the opposite direction to its normal rotation to take up any free play while doing this. If the ignition timing is correct, the notch on the crankshaft will be aligned with the appropriate pointer on the timing scale (3⁰ BTDC for 1098 cc engine). The 948 cc crankshaft pulley timing mark is at TDC, although the timing should be set at 4⁰ BTDC, or 5⁰ BTDC for High Compression engines. The 4⁰ mark can be calculated by making a mark 0.1875 in (4.76 mm) to the left of the pulley notch.

If the timing is incorrect, turn the knurled nut on the side of the distributor body (Fig. B:7). One graduation on the vernier scale represents approximately 5⁰ of timing movement and is equal to fifty-five clicks of the adjuster nut. Turn the adjuster nut towards the 'A' cast on the distributor body if the timing notch is after the timing pointer, or towards the 'R' if the mark is before the pointer.

If a large correction is required, turn the knurled nut until the vernier scale is in the central position. Turn the crankshaft until the notch is aligned with the mark on the timing scale. Slacken the distributor clamp bolt and rotate the distributor body anti-clockwise past the point where the test lamp illuminates, then carefully rotate it clockwise until the lamp just goes out. Tighten the clamp bolt without disturbing the body setting, then recheck the setting as described above.

AIR CLEANER. . . . . [8]

Oil Bath Type (Fig. B:14 & B:15)

An oil bath air cleaner is fitted to all earlier models. The cleaner should be cleaned and filled with new oil at the specified intervals, or more frequently if inspection shows this to be necessary.

Wash the filter element in a bowl of paraffin and allow it to drain and dry thoroughly.

Lift out the oil container, empty the oil, and scrape out the accumulated sludge. Wash the entire oil container in paraffin and fill to the level with engine oil. It is not necessary to oil the filter element; it is done automatically when the engine starts up.

Dry Type Air Cleaner

Two types of dry air cleaner were fitted to the later Morris 1000 models, both similar in construction.

To remove the element, unscrew the wing nut from the top of the cleaner (Fig. B:8), remove the body, and extract the element. Collect the base and rubber washer, remove the screws securing the air cleaner tie-rod casting to the carburettor body, and lift away the tie-rod casting and joint washer. Reverse the removal procedure to refit the cleaner.

NOTE: The air cleaner intake should be positioned adjacent to the exhaust manifold during winter operating conditions in order that the possibility of carburettor icing is reduced to the minimum. It is advisable to move the intake away from the manifold in warmer weather.

FUEL PUMP. . . . . [9]

Cleaning the Filter

The SU electric fuel pump is situated on the wing valance inside the engine compartment and incorporates

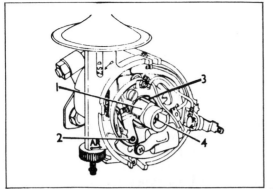

1. Cam
2. Contact breaker pivot
3. Automatic advance weights
4. Cam spindle screw

Fig. B:4 Distributor lubrication

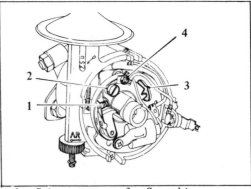

1. Points gap
2. Securing screw
3. Screwdriver cutout
4. Spring securing nut

Fig. B:5 Contact breaker assembly

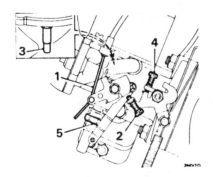

Fig. B:6 Inside view of distributor cap showing contacts

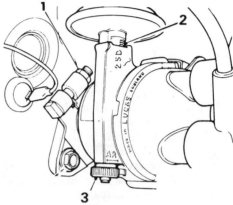

1. Clamp bolt nut   2. Vernier scale   3. Knurled adjuster nut

Fig. B:7 Ignition timing adjustment

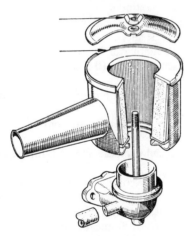

Fig. B:8 The early type dry air cleaner

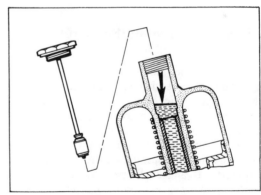

Fig. B:9 Piston damper oil level

1. Choke cable
2. Fast idle screw
3. Piston lifting pin
4. Throttle adjusting screw
5. Mixture adjusting nut

Fig. B:10 Carburettor idle adjustment

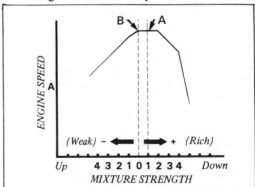

Fig. B:11 Mixture setting graph

a filter at the pump inlet nozzle.

To remove the filter, remove the two screws securing the clamp plate to the pump body. Detach the inlet nozzle and remove the filter.

Wash the filter in petrol to remove any dirt, fluff, etc. Examine the inlet nozzle for any signs of dirt and wash if necessary.

Refit the filter screen and nozzle, ensuring that the sealing ring is correctly positioned. Secure the nozzles in position. Switch on the ignition and check for fuel leaks at the pump. On early models, a filter is incorporated in the float chamber assembly (Fig. B:16).

CARBURETTOR . . . . [10]

Damper Oil Level (Fig. B:9)

The oil level in the carburettor damper reservoir must be maintained approximately 0.5 in (13 mm) above the top of the hollow piston rod.

To check the level, unscrew the damper cap from the top of the suction chamber and withdraw the cap and damper. Top up if necessary with light oil (preferably SAE 20 grade). Push the damper assembly back into position and screw the cap firmly into place.

Failure to maintain the oil at the correct level will cause the piston to flutter and reduce acceleration.

Slow Running Adjustment (Fig. B:10)

Before attempting to adjust the carburettor slow-running setting, ensure that all other items relevant to good engine performance are in good condition and/or correctly adjusted (e.g. contact breaker points, ignition timing, spark plugs, valve clearances, etc.). Also check the air cleaner to ensure that the element is clean, and check that the throttle operation is free and unrestricted.

Carburettor tuning should be confined to setting the idling and fast idling speeds and the mixture at idle speed. A reliable tachometer should be used if possible. To tune the carburettor, proceed as follows:-

1. Check the oil level in the piston damper, as detailed above, and top up if necessary.
2. Check that the throttle moves freely without signs of sticking and returns fully when released.
3. Check that the mixture control returns fully when the choke cable is pushed fully home. Also check that the cable has about 1/16 in (2 mm) free-play before it starts to pull on the lever.
4. Check that a small clearance exists between the end of the fast idle screw and the fast idle cam.
5. Raise the carburettor piston and check that it falls freely on to the carburettor bridge with a distinct metallic click when released. The piston can be raised for this purpose either with the piston lifting pin at the side of the

carburettor, or directly with a finger at the air intake. In this latter case the air cleaner must first be removed to gain access. If the piston fails to fall freely, the jet must be centred as detailed in the Fuel System section.
6. Connect a suitable tachometer to the engine if available.
7. Start the engine and run it at fast idle until it has attained its normal running temperature. Continue to run it for a further five minutes.
8. Temporarily increase the engine speed to approximately 2,500 rpm, and maintain this speed for about half a minute to clear the inlet manifold of excess fuel. Repeat this procedure at three minute intervals if the remainder of the adjustments cannot be completed within this period of time.
9. Check the idle speed and adjust if necessary by turning the throttle adjusting screw. The idle speed should be about 500 - 650 rpm. Refer to 'Tune-Up Data' at the end of the section for a list of the precise specified figures, if required.
10. Now adjust the idle mixture by turning the jet adjusting nut one flat at a time, up or down, until the fastest idle speed consistent with smooth running is achieved (Point A on graph in Fig. B:11). Turning the nut up will weaken the mixture, and down will enrich it. Now turn the nut up slowly (weakening) until the engine speed just starts to fall (Point B on graph). This should give the weakest position for maximum speed.
11. Recheck the idle speed and adjust if necessary to obtain the specified idle speed.
12. The mixture strength can be checked by lifting the piston approximately 1/32 in (0.8 mm) with the lifting pin.
a) If the engine speed momentarily increases very slightly, the mixture is correct.
b) If the engine speed increases, and continues to do so, the mixture is too rich.
c) If the engine speed decreases, the mixture strength is too weak.
13. When the mixture is correct, the exhaust note should be regular and even. If it is irregular, with a splashy type of misfire and colourless exhaust, the mixture is too weak. If there is a regular or rhythmical type of misfire in the exhaust beat, together with a blackish exhaust, then the mixture is too rich.
14. To check the fast idle speed, pull out the choke knob until the linkage is just about to move the mixture jet and lock the knob in this position. The fast idle speed should be about 750 - 900 rpm. Again refer to 'Tune-Up Data' for the precise specified figures, if required. If adjustment is necessary, turn the fast idle screw until the correct fast idle speed is obtained. Push the choke knob fully in and check that a clearance exists between the end of the fast idle screw and the fast idle cam.

NOTE: When adjustment has been made, it is advisable to be sure the choke cable is correctly positioned. With the choke control in, the carburettor end of the cable should be tight, but not interfering with the position of the jet assembly (Fig. B:17).

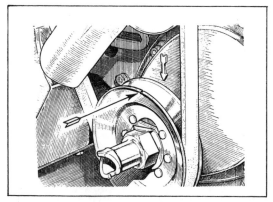

Fig. B:12 Timing mark arrangement on early models

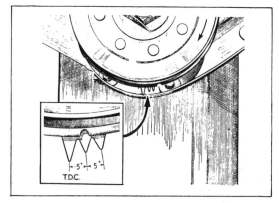

Fig. B:13 Later timing mark arrangement

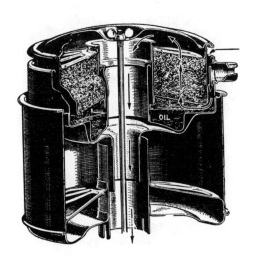

Fig. B:14 Early type oil bath air cleaner

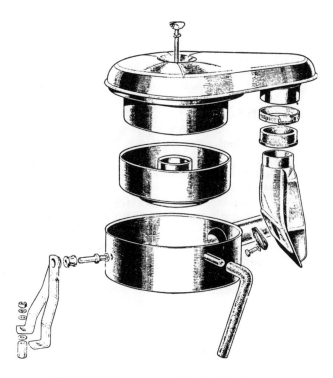

Fig. B:15 Late type oil bath air cleaner

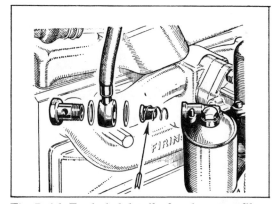

Fig. B:16 Exploded detail of carburettor filter

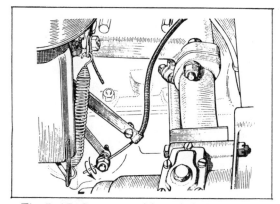

Fig. B:17 Correct position of choke cable

Tune-up Data

ENGINE

Compression ratio
948 cc APJM 8.3:1
948 cc 9M 7.2:1
1098 cc, 10MA, 10ME or 10V . . . . 8.5:1 or 7.5:1

Compression pressure
1098 cc HC . . . . 160 lb/in^2 (11.25 kg/cm^2)
1098 cc LC . . . . 130 lb/in^2 (9.14 kg/cm^2)
Firing order . . . . 1 - 3 - 4 - 2
Valve clearances
Inlet . . . . 0.012 in (0.3 mm) cold
Exhaust . . . . 0.012 in (0.3 mm) cold

IGNITION

Spark plugs . . . . Champion N5
Plug gap . . . . 0.024-0.026 in (0.625-0.660 mm)
Distributor contact gap . . . . 0.014-0.016 in (0.35-0.40 mm)
Dwell angle
Distributor type Lucas 25D4 . . . . 60° ± 3°
Distributor rotation (viewed from above) . . . . Anti-clockwise
Static timing
948 cc HC . . . . 5° BTDC
948 cc LC . . . . 4° BTDC
1098 cc . . . . 3° BTDC
Timing marks . . . . Pointers on timing cover, notch on
crankshaft pulley

CARBURETTOR

Type . . . . SU H2 or SU HS2
Idling speed . . . . 500 rpm

NON-START
Trouble Shooter

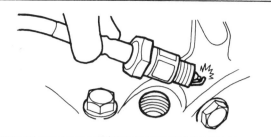

FAULT	CAUSE	CURE
Starter will not turn engine (headlights dim)	1. Battery low 2. Faulty battery 3. Corroded battery cables or loose connections 4. Starter jammed 5. Seized engine	1. Charge battery and check charging system. 2. Fit new battery. 3. Clean battery connections or replace battery leads. Tighten battery and starter-motor connections. 4. Free starter. 5. Remove spark-plugs to confirm.
Starter will not turn engine (headlights bright)	1. Faulty starter solenoid 2. Faulty starter engagement (starter-motor whine) 3. Faulty starter 4. Faulty ignition switch	1. Replace solenoid. 2. Clean or replace starter bendix. 3. Repair or replace starter motor. 4. Fit new switch.
Engine turns slowly but will not start	1. Battery low 2. Faulty battery 3. Corroded battery leads or loose connections 4. Faulty starter	1. Charge battery and check charging system. 2. Replace battery. 3. Clean battery connections or replace battery leads. Tighten connections. 4. Repair or replace starter motor.
Engine turns but will not fire	1. Ignition fault 2. No spark at plug lead 3. Spark at plug lead 4. Fuel reaching carburettor 5. No fuel to carburettor 6. Car with electric fuel pump 7. Car with mechanical pump	1. Check for spark at plug lead. 2. Check coil output to confirm high or low-tension fault. If spark from coil, check HT leads, distributor cap and rotor arm, particularly for cracks, tracking or dampness. If no spark from coil, check ignition-coil connections and contact-breaker points for short circuits or disconnection. 3. Remove air cleaner from carburettor and check choke operation. Loosen petrol-pipe union at carburettor. Turn engine by starter for a mechanical pump, or switch on ignition for electric pump. Check if petrol is being delivered. 4. Look into carburettor mouth. Operate throttle and observe whether damp or dry. If dry, clean jets and needle valve. If damp, remove spark-plugs, dry, clean and check gaps. 5. Remove petrol-tank cap and check for fuel. 6. Check pump has a good earth and give pump a sharp tap. If it starts pumping, which will be heard, replace pump. If not fuel lines may be blocked. 7. Remove pump-top cover, clean pump filter and make sure the cover, when refitted, is airtight. Check flexible pipe to pump for air leaks.
Engine backfires	1. Ignition timing faulty 2. Damp distributor cap and leads	1. Check and reset ignition timing. 2. Dry thoroughly and check firing order.

Engine

VALVE CLEARANCES . . . . [1]

The valve rocker clearances should be checked with the engine cold. Disconnect the engine breather hose between the rocker cover and air cleaner. Unscrew the two sleeve nuts securing the rocker cover and remove the nuts together with their cup washers and seals. Lift off the rocker cover, taking care not to damage the cork gasket, otherwise it will have to be renewed.

It will facilitate turning over the engine if the spark plugs are removed at this point.

The crankshaft can be rotated using a suitable size of socket on the crankshaft pulley nut. Alternatively, this can be achieved by engaging third or top gear and pushing the car forwards.

Check the clearance between each valve stem and its respective rocker arm with a 0.012 in (0.3 mm) feeler gauge, when the valve is in the fully closed position. The gauge should be a neat sliding fit. Check the clearances in the following order:-

Check No. 1 valve with No. 8 fully open
Check No. 3 valve with No. 6 fully open
Check No. 5 valve with No. 4 fully open
Check No. 2 valve with No. 7 fully open
Check No. 8 valve with No. 1 fully open
Check No. 6 valve with No. 3 fully open
Check No. 4 valve with No. 5 fully open
Check No. 7 valve with No. 2 fully open

If adjustment is necessary, slacken the adjusting screw locknut with a ring spanner and turn the adjusting screw until the correct gap is obtained (Fig. C:1). Turn the screw clockwise to reduce the clearance, or anti-clockwise to increase it. Retighten the locknut while holding the adjusting screw with the screwdriver to stop it turning, then recheck the gap.

When adjustment is complete, refit the rocker cover, using a new cork gasket if necessary. In this case, ensure that all traces of old gasket are removed from the cover and cylinder head mating faces. Tighten the two retaining nuts evenly. Refit the spark plugs.

CYLINDER HEAD . . . . [2]

Removal

1. Raise the bonnet and remove the split pin and clevis pin securing the bonnet prop to the bonnet lid and secure the bonnet open.
2. Disconnect the battery leads.
3. Drain the cooling system with the drain tap on the radiator base.
4. Remove the air cleaners. Disconnect the throttle and mixture (choke) control cables, the distributor vacuum pipe, and the fuel hose from the carburettor.
5. Remove the nuts and spring washers securing the carburettor to the inlet manifold studs, and lift off the carburettor assembly.
6. Disconnect the radiator top hose from the thermostat housing. Disconnect the heater hose from the rear end of the heater water pipe at the inlet manifold and the radiator bottom hose from the front end of the pipe. Disconnect the heater inlet hose from the hot water control valve at the rear of the cylinder head.
7. Slacken the top clip on the small by-pass hose between the cylinder head and the water pump.
8. Remove the distributor vacuum pipe clip from its fixture on the hot water control valve.
9. Disconnect the exhaust down pipe from the exhaust manifold.
10. Remove the inlet and exhaust manifold from the cylinder head. The heater water pipe is also secured by two of the manifold nuts.
11. Disconnect the HT leads from the spark plugs and remove the spark plugs.
12. Remove the rocker cover.
13. Slacken the rocker shaft bracket securing nuts and the external cylinder head nuts evenly, a turn at a time, in the order shown in Fig. C:2. Remove the nuts and lift off the rocker assembly together with its brackets. Withdraw the pushrods, keeping them in their installed order, to ensure replacement in their original positions.

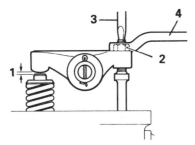

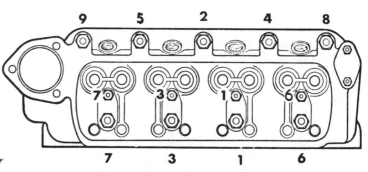

1. 0.012 in (0.3 mm) clearance - cold   3. Screwdriver
2. Adjusting screw and locknut   4. Ring spanner

Fig. C:1 Adjusting valve rocker clearances

Fig. C:2 Cylinder head nut loosening and tightening sequence

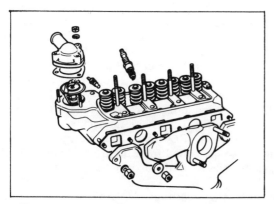

Fig. C:3 Details of cylinder head assembly

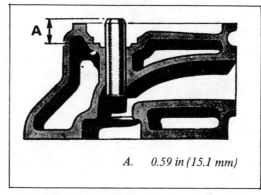

1. Early type with cotter clip
2. Later type

Fig. C:4 Valve assembly

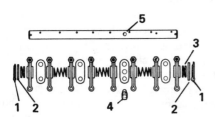

1. Split pins   4. Shaft locating screw
2. Plain washers   5. Screw locating hole
3. Double coil spring washers

Fig. C:5 Dismantling and reassembly sequence of rocker shaft

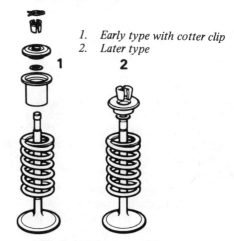

A.   0.59 in (15.1 mm)

Fig. C:6 Valve guide installed in position

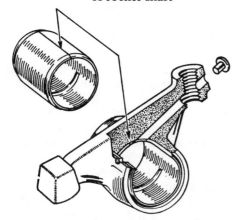

Fig. C:7 Forged type rocker arm with replaceable bush

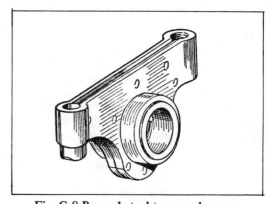

Fig. C:8 Pressed-steel type rocker arm

14. Lift off the cylinder head. It may be necessary to tap each side of the head gently with a hide-faced hammer to break the joint. Lift the head squarely to prevent the studs binding in their holes. Remove the cylinder head gasket.

Installation

Installation is a reversal of the removal procedure, with special attention to the following points.
a) Ensure that all joint surfaces, especially the mating surfaces of the cylinder head and block, are perfectly clean and free from old gasket material.
b) If the cylinder head was removed to replace a leaking or blown head gasket, check the mating faces on both the head and block for distortion before reassembly.
c) Use new gaskets where appropriate. A cylinder head gasket set should be obtained, as this will contain all the necessary gaskets.
d) Do not use grease or jointing compound of any type on the cylinder head gasket when fitting.
e) Ensure the head gasket is correctly positioned. The gasket is normally marked 'TOP' and 'FRONT'.
f) Ensure that the push rods are installed in their original positions. Dip the ends of the rods in clean engine oil prior to installing them.
g) When fitting the rocker shaft assembly, ensure that the rocker arm adjusting screws locate correctly in the cupped end of their respective push rods. If any work has been carried out on the valves (e.g. recutting the valve seats) the rocker arm adjusting screws should be released slightly before installing the rocker shaft assembly. Lubricate the rocker assembly with clean engine oil.
h) Tighten the cylinder head and rocker shaft pedestal nuts evenly, following the sequence shown in Fig. C:2. The cylinder head nuts and the rocker pedestal nuts must be tightened to the specified Torques. See Tightening Torques at the end of the book.
i) Check the valve clearances, as described previously, and adjust if necessary.
j) When installation is complete, refill the cooling system, then run the engine and check for oil, water or exhaust leaks.
k) Finally, with the engine at normal operating temperature, check the ignition timing and engine idle settings as detailed in the Tune-up section at the beginning of this manual.

Dismantling

1. Unscrew the spark plugs from the cylinder head.
2. Remove the inlet and exhaust manifolds.
3. Remove the water outlet housing and remove the thermostat cover from the recess in the head (Fig. C:3).
4. Remove all carbon deposits from the combustion chambers, valve heads and valve ports using a suitable scraper, such as a screwdriver, and a wire brush. Take care to avoid damaging the machine surface of the cylinder head.
5. Similarly, clean all deposits from the cylinder block face and piston crowns, but leave a ring of carbon around the outside of each piston and the top of each bore. Ensure that carbon particles are not allowed to enter the oil or water ways in the block. This can be prevented by plugging the passages with small pieces of cloth while the carbon is being removed.
6. At each valve in turn, remove the spring clip from the collets (early models only). Compress the valve spring, using a suitable spring compressor tool, and extract the two split tapered collets from around the valve stem. Take care to ensure the valve stem is not damaged by the spring retainer when pressing it down. Release the compressor tool and remove the spring retainer, shroud (early models only) and valve spring (Fig. C:4). Remove the rubber oil seal (where fitted) from the valve stem and withdraw the valve from the cylinder head. Suitably mark the valve and associated components to identify their position in the cylinder head.
7. To dismantle the rocker assembly, remove the shaft locating screw from the No. 2 rocker shaft bracket. Remove the split pins from each end of the rocker shaft, and slide the washers, springs, rocker arms and support brackets of the shaft (Fig. C:5). Note the relative position of the components for reassembly. If necessary, the blanking plug can be unscrewed from the front end of the shaft to enable the oilways of the shaft to be cleaned out.

Inspection & Overhaul - Valves

Clean the valves and seatings and examine them for signs of pitting, burning or other damage.

A simple method of removing carbon from the valves is to insert the valve stem in the chuck of an electric drill and, using as slow a speed as possible, scrape the deposits off with a file or screwdriver. The valve can then be finished off with emery cloth.

Inspect the valve face and edges for pits, grooves, scores, or other damage. Valves in reasonable condition may be resurfaced on a valve grinding machine, but only sufficient metal to true up the face should be removed. If the thickness of the valve head is reduced to 0.020 in (0.5 mm) or less after grinding, then the valve should be discarded as it will run too hot in use.

Examine the valve stem for excessive or abnormal wear, and renew the valve if necessary.

If the valves are in poor condition, they should be renewed.

Valve Guides

Check the stem to guide clearance of each valve in turn in its respective guide. Raise the valve slightly from its seat and rock the head from side to side. If the movement across the seat is excessive, this indicates a worn guide and/or valve stem. Repeat the check using a new valve. If the movement is still excessive, the guide is worn and should be renewed.

Remove the old guide by drifting it downwards into the combustion chamber (Fig. C:6). Ensure the bore in the cylinder head is clean, then drive the new guide into position in the head so that its top end protrudes 0.594 in

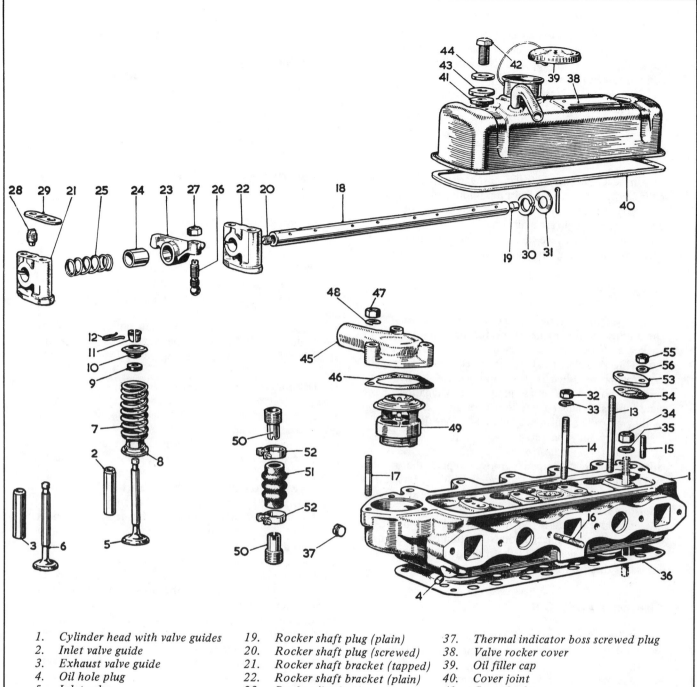

1. Cylinder head with valve guides
2. Inlet valve guide
3. Exhaust valve guide
4. Oil hole plug
5. Inlet valve
6. Exhaust valve
7. Outer valve spring
8. Shroud for valve guide
9. Valve packing ring
10. Valve spring cup
11. Valve cotter
12. Valve cotter circlip
13. Rocker bracket stud (long)
14. Rocker bracket stud (short)
15. Cover-plate stud
16. Manifold stud
17. Water outlet elbow stud
18. Valve rocker shaft (plugged)

19. Rocker shaft plug (plain)
20. Rocker shaft plug (screwed)
21. Rocker shaft bracket (tapped)
22. Rocker shaft bracket (plain)
23. Rocker (bushed)
24. Rocker bush
25. Rocker spacing spring
26. Tappet adjusting screw
27. Locknut
28. Rocker shaft locating screw
29. Rocker shaft bracket plate
30. Spring washer
31. Washer
32. Nut
33. Spring washer
34. Cylinder head nut
35. Washer
36. Cylinder head gasket

37. Thermal indicator boss screwed plug
38. Valve rocker cover
39. Oil filler cap
40. Cover joint
41. Cover bush
42. Nut
43. Distance piece
44. Cup washer
45. Water outlet elbow
46. Joint
47. Nut
48. Spring washer
49. Thermostat
50. By-pass adaptor
51. By-pass connector (rubber)
52. By-pass clip
52. Cover plate
54. Joint (plate to cylinder head)
55. Cover nut
56. Spring washer

Fig. C:9 Details of cylinder head assembly

© BLUK

Engine

(15.09 mm) above the machined face of the valve spring seating. The inlet valve guide must be fitted with the largest chamfer at the top, and the exhaust guide with the counterbore at the bottom.

NOTE: The valve seats should be recut after fitting new valve guides to ensure the seat is concentric with the guide bore.

Valve Seats

Inspect the seating surface on each valve seat in the cylinder head for signs of pitting, burning or wear. Where necessary, the seat can be recut as long as the seat width and correction angle are maintained.

The seating surface must be recut when fitting a new valve, or after fitting new valve guides.

Rocker Gear

Inspect the bearing surface on the rocker shaft and the bushes in the rocker arms for wear. Two types of rocker arm are used; a pressed-steel type and a forged type (Fig. C:7 and C:8). If the latter type is fitted, the arm can be rebushed if worn, but the pressed-steel type must be renewed as an assembly. The installation of the new bushes should be left to a Specialist Machine Shop as they must be burnish-reamed to size after fitting.

Inspect the contact pad at the valve end of each rocker arm for indications of scuffing or excessive or abnormal wear. If the pad is grooved, replace the arm. Do NOT attempt to true the surface by grinding. Check that all oil passages are clear. Replace any damaged or worn adjusting screws or locknuts.

Inspect each push rod for straightness. If bent, the push rod must be replaced - do NOT attempt to straighten it. Also inspect the ends of the rods for nicks, grooves or signs of excessive wear.

Reassembly (Fig. C:9)

Reassemble the cylinder head in the reverse order of dismantling, with special attention to the following points:-

a) Assemble the rocker shaft assembly in the reverse order of dismantling. The plugged end of the shaft must be located at the front of the engine. Ensure that the double coil spring washers are fitted at either end of the rocker shaft (Fig. C:5).

b) Lap in each valve in turn using coarse, followed by fine grinding paste until a gas-tight seal is obtained at the seat. This will be indicated by a continuous matt-grey ring around the valve face and seat. When this has been achieved, clean all traces of paste from the cylinder head and valves - this is most important.

c) Lubricate the valve guides and valves with clean engine oil before installing the valves.

d) Fit new valve stem oil seals over the valve stem and on to the valve guide, where applicable. Lubricate the seal with oil to make fitting easier. On early models with the valve spring shroud and collet spring, the oil seal is located

on the valve stem at the bottom of the collet groove.

e) Ensure that the valve stem is not damaged by the spring retainer when compressing the valve spring, and that the split tapered collets engage correctly in the valve stem and spring retainer when the spring is released. Refit the spring clip to the collet, where applicable.

f) Use new gaskets when refitting the manifolds and water outlet housing.

TIMING COVER OIL SEAL . . . . [3]

Replacement

1. Drain the cooling system and remove the radiator as detailed in the Cooling System section.
2. Slacken the dynamo mounting bolts and remove the fan belt.
3. Knock back the lock washer tab on the crankshaft starter dog bolt and unscrew the dog using a suitable size of socket. Carefully lever the dog pulley from the crankshaft.
4. Disconnect the crankcase breather pipe from the oil separator (where fitted).
5. Remove the bolts securing the timing cover to the engine front plate and detach the cover.
6. Inspect the oil seal for signs of wear or damage; if either of these conditions is present, the seal should be replaced.
7. Press or lever the old oil seal from the timing cover. Ensure that the bore is clean and free from burrs.
8. Lubricate the new oil seal with engine oil and press it into position in the cover bore. The lips of the seal must face into the timing cover.
9. Clean all old gasket material from the timing cover and front plate mating faces.
10. Position a new gasket on the engine front plate, using grease to retain it in position.
11. Ensure that the oil thrower is in place on the crankshaft in front of the timing sprocket, with the face marked 'F' or the concave side (early type) facing outwards.
12. Fill the groove between the lips of the seal with grease. Lubricate the seal contact surface on the crankshaft pulley and insert the pulley hub into the seal, turning the pulley clockwise to avoid damaging the lip of the seal.
13. Fit the timing cover and pulley together to ensure the seal is correctly centralised. Align the pulley with the key in the crankshaft, then push the cover and pulley into position.
14. Fit the cover retaining bolts and tighten them evenly.
15. Fit the bolt with a new lock washer. Tighten the bolt to 70 lb.ft (9.6 kgm), then secure with the lock washer tab.
16. Refit the fan belt and adjust the tension so that a deflection of approximately 0.5 in (13 mm) is possible at at point midway along the longest run, then tighten the dynamo mounting bolts securely.
17. Refit the radiator and refill the cooling system as detailed in the Cooling chapter.

Fig. C:10 Timing gear alignment marks

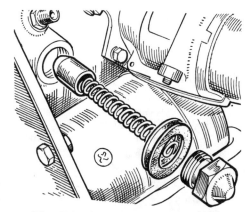

Fig. C:11 Oil pressure relief valve

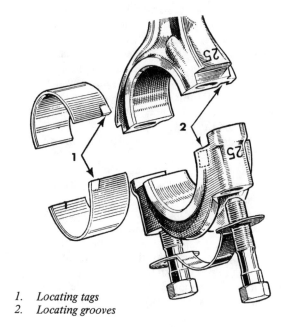

1. Locating tags
2. Locating grooves

Fig. C:12 Component parts of the big ends

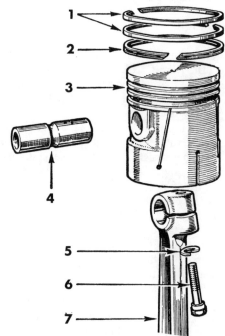

1. Piston rings (compression)   4. Gudgeon pin
2. Piston ring (oil return)   5. Spring washer
3. Piston   6. Clamp screw
                                 7. Connecting rod

Fig. C:13 Component parts of the piston and
connecting rod small end

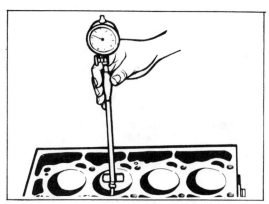

Fig. C:14 Measuring cylinder bores with
internal micrometer

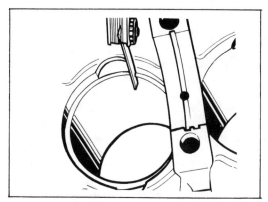

Fig. C:15 Checking piston ring end gap
with ring positioned squarely in bore

TIMING CHAIN & GEARS. . . . . [4]

Removal

1. Remove the timing cover as detailed above.
2. Remove the oil thrower from the crankshaft.
3. Release the lockwasher tab and remove the camshaft gear retaining nut and lockwasher.
4. Rotate the crankshaft until the two timing marks on the gears are opposite each other (Fig. C:10).
5. Remove both the camshaft and crankshaft sprockets together with the timing chain, by easing each gear wheel forward a fraction at a time with suitable small levers or two screwdrivers.
6. Retain the packing shims fitted immediately behind the crankshaft sprocket.

Installation

7. Rotate the crankshaft if necessary so that its keyway is at TDC (Fig. C:10). Similarly, rotate the camshaft if necessary so that its keyway is in the two o'clock position.
8. Fit the crankshaft and camshaft sprockets without the timing chain.
9. Check the alignment of the gears by placing a straight-edge across the teeth of both gears and measuring the gap between the straight edge and the crankshaft sprocket with feeler gauges.

Adjust if necessary by altering the thickness of the shim pack behind the crankshaft sprocket. The driving key in the crankshaft will have to be removed before the shim pack can be withdrawn. Refit the key once the correct shim thickness has been determined.

10. Remove both sprockets and assemble them in the timing chain with their alignment marks opposite each other (Fig. C:10).
11. Keeping the gears in this position, fit the sprocket on the crankshaft, then rotate the camshaft as necessary to align the key with the keyway in the sprocket. Push both gears as far on to the shafts as they will go and secure the camshaft sprocket with the nut and a new lock washer. Note that the locating tag on the lock washer fits into the keyway of the camshaft sprocket.
12. Refit the oil thrower, noting that the face marked 'F' or the concave side (early type) should face outwards.
13. Refit the timing cover as detailed previously.

OIL PRESSURE RELIEF VALVE . . . . [5]

The oil pressure relief valve prevents excessive oil pressure from building up when starting the engine from cold. The valve is non-adjustable and is located under the hexagon domed nut on the right-hand side of the cylinder block directly above the starter motor (Fig. C:11).

To examine the valve, unscrew the domed nut and washer(s), and withdraw the coil spring and valve plunger.

Check that the face of the valve is not badly pitted and that the valve is seating correctly. If the valve is only lightly pitted, lap the valve on to its seating using metal polish. Service Tool 18G 69 is useful for this purpose, as this is a mandrel which fits neatly into the end of the valve, but it is not essential.

Check the length of the coil spring. Its free length should be 2.86 in (72.64 mm). Renew if it is worn or weak.

Refit the components of the valve in the reverse order of removal.

PISTONS & CONNECTING RODS. . . . . [6]

Removal

Remove the cylinder head as detailed under the appropriate heading previously.

Drain the engine oil into a suitable container. Remove the sump retaining screws together with their spring washers, and detach the sump.

For each piston and connecting rod in turn:-
a) Turn the crankshaft as necessary to bring the connecting rod to the bottom of its travel.
b) Inspect the top of the cylinder bore for any carbon formation or wear ridge and remove if present.
c) Check that both the connecting rod and cap are suitably marked with their respective cylinder number.
d) Tap back the lock washer tabs, unscrew the big end bolts two or three turns and tap them to release the big end bearing cap. Completely remove the bolts and locking plate and detach the bearing cap from the connecting rod. It should be noted that the big ends are split diagonally (Fig. C:12).
e) Push the piston and connecting rod assembly up the cylinder bore, and carefully withdraw the assembly from the top of the cylinder block.
f) Remove the bearing shells from the cap and rod. Identify the shells if they are to be re-used.
g) If required, the piston can be separated from the connecting rods by removing the retaining bolt from the small end of the rod and sliding out the piston pin. Once the bolt has been removed, it may be easier to immerse the piston in hot water, before sliding the pin out (Fig. C:13).

Inspection and Overhaul

Cylinder Bores

Inspect the cylinder walls for signs of scoring, scuffing or roughness. Inspect the top and bottom of the bore at the limit of piston travel for evidence of a ridge or step indicating bore wear.

If the bores look in reasonable condition, check them for wear using an accurate internal micrometer (Fig. C:14). Measure the diameter of each bore at three different levels with the gauge placed first in line with the crankshaft axis, then across it. The difference between the two measurements at the same level will give the out-of-round or ovality of the bore, and the difference between the measurements at the top and bottom of the bore in the same plane will give the bore taper.

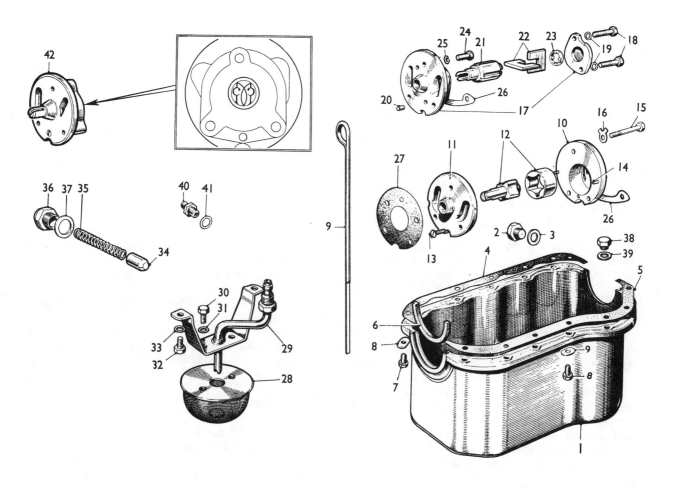

1.	Sump
2.	Sump drain plug
3.	Washer
4.	Sump to crankcase joint - RH
5.	Sump to crankcase joint - LH
6.	Main bearing cap oil seal
7.	Screw and captive washer
8.	Washer
9.	Dipstick
10.	Oil pump body
11.	Cover (plain hole)
12.	Driving shaft with inner and outer rotors
13.	Cover to body screws
14.	Dowel
17.	Body and cover assembly
18.	Screw
19.	Shakeproof washer
20.	Dowel
21.	Rotor
22.	Vane
23.	Sleeve
24.	Pump to crankcase screw
25.	Spring washer
26.	Lock plate (for all pumps)
27.	Pump to crankcase joint
28.	Oil strainer
29.	Suction pipe with oil strainer bracket
30.	Screw
31.	Shakeproof washer
32.	Screw
33.	Shakeproof washer
34.	Oil relief valve
35.	Spring for oil relief valve
36.	Cap nut
37.	Washer
38.	Oil priming plug
39.	Washer (copper)
40.	Oil pressure union
41.	Washer (fibre)
42.	Pump assembly - Concentric type

Fig. C:16 Details of oil pump and sump

It may be possible to remove minor imperfections by honing, but cylinders which are deeply scored, stepped or excessively worn must be rebored to the next oversize.

Cylinders which are already over-bored to the maximum, or which cannot be rebored within the maximum specified limit may be restored by fitting liners. If liners have not previously been fitted, the cylinder block must be suitably machined to accept the liners.

Needless to say, both the boring and lining operations must be entrusted to a Specialist Engineering Firm who will have the necessary skill and equipment required to carry out work of this nature.

NOTE: All main bearing caps must be in position during the boring operation to avoid distortion of the main bearing bores; the main bearing caps should therefore be fitted when delivering the block for reboring or lining.

After any reboring, honing or de-glazing operation, the cylinder bores should be washed with soap or detergent and water, then rinsed thoroughly with clean water and wiped dry with a clean lint-free cloth. Finally, smear the bores with engine oil to prevent corrosion.

Pistons

If not already removed, remove the piston rings from each piston. The rings must always be removed or refitted over the crown of the piston - NEVER over the piston skirt.

Clean all deposits from the piston surfaces. Carbon deposits can be scraped off, while gum and varnish can be cleaned off with solvent. Do NOT use caustic cleaning solution or a wire brush to clean the pistons.

Carbon deposits should be removed from the ring grooves. If a proper ring groove cleaner tool is not available, use a piece of old piston ring as a scraper. Take great care to avoid damaging the side of the groove, otherwise excessive side-play will result, with consequent loss of gas tightness and excessive fuel consumption. Ensure that the oil drain holes in the oil control grooves are clear.

Inspect each piston for cracks or fractures, or signs of scoring, scuffing or roughness indicating abnormal wear. Spongy, eroded areas near the edge of the piston crown are usually caused by detonation or pre-ignition. Inspect the piston grooves for high steps at the inner portion of the lower lands. Replace any piston which shows signs of wear or damage.

Piston Rings

It is recommended that new piston rings be fitted as a matter of course when overhauling the engine. Where new rings are being installed in a used cylinder, the glaze must first be removed from the cylinder walls. A proper glaze breaker tool should be used for this purpose, but in its absence fine emery cloth can be used instead. In this latter case ensure that all traces of abrasive are cleaned off the cylinder walls when the job is completed.

Check the end gap of each piston ring in its respective cylinder bore, using feeler gauges (Fig. C:15). Use the inverted piston to position the ring squarely in the bore. With worn bores, the ring should be located at the lower limit of travel of the piston rings, as this portion of the bore will be least worn. If the gap is outside the specified limits, try another ring set.

Check the side clearance of each ring in its respective piston groove with a feeler gauge inserted between the ring and the land of the groove (Fig. C:26). The gauge should slide freely around the entire circumference without binding.

Piston Pins

Inspect each piston pin for wear, fracture, or signs of etching. If any pin is worn or damaged, it must be renewed together with its respective piston. The piston pin must NOT be renewed independently.

Connecting Rods

Clean the connecting rods and bearing caps with petrol or other suitable solvent and dry thoroughly. Blow out the oil passages with compressed air.

Inspect the rods for signs of fracture, and the big end bearing bores for out-of-round or taper. Renew any rod which is unsatisfactory.

Inspect the small end bush for wear or damage. The bush cannot be renewed on its own, so if worn or damaged the complete connecting rod assembly must be renewed, together with its piston pin.

Big End Bearing Shells

Clean the bearing shells with petrol or other suitable solvent and dry thoroughly. Do NOT scrape gum or varnish from the shells.

Inspect the bearing surface of each shell carefully. Bearings which have worn, scored, chipped or pitted surfaces should be replaced. The bearing base may be visible, but this does not necessarily mean that the bearing is worn. It is not necessary to fit new bearing shells in this case unless the bearing clearance is outside the specified limits.

Check the clearance of bearings which appear satisfactory as described below.

Checking the Bearing Clearances

1. Ensure that the crankpin surface, bearing shells and bearing cap are perfectly clean and free from oil or dirt.
2. Fit the bearing shells into their locations in the connecting rod and cap, ensuring that the retaining tab on each shell correctly engages the corresponding notch in the housing. (Fig. C:12).
3. Place a piece of Plastigage across the full width of the crankpin and about 0.25 in (6 mm) off-centre.
4. Plastigage is available in three different diameters for the range between 0.001 and 0.009 in.

Type	Colour	Range
PG 1	Green	0.001-0.003 in (0.025-0.075 mm)
PR 1	Red	0.002-0.006 in (0.05-0.15 mm)
PB 1	Blue	0.004-0.009 in (0.10-0.23 mm)

In most cases the middle range RED pack will suffice.

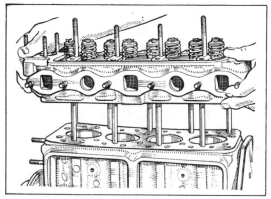

Fig. C:17 Replacing the cylinder head.

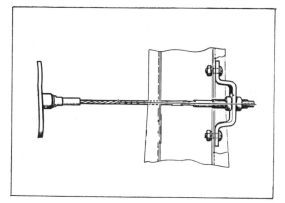

Fig. C:18 Early type engine steady cable

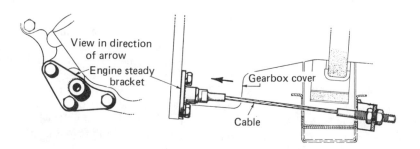

Fig. C:19 Later type engine steady cable

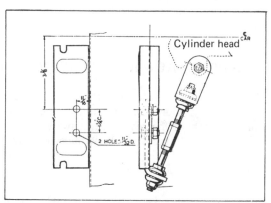

Fig. C:20 Engine tie rod and bracket assembly

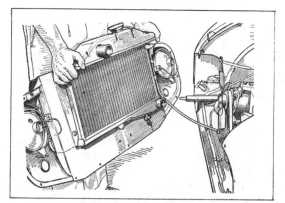

Fig. C:21 Removing radiator and grille

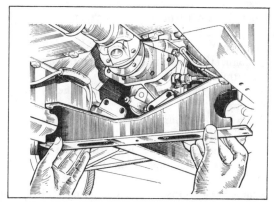

Fig. C:22 Removing body crossmember

Fig. C:23 Withdrawing the power unit

© BLUK

5. Assemble the connecting rod and cap on the crankpin and tighten the bearing cap bolts or nuts to their specified torque.

6. Release the bolt or nuts and remove the bearing cap. It should be noted that the connecting rod must not be moved on the crankpin while the Plastigage is in position.

7. Measure the width of the compressed Plastigage filament, using the scale provided on the Plastigage pack. The widest point will give the minimum clearance, and the narrowest point the maximum clearance. The difference between the two readings will therefore give the taper on the journal.

8. To check the journal for out-of-round, clean all traces of Plastigage material from the journal and bearing shells. Repeat the measuring procedure 90º further round on the journal. The difference between the two readings will indicate the out-of-round of the journal.

9. When measurement is completed, clean all Plastigage material off the bearing shell and crankpin.

Reassembly

NOTE: The connecting rod assemblies for No. 1 and 3 cylinders are identical and are interchangeable when new, as are those for No. 2 and 4 cylinders. However, when refitting used parts it is essential that they should be refitted in their original positions. The odd and even pairs of rods differ in that the big end bosses are offset to different sides of the assembly in relation to the rod centre-line; the odd pairs have the large offset to the rear, and the even pairs have it to the front (Fig. C:24).

For each piston and connecting rod in turn:-

a) Assemble the connecting rod to its piston with the 'FRONT' marking on the piston crown to the front, and the big end joint face biased towards the left-hand side of the assembly. Also check that the big end boss has the correct offset for the respective rod, as noted above. Apply a light coat of graphited oil to the piston pin and the bores in the piston and connecting rod. The pin should be a thumb push-fit at a room temperature of 20ºC (68ºF). Secure the pin by refitting the retaining bolt and spring washer through the small end of the connecting rod.

b) Fit the piston rings to the pistons, following the instructions supplied with the new rings. The rings must be fitted from the top of the piston. Fit the oil control ring in the lower groove first, followed by the lower, the middle and then the upper compression rings.

Service rings for use in worn bores normally have a stepped top ring to avoid the wear ridge at the top of the bore. It is obviously important that the ring is fitted with the stepped portion uppermost, otherwise breakage of the rings will result.

Where possible, proper piston ring pliers should be used to expand the rings when installing them as this will eliminate the possibility of ring breakage or damage to the piston.

Installation

For each piston and connecting rod in turn:-

a) Check that the piston is correctly assembled to its respective connecting rod.

b) Position the piston rings so that their gaps are set at approximately 90º to each other.

c) Lubricate the cylinder bore and piston rings liberally with engine oil.

d) Lubricate the piston pin with graphited oil.

e) Install the assembly in its correct respective bore, with the 'FRONT' marking on the piston crown towards the front of the engine.

f) Compress the piston rings using a proper piston ring compressor tool. Do not attempt to fit the pistons by hand, otherwise breakage of the rings may result. Push the piston into the cylinder bore using the handle end of a hammer until the piston crown is slightly below the top of the cylinder. Take great care to avoid hitting the crankshaft with the connecting rod.

g) Fit the bearing shells dry in the connecting rod and cap. Ensure that the retaining tab on each shell correctly engages the corresponding notch in the bearing housing.

h) Coat the crankshaft journal and bearing shells liberally with engine oil, then pull the connecting rod assembly down firmly on to the journal and fit the cap to the rod.

i) Check that the identification numbers on the rod and cap match and are on the same side of the assembly.

j) Fit the big end bolts with a new locking plate. Tighten the bolts to 35 lb.ft (4.8 kgm) and secure with the locking plate tabs.

Refit the sump, using a new joint gasket. Tighten the retaining screws securely, but do not overtighten them.

Refit cylinder head as detailed previously (Fig. C:17).

Finally, refill the sump with the specified grade of engine oil.

ENGINE REMOVAL & INSTALLATION . . . [7]

The engine can be removed with or without the gearbox on very early models. On later models, the engine has to come out without the gearbox. In any case, removing the engine without the gearbox follows the same procedure.

Removal Without Gearbox

1. Remove the clevis pin securing the bonnet prop to the bonnet lid and secure the bonnet in the open position. It may be easier to remove the bonnet completely.

2. Drain the oil from the engine.

3. Drain the water from the cooling system. If anti-freeze mixture is in use it should be drained into a clean container so that it may be used again.

4. Disconnect the battery by removing the lead from the positive terminal.

5. Release the flexible petrol pipe from the union on the petrol pump.

6. Remove the carburettor and air cleaner as described in the Fuel chapter.

7. Disconnect and remove the bottom and top radiator hoses, and the heater pipe connection at the radiator (if fitted).

8. Remove the four set bolts and spring washers which attach the radiator to the grille and lift out the radiator.

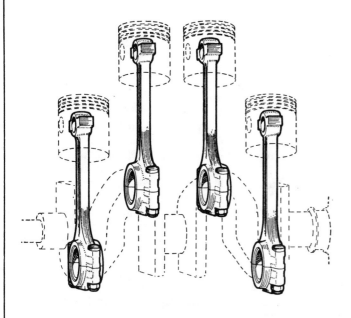

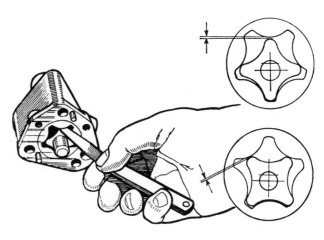

Fig. C: 24 Correct offsets for big ends on crankshaft

Fig. C: 25 Checking oil pump rotor clearances - Hobourn-Eaton pump

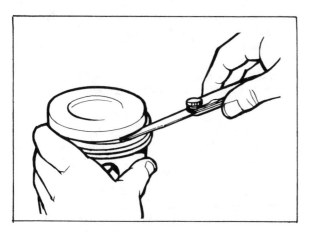

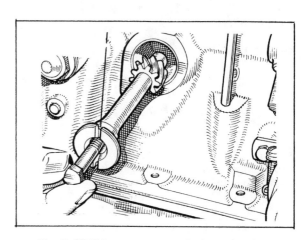

Fig. C: 26 Checking piston ring clearance in groove

Fig. C: 27 Using tappet cover bolt to withdraw distributor drive shaft

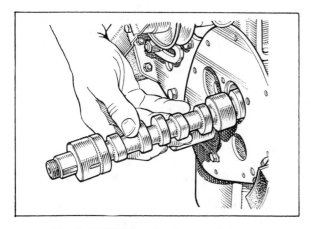

Fig. C: 28 Withdrawing the camshaft

Fig. C: 29 Withdrawing the crankshaft

©BLUK

9. Disconnect the heater pipe from the control valve (if fitted).

10. Slacken the two exhaust flange clamp bolts and disconnect the exhaust pipe.

11. Disconnect the dynamo and starter leads, and the low-tension lead from the distributor.

12. Remove the high-tension lead from the coil.

13. Disconnect the oil gauge pipe from the cylinder block.

14. Support the engine with suitable lifting tackle.

15. Remove the four nuts, bolts, and spring washers securing the left-hand front engine mounting bracket to the tie-plate.

16. Remove the two nuts and washers which secure each of the two front engine mounting brackets to the mounting rubbers.

17. Disconnect the clutch lever return spring from the rear engine mounting plate.

18. Support the front end of the gearbox by means of a suitable support.

19. Remove the set bolts and nuts and bolts which secure the gearbox to the engine, noting that two nuts and bolts also attach the starter.

20. Move the engine forward clear of the clutch and then lift it upwards, turning it at right angles to clear the radiator grille.

Installation

Installation is a reverse of the removal procedure.

Removal - With Gearbox

1. Remove the bonnet as described in the previous section.

2. Drain the oil from the engine and gearbox. Drain the water from the cooling system. If anti-freeze mixture is in use it should be drained into a clean container so that it may be used again.

3. Disconnect the battery by removing the lead from the positive terminal.

4. Release the flexible petrol pipe from the union of the petrol pump. Remove the carburettor and air cleaner as described in the Fuel chapter.

5. Slacken the two exhaust flange clamp bolts and disconnect the exhaust pipe.

6. Disconnect and remove the bottom and top radiator hoses. If the car is fitted with a heater disconnect the heater pipes from the radiator base tank and the control valve on the rear end of the cylinder head.

7. Disconnect the dynamo and starter leads and the low-tension lead from the distributor. Remove the high-tension lead from the coil.

8. On later models where the coil is mounted on the dynamo only disconnect the two low-tension wires to 'CB' and 'SW' on the coil.

9. Disconnect the oil gauge pipe from the cylinder block. Remove the front bumper assembly, which is secured to the frame by two nuts.

10. Release the radiator mask by removing the nuts, bolts, and washers securing the grille surround to the wings and frame. The plated surround each side of the radiator is secured by three 2 B.A. nuts, accessible beneath the wing.

11. Remove the split pin and spring washer from the bonnet catch-operating arm and disconnect the operating rod.

12. Disconnect the sidelamps from the snap connectors attached to the side valances.

13. Lift out the radiator and grille assembly (Fig. C:21).

14. Disconnect the clutch lever return spring from the rear engine mounting plate.

15. Disconnect the two operating rods from the clutch relay lever by removing the split pins and anti-rattle washers. Withdraw the operating rod from the clutch lever.

16. Disconnect the speedometer cable from the gearbox.

17. Take out the two set bolts and spring washers securing the relay lever bracket to the main frame. Remove the packing plate, bracket, and bushes. Take care not to lose the washer between the inner bush and the lever.

18. Remove the thrust spring from the opposite end of the lever.

19. Support the weight of the power unit with suitable lifting tackle. Remove the front carpet and felt and the gearbox cover-plate. Note that the two innermost screws on either side of the gearbox tunnel are longer than the rest and screw into the gearbox support member.

20. Take out the three set bolts and remove the gear lever assembly.

21. Remove the engine steady cable or bracket (Figs. C: 18, 19 or 20) by removing the locknut and adjusting nut at the bulkhead end of the cable.

22. Remove the nuts with spring and flat washers which secure the rear mounting rubbers to the crossmember.

23. Take out the four set bolts securing the crossmember to the frame, noting that the forward one on the left-hand side also secures the earthing cable.

24. Lower the rear of the power unit carefully until the crossmember can be removed (Fig. C:22).

25. Remove the four nuts, bolts, and spring washers which secure the front left-hand engine mounting bracket to the tie-plate.

26. Remove the nuts and washers which secure the front engine mounting rubbers to each side of the mounting plate.

27. Raise the power unit and remove the left-hand mounting bracket and rubber assembly.

28. Move the unit sideways to clear the right-hand mounting rubber studs, then raise the unit and manœuvre it forward clear of the car (Fig. C:23).

Installation

Installation is carried out in the reverse order. It should be noted, however, that when reconnecting the clutch-operating mechanism the longest end of the relay lever shaft carries the thrust spring as it is fitted into the spherical bush.

It will be found to be easier to re-engage the gearbox mainshaft splines with the propeller shaft if the car is rolled backwards as the power unit is offered into position. Do not fully tighten the engine mounting rubber bolts

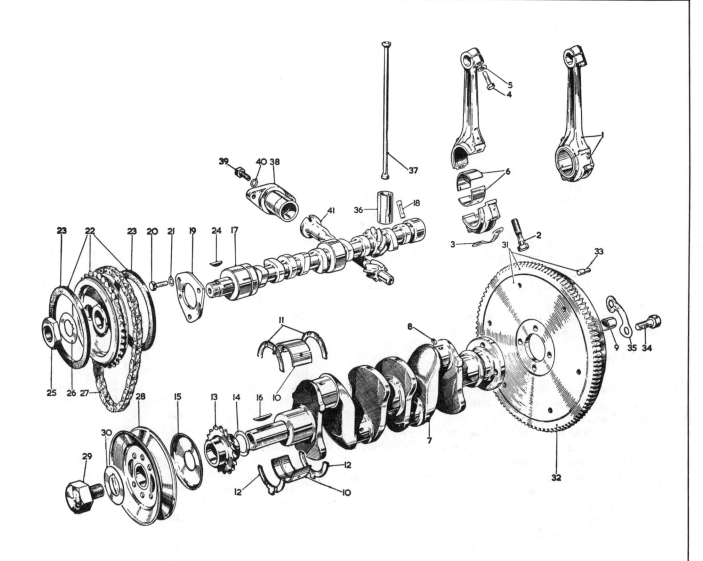

1.	Connecting rod cap	
2.	Cap bolt	
3.	Lock washer	
4.	Clamping screw	
5.	Spring washer	
6.	Big-end bearing	
7.	Crankshaft	
8.	Oil restrictor	
9.	First motion shaft bush	
10.	Main bearing	
11.	Upper thrust washer	
12.	Lower thrust washer	
13.	Crankshaft gear	
14.	Packing washer	

15.	Oil thrower
16.	Gear and crankshaft key
17.	Camshaft
18.	Oil pump driving pin
19.	Locking plate
20.	Screw
21.	Shakeproof washer
22.	Camshaft gear
23.	Tensioner ring
24.	Gear key
25.	Gear nut
26.	Lock washer
27.	Camshaft driving chain
28.	Crankshaft pulley

29.	Pulley retaining bolt
30.	Lock washer
31.	Flywheel
32.	Starter ring
33.	Dowel
34.	Screw
35.	Lock washer
36.	Tappet
37.	Pushrod
38.	Distributor housing
39.	Screw
40.	Shakeproof washer
41.	Distributor driving spindle

Fig. C:30 Details of engine internal components

until the mountings are supporting the full weight of the power unit.

FLYWHEEL . . . . [8]

Removal

The flywheel can be removed only after the engine has been removed from the car and has been separated from the gearbox.

Slacken the six clutch assembly retaining bolts evenly, working in diagonal sequence. Hold the pressure plate cover, remove the bolts and detach the pressure plate assembly and clutch disc from the flywheel. Note that two dowels locate the pressure plate cover on the flywheel.

Tap back the lock plate tabs and remove the flywheel retaining bolts. Gently tap the flywheel off the crankshaft flange.

If required, the engine rear plate may now be withdrawn after removing the retaining set screws.

Installation

If the engine rear plate was removed, it should be checked for distortion before refitting. Use a new joint gasket if necessary.

Ensure that the mating surfaces on the flywheel and crankshaft flange are perfectly clean and free from burrs. Locate the flywheel squarely on the crankshaft flange and tap it into place. Fit the retaining bolts with new locking plates and tighten to 40 lb.ft (5.5 kg m). Secure with the locking plate tabs.

Place the clutch disc in position on the flywheel. The flywheel side of the disc is appropriately marked near the centre. The long side of the hub must face away from the flywheel.

Centralise the clutch disc using a suitable clutch aligning tool, and locate the pressure plate assembly on the flywheel face. Fit the clutch assembly retaining bolts, and tighten them evenly. Remove the aligning tool.

OIL PUMP. . . . . [9]

Removal (Fig. C:16)

Remove the flywheel, clutch assembly and engine backplate as detailed above.

Release the lock washer tabs and remove the bolts securing the oil pump to the rear face of the cylinder block. Withdraw the pump together with its gasket. Note the position of the slot in the pump drive shaft in order to facilitate installation.

Installation

Clean all traces of old gasket material from the joint faces of the oil pump and cylinder block.

Install the pump in the reverse order of removal. Use a new gasket and lock washers. Ensure that the pump

intake and delivery ports are not obstructed by the gasket when fitting.

Overhaul

The oil pump may be of either Burman or Hobourn-Eaton manufacture. The latter type is serviced as a complete assembly only. Either type can be used on all engines.

Burman Type

Remove the cover retaining screws and detach the cover. Withdraw the rotor and vane assembly. Remove the retaining sleeve from the end of the rotor and extract the vanes.

Inspect the internal components for wear or damage. In most cases it will be more expedient to obtain a replacement pump rather than attempt to repair the existing unit by fitting new parts. Reassembly is a reversal of the dismantling procedure.

Hobourn-Eaton Type (Fig. C:25)

Remove the screw securing the cover to the pump body and detach the cover. Note that the cover is also located by two dowels on the pump body. Withdraw the rotors and pump shaft from the body.

Wash all parts in petrol and dry thoroughly. Visually inspect the rotors and interior of the pump body for signs of scoring, etc. If the pump appears satisfactory, refit the rotors in the pump body.

Using feeler gauges, measure the clearance between the lobes of the inner and outer rotor. If the clearance exceeds 0.006 in (0.15 mm), both rotors must be replaced.

Check the rotor endfloat by placing a straight-edge across the face of the pump body, and measuring the clearance between the underside of the straight-edge and the top face of the rotors (Fig. C:25). The clearance should not exceed 0.005 in (0.13 mm). If the endfloat is excessive, this may be remedied by carefully lapping the face of the pump body on a flat surface, after removing the two cover locating dowels.

Check the diametrical clearance between the outer rotor and the pump body. If the clearance exceeds 0.010 in (0.25 mm), the rotors, pump body, or the complete assembly must be renewed.

Reassemble the pump in the reverse order of dismantling, then check the pump for freedom of action. Fig. C: 32 shows how the Minor engine is lubricated.

CAMSHAFT AND CAM FOLLOWERS . . . . [10]

Removal

1. Remove the radiator as described in the Cooling chapter and take off the rocker assembly as described previously.
2. Remove the inlet and exhaust manifold assembly as described previously.
3. Lift the push-rods out of the engine, keeping them in order for correct reassembly.

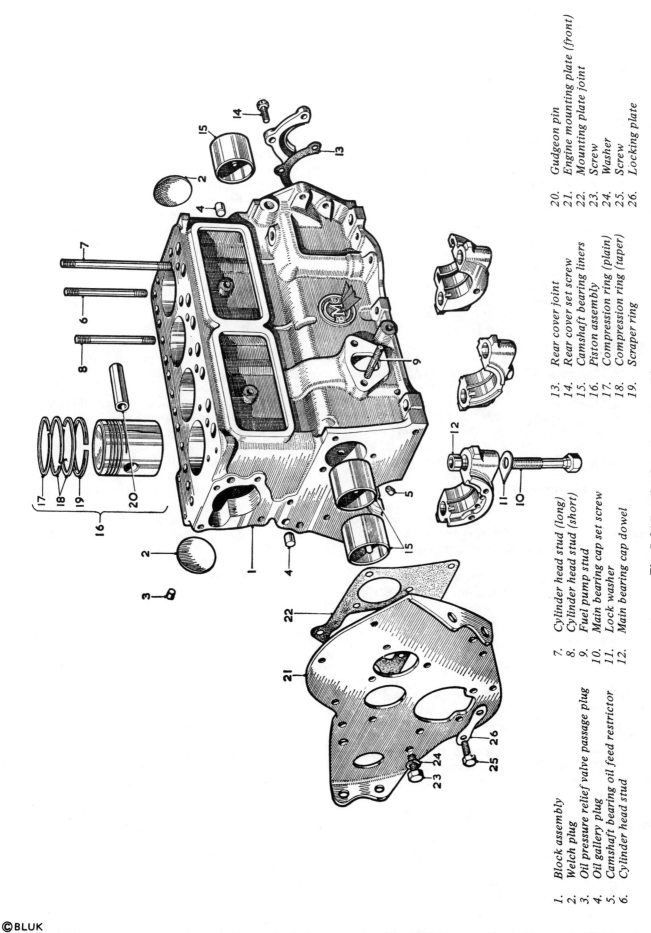

1. Block assembly
2. Welch plug
3. Oil pressure relief valve passage plug
4. Oil gallery plug
5. Camshaft bearing oil feed restrictor
6. Cylinder head stud

7. Cylinder head stud (long)
8. Cylinder head stud (short)
9. Fuel pump stud
10. Main bearing cap set screw
11. Lock washer
12. Main bearing cap dowel

13. Rear cover joint
14. Rear cover set screw
15. Camshaft bearing liners
16. Piston assembly
17. Compression ring (plain)
18. Compression ring (taper)
19. Scraper ring

20. Gudgeon pin
21. Engine mounting plate (front)
22. Mounting plate joint
23. Screw
24. Washer
25. Screw
26. Locking plate

Fig. C:31 Details of crankcase assembly

4. Remove the two tappet covers from the side of the cylinder block and lift out the tappets, making sure they are marked for correct reassembly.

5. Remove the timing cover, timing chain, and gears as already described.

6. Disconnect the high-tension leads from the coil and sparking plugs and the low-tension wire from the side of the distributor.

7. Disconnect the suction advance unit pipe from the distributor and take out the two bolts with flat washers securing the distributor to the housing. Do not slacken the clamping plate bolt or the ignition timing setting will be lost.

8. Withdraw the distributor.

9. Take out the bolt securing the distributor housing to the cylinder block. Using one of the tappet cover bolts as an extractor screwed into the tapped end of the distributor drive spindle, withdraw the spindle (Fig. C:20).

10. Take out the three set screws and shakeproof washers which secure the camshaft locating plate to the cylinder block and withdraw the camshaft (Fig. C:21).

Inspection (Camshaft)

Clean the camshaft thoroughly with petrol or other suitable solvent, then wipe dry. Inspect the cam lobes and journals for scoring or signs of abnormal wear.

Check the skew gear teeth for wear or damage. If either of these conditions is present, the camshaft must be renewed. In this case, the skew gear on the distributor drive spindle should also be checked. Refer to Fig. C:20.

Inspection (Camshaft Bearings)

Inspect the bearing liners in the cylinder block, especially at the front bearing, for wear. If the bearings are worn, or the clearance at the front bearing is excessive, new bearing liners must be fitted.

The new bearings must be line-reamed after fitting, and as several special tools are required for the installation and reaming operations, it is recommended that this work be entrusted to an Authorised Dealer or Specialist Machine Shop.

Inspection (Cam Followers)

Inspect the cam followers for wear or scoring. Followers which are only slightly worn on their lower face may be used again with the same camshaft, but replacement is preferable.

New cam followers must be used when fitting a new camshaft. Fit new followers by selective assembly so that they just fall in their bores under their own weight, when lubricated.

Installation

Replacement of the camshaft is a reversal of the removal procedure. Remember to align and engage the drive pin in the rear end of the camshaft with the slot in the oil pump drive shaft when replacing the camshaft in its housing.

CRANKSHAFT & MAIN BEARINGS......[11]

Removal

The engine must be removed from the car to carry out this operation.

1. If not already drained, drain the engine oil from the sump, and remove the sump.

2. Unscrew the oil pick-up pipe at its connection with the crankcase. Remove the two screws securing the strainer support bracket to the main bearing cap. Remove the strainer and support bracket from the crankcase. Refer to Fig. C:16.

3. Remove the flywheel, clutch and engine rear plate as detailed previously.

4. Remove the timing cover, timing chain and gears as detailed previously.

5. Remove the spark plugs to facilitate turning over the engine.

6. Ensure that all bearing caps for both main bearings and connecting rods are suitably marked so that they can be refitted in their original locations.

7. At each connecting rod in turn:-

a) Turn the crankshaft as necessary to bring the connecting rod to the bottom of its travel.

b) Tap back the lock washer tabs, unscrew the big end bolts two or three turns and tap them to release the big end bearing cap from the connecting rod.

c) Push the piston and connecting rod up the cylinder bore sufficiently to clear the crankshaft.

8. Release the main bearing cap bolts evenly, and detach each of the main bearing caps. The bottom halves of the two crankshaft thrust washers will be removed with the centre main bearing cap.

9. Remove the screwed plug from the rear bearing cap oil return pipe and withdraw the pipe.

10. Carefully lift the crankshaft out of the crankcase (Fig. C:29).

11. Remove the upper halves of the thrust washers from their locations on either side of the centre main bearing.

12. Remove the bearing shells from their housings in the crankcase and the main bearing caps. Identify the shells if they are to be re-used.

13. If required, remove the bearing shells from the connecting rods and big end bearing caps. Identify the shells if they are to be re-used.

Inspection (Crankshaft)

Wash the crankshaft with petrol or other suitable solvent, and dry thoroughly. Take great care to avoid damaging the machined surfaces. Blow out the oil passages with compressed air. In some cases it may be necessary to probe the passages with a piece of wire to ensure they are clear.

Inspect each bearing journal for scratches, scores, grooves, or other damage. Refer to Fig. C:30.

Measure the diameter of each journal in at least four

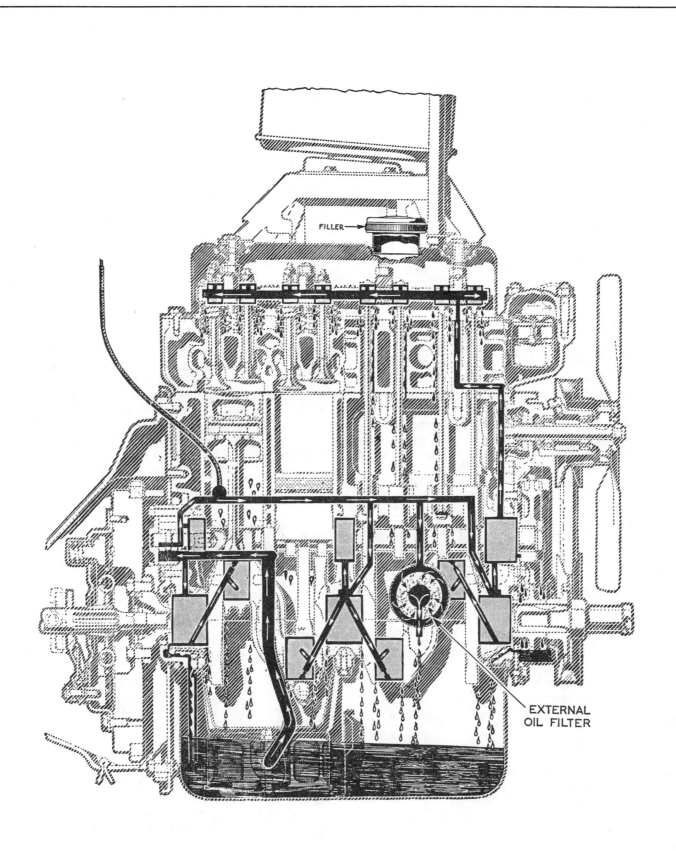

FILLER

EXTERNAL
OIL FILTER

Fig. C:32 Cross section of Minor engine showing lubrication

places with an accurate micrometer to determine out-of-round, taper or undersize. If the taper or out-of-round is excessive, or if any of the journal surfaces are severely marked, the crankshaft should be re-ground or replaced. If any journals will not clean up within the minimum specified regrind diameter, the crankshaft must be replaced.

Inspection (Main Bearings)

Clean and inspect the main bearing shells in a similar manner to that described for the Big End Bearing Shells under the heading 'PISTONS & CONNECTING RODS' previously.

The clearance of each bearing should also be checked as detailed under that heading.

Thrust Washers

Clean and inspect the thrust washers in a similar manner to that for the bearing shells. Renew the thrust washers if worn or damaged. See Fig. C:22.

Installation

Assemble the components in the reverse order of removal, with special attention to the following points:-
a) Tighten all nuts and bolts to their specified torques.
b) Ensure all bearing surfaces are perfectly clean, and lubricate them with engine oil before assembly.

c) If the bearing shells are being re-used, ensure that they are refitted in their original locations.
d) Ensure that the locating tag on each bearing shell correctly engages the corresponding notch in the bearing housing.
e) Ensure that all bearing caps are fitted in their correct positions, indicated by the identification marks.
f) Ensure that the thrust washers are located the correct way round on each side of the centre main bearing. The oil grooves on the thrust washers should face outwards. Also ensure that the tab on the lower thrust washers locates correctly in the slot in the main bearing cap.
g) The rear main bearing cap horizontal joint surfaces should be cleaned thoroughly and lightly covered with jointing compound before the cap is fitted to the cylinder block. This ensures a perfect oil seal when the cap is bolted down to the block.
h) Lubricate the rear main bearing cap joint seal liberally with oil before refitting.
i) Check the crankshaft endfloat either with a dial gauge or feeler gauges. In the former case, locate the dial gauge with the stylus in contact with the machined surface of the crankshaft throw, then lever the crankshaft fully forward and zero the gauge. Lever the crankshaft in the opposite direction and note the gauge reading. If the endfloat exceeds the specified limits of 0.002 - 0.003 in (0.051 - 0.076 mm), fit new thrust washers.

If feeler gauges are being used, measure the clearance between the thrust washers and the crankshaft face with the crankshaft pushed fully in one direction.

Technical Data

GENERAL

	948 cc	1098 cc
Type	APJM or 9M	10MA, 10ME or 10V
Bore/stroke	62.94/83.72 mm	64.58/83.72 mm
Capacity	948 cc	1098 cc
Compression ratio	8.3 or 7.2:1	8.5 or 7.5:1
Firing order	1 - 3 - 4 - 2	1 - 3 - 4 - 2
Idling speed	500 rpm	500 rpm

CRANKSHAFT

Main journal diameter	1.7505-1.7510 in (44.46-44.47 mm)
Crankpin journal diameter	1.6254-1.6259 in (41.28-41.29 mm)
Max. permissible regrind, main and crankpin journals	0.040 in (1.01 mm) below std. diameter
Crankshaft endfloat	0.002-0.003 in (0.051-0.076 mm)

MAIN BEARINGS

Length	1.0625 in (27 mm)
Diametrical clearance	0.0010-0.0025 in (0.025-0.063 mm)

VALVE TIMING

Inlet valve:
    Opens . . . . 5° BTDC
    Closes . . . . 45° ABDC
Exhaust valve:
    Opens . . . . 51° BBDC
    Closes . . . . 21° ATDC
Rocker checking clearance . . . . 0.02 in (0.51 mm)
Rocker running clearance . . . . 0.012 in (0.30 mm) cold

VALVE GUIDES

Fitted height above spring seat . . . . 0.594 in (15.1 mm)

LUBRICATION SYSTEM

Oil pump . . . . Internal gear or vane type
Relief valve opening pressure . . . . 60 lb/in^2 (4.2 kg/cm^2)
Oil pressure:
    Running . . . . .30-60 lb/in^2 (2.1-4.2 kg/cm^2)
    Idling . . . . .10-25 lb/in^2 (0.7-1.7 kg/cm^2)
Sump capacity (inc filler) . . . . 6.5 pts (3.7 litres)

BIG-END BEARINGS

Diametrical clearance . . . . 0.0010-0.0025 in (0.0254-0.063 mm)
Endfloat on crankpin
    1098 cc . . . . .0.008-0.012 in (0.203-0.305 mm)

PISTONS

Clearance in cylinder
    Bottom of skirt . . . . 0.0005-0.0011 in (0.013-0.028 mm)
    Top of skirt . . . . 0.0021-0.0037 in (0.053-0.094 mm)

PISTON RINGS

Compression: - Type
    Top . . . . .Plain, internally chamfered
    Second and third . . . . Tapered
Clearance in groove . . . . 0.002-0.004 in (0.051-0.102 mm)
Fitted gap . . . . .0.007-0.012 in (0.178-0.30 mm)
Oil control: Type
    Early engines . . . . .Slotted scraper
    Later engines . . . . .Wellworthy - Duraflex 61
    Fitted gap:
        Rails . . . . .0.012-0.028 in (0.31-0.7 mm)
        Side spring . . . . 0.10-0.15 in (2.54-3.81 mm)

CAMSHAFT

Diametrical clearance . . . . 0.001-0.002 in (0.025-0.051 mm)
Endfloat . . . . 0.003-0.007 in (0.076-0.178 mm)

VALVES

Seat angle . . . . .45°
Stem to guide clearance
    Inlet . . . . 0.0015-0.0025 in (0.038-0.063 mm)
    Exhaust . . . . .0.002-0.003 in (0.051-0.076 mm)

ENGINE
Trouble Shooter

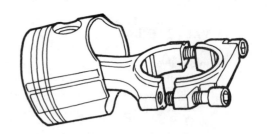

FAULT	CAUSE	CURE
Noisy tappet (with correct clearance)	1. Wear in rocker pad face and/or rocker sleeve and shift (OHV). 2. Worn cam follower (OHC).	1. Reface pad surface, replace rockers or shaft (OHV). 2. Fit new followers (OHC).
Lack of compression	1. Faulty valve seat, excessive wear in stem or guide. 2. Faulty head gasket. 3. Worn pistons, rings and bores.	1. Recut seat and valve, fit new guide and valve. 2. Fit new gasket or reface head. 3. Either fit new rings, pistons and rings and rebore. If engine badly worn then recon. engine.
Smoke from exhaust. Lack of power	1. As above. 2. Blocked crankcase breather.	1. As above. 2. Check breathing apparatus as above.
Piston slap	1. As above (except blocked breather).	1. As above
Big-end knock	1. Wear between big-end shell and crankcase. Wrong torque on bolts.	1. Depending on wear, fit new shells, regrind crankshaft and check torque.
Mains rumble	1. Wear between main bearing shells and crankshaft.	1. As above.
Cam follower tap	1. Camshaft worn or follower dished.	1. Examine and replace followers or camshaft. Or both.
Knocking when clutch depressed. Movement at crank pulley	1. Excessive crankshaft end-float. Wear between crank and thrust washer.	1. Fit new thrust washers and recheck clearance.
Clattering from front of engine	1. Worn or slack timing chain, worn chain tensioner.	1. Fit new chain and tensioner. Adjust chain where necessary.
Small-end or gudgeon pin knock	1. Excessive wear between gudgeon pin and con-rod.	1. Fit new bush to con-rod.
Lack of oil pressure	1. Excessive wear in crankshaft journals. 2. Faulty oil pump. 3. Blocked oil pick-up strainer. 4. Faulty pressure-relief valve. 5. Blocked oil filter. 6. Lack of Oil.	1. Overhaul engine. 2. Fit new pump. 3. Clean pick-up. 4. Fit new relief valve. 5. Fit new filter. 6. Install fresh oil.
Oil leaks	1. Sump gaskets or packings. 2. Front and rear crankshaft oil seal. 3. Rocker or camshaft gasket. 4. Oil filter.	1. Fit new gaskets. 2. Fit new seals. 3. Fit new gasket. 4. Check filter seal.
Lack of power (engine in good condition)	1. Faulty ignition timing. Faulty sparking plugs, points or condenser. Wrong valve clearance.	1. Tune engine.

Engine Electrics

DISTRIBUTOR. . . . .[1]

Distributor lubrication and replacement of the contact breaker points has already been covered in the 'Tune-up' section previously, and reference should be made for details, if required.

Removal (Fig. D:1)

Disconnect the HT leads from the spark plugs and the ignition coil. If necessary, label the spark plug leads with their respective cylinder numbers to ensure correct fitment on reassembly. Remove the distributor cap from the distributor body.

Disconnect the distributor low tension lead from the terminal blade on the distributor body. Disconnect the vacuum pipe from the vacuum control unit on the distributor.

Remove the two bolts securing the distributor clamp plate to the pedestal on the cylinder block and withdraw the distributor, complete with its clamp plate.

Installation

Install the distributor in the reverse order of removal, paying special attention to the following points:-
a) When offering up the distributor to the engine, position it with the vacuum control unit pointing upwards towards the No. 3 spark plug.
b) Rotate the distributor shaft until the lugs on the driving dog engage in the slots in the distributor gear. The slots in the gear and the lugs on the dog are offset and can only engage each other in one position.
c) Turn the distributor body until the clamp plate holes are aligned with those in the pedestal, then fit the two securing bolts.
d) When installation is completed, check the ignition timing and reset if necessary, as detailed in the Tune-up section previously.

Overhaul

In most cases of wear or damage to the main components of the distributor (distributor shaft, cam assembly, advance mechanism, bearings etc.) it will probably be more economical and convenient to exchange the complete distributor, rather than attempt to overhaul or repair it. This will be particularly applicable if the unit has seen a long period of use.

The components of the distributor assembly are shown in Fig. D:1.

DYNAMO . . . .[2]

Removal & Installation (Fig. D:2)

Dynamo removal is a straight-forward operation and is merely a matter of disconnecting the two leads from the rear of the unit and removing the mounting bolts. The unit can then be lifted away from the engine.

When installing the dynamo, set the drive belt tension so that a free-play of approximately 0.5 in (13 mm) exists at the midway point along the longest belt run.

If a replacement unit has been fitted, it should be 'polarised' before reconnecting the leads to the two terminals. To do this, connect a short lead between the two terminals on the dynamo and connect another longer lead to one of the terminals. At the starter solenoid, touch the other end of the long lead to the large battery feed terminal (opposite terminal to starter lead attachment) several times. The dynamo will now be correctly polarised to suit the electrical system. Remove the temporary leads and connect up the two dynamo leads to the large and small terminal respectively on the rear of the unit.

Brushes (Fig. D:4)

Most faults associated with the dynamo are normally due either to the brushes or the rear bearing. In the latter case, excessive wear at the rear bearing bush allows the armature shaft to run eccentric and touch the field coils, in which case the complete unit is best exchanged. This condition is easily identified as excessive side movement at the rear end of the shaft when the drive pulley is moved side-to-side.

To examine the brushes, unscrew the two through-bolts at the rear end bracket and withdraw the end bracket from the dynamo yoke.

Check the condition and length of the two carbon brushes in the end bracket, and the condition of the surface on the commutator. If the brushes are worn to or are approaching their minimum length of 0.25 in (6 mm), they should be renewed.

To renew the brushes, detach the old brush leads from the holders on the end bracket by removing the screw and lock washer. Note the positions of the terminal tags before disconnecting the leads. Ensure that the replacement brushes are of the correct type and length. Secure the new brushes in position on the end bracket.

Inspect the contact surface on the commutator for signs of wear, burning or blackening of the segments. The latter indicates a short circuit. An open circuit will cause burned spots between the segments. Ideally the commutator surface should be smooth with a dark grey colour. If blackened or dirty, it can be cleaned up with a petrol-moistened cloth. Slight imperfections can be removed with fine glass paper - not emery cloth. Use the glass paper over the whole surface of the commutator.

If the commutator is grooved, scored, pitted or badly worn, it must be skimmed down or replaced.

Fit each brush into its holder in turn and check for freedom of movement. If a brush sticks, it can usually be freed by cleaning both the brush and the holder with a petrol-moistened cloth, or by lightly polishing the sides of the brush with a smooth file.

Locate the brush springs on the side of each brush to hold them in the raised position. Check that the fibre thrust washer is in position on the end of the armature shaft, then refit the commutator end bracket. Ensure that the locating pip on the end bracket correctly engages the notch in the dynamo yoke. Fit the two through-bolts and tighten securely.

Release the brushes on to the commutator by inserting a thin screwdriver through the ventilation hole in the end bracket adjacent to the brush holders and gently levering up the spring end on to the top of the brush.

Before refitting the dynamo on the car, add one or two drops of light oil to the rear bearing through the hole in the centre of the end bracket. Do not over-lubricate the bearing otherwise oil may be thrown on to the brush gear in use.

Overhaul (Fig. D:4)

If any repair work, other than replacing the brushes, is necessary it will probably be more economical and convenient to have the dynamo repaired by an electrical specialist, or to exchange it for a replacement unit.

If the unit is being exchanged, it will be necessary to remove the drive pulley as this will not normally be supplied with the new unit. After removing the pulley nut, the pulley can be levered off the keyed shaft, but care should be taken to avoid damaging the rim of the pulley.

VOLTAGE REGULATOR . . . . [3]

A two-bobbin voltage control regulator - Lucas type RB 106/2 - is used to control the generator output and this is mounted in the engine compartment (Fig. D:3). If there is a charging fault and the dynamo is found to be working satisfactorily then it is likely that the regulator is at fault. Rather than attempt to clean or adjust the unit it is advised that the unit be exchanged at your local dealer, accessory shop or auto-electrician. Unless completely overhauled (requiring special tools and meters), it is likely that any adjustment would only be a temporary cure.

Removal and Installation

1. Disconnect the battery leads.
2. Remove the leads from the regulator, noting all of the various connections.
3. Unscrew two screws securing the unit to the engine compartment.
4. Replace the regulator and secure it with two screws.
5. Reconnect the leads in the same positions as removed.
6. Reconnect the battery.

ALTERNATOR . . . . [4]

The latest Morris 1000 models were all fitted with the Lucas type 11AC alternator shown in Fig. D:5. It is a conventional type unit with a separate control box.

Most faults allied to the alternator charging system are due either to worn or damaged brushes, or a defective regulator. Replacement of both the brushes and the regulator unit is detailed under the appropriate headings below. If anything more involved, such as the rectifier diodes, slip rings, bearings, etc., is at fault, it is recommended that the alternator be given to an Electrical Specialist for repair, or an exchange unit obtained. In most cases this will be found to be the most economical and convenient solution rather than attempt to obtain replacement parts and repair it.

It should be noted that the battery should ALWAYS be disconnected before starting work on the charging system to avoid the possibility of damage to the semi-conductor devices in the alternator.

Removal and Installation

Removal and installation of the alternator is a straightforward operation, similar to that described for the dynamo previously. However, in this case it is most important that the battery must be disconnected before starting work on the alternator as the alternator main feed cable is live at all times. Do not reconnect the battery until installation is complete and all leads have been properly reconnected.

It should be noted that 'polarisation' of the alternator is not necessary and in fact, if carried out, will probably cause damage to some of the semi-conductor devices in the charging circuit.

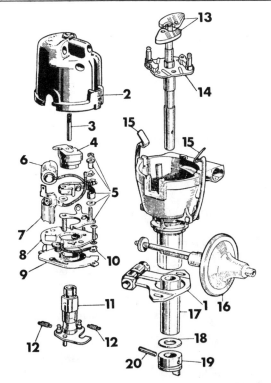

Fig. D:2 Details of generator mounting bolts

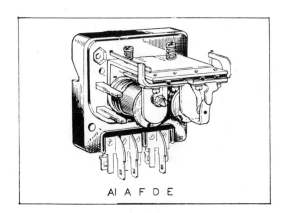

Fig. D:3 Voltage control box with cover removed

1. Clamping plate	11. Cam assembly
2. Moulded cap	12. Automatic advance springs
3. Brush and spring	13. Weight assembly
4. Rotor arm	14. Shaft and action plate
5. Contacts (set)	15. Cap-retaining clips
6. Capacitor	16. Vacuum unit
7. Terminal and lead (low-tension)	17. Bush
8. Moving contact breaker plate	18. Thrust washer
9. Contact breaker base plate	19. Driving dog
10. Earth lead	20. Taper pin

Fig. D:1 Exploded view of the Lucas 25D4 distributor

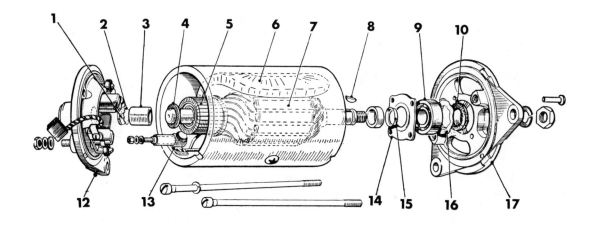

1. Oiling pad	7. Armature	13. Field terminal post
2. Aluminium disc	8. Key	14. Bearing plate
3. Bush	9. Ball bearing	15. Cap washer
4. Fibre washer	10. Felt washer	16. Corrugated washer
5. Commutator	12. Commutator end bracket	17. Drive end bracket
6. Field coils		

Fig. D:4 Exploded view of the Lucas C40/1 dynamo

Brushes (Fig. D:5)

Remove the nuts, washers and insulating pieces from the output terminal at the rear of the alternator.

Remove the two brush box retaining screws and withdraw the brush box assembly from the rear end bracket. Take care not to lose the two washers fitted between the brush box moulding and the end bracket as these must be refitted in their original locations on reassembly.

To remove the brushes from the brush box, close up the retaining tongue at the base of each field terminal blade and withdraw the brush, spring and terminal assembly from the brush box.

Check the brushes for wear. The brush length when new is 0.30 in (8 mm). If worn to, or approaching the wear limit of 0.16 in (4 mm) the brush assemblies should be renewed. New brush assemblies are supplied complete with their spring and 'Lucar' field terminal blade.

It should be noted that the brush which bears on the inner slip ring is always connected to the positive side of the electrical system, since the lower linear speed of the inner slip ring results in reduced mechanical wear and helps to offset the higher rate of electrical wear peculiar to the positive connected brush.

If the original brushes assemblies are to be re-used, clean them with a cloth moistened in petrol or white spirit, then dry thoroughly.

Check the brushes for freedom of movement in their holders. If necessary lightly polish the brush sides on a smooth file, then clean off and refit.

To reassemble the brushes to their holders, push each brush complete with its spring and terminal blade into its holder until the tongue on the terminal blade registers in the brush box. To ensure the terminal blades are properly retained, the tongue should be levered up with a small screwdriver to make an angle of about 30° with the terminal blade.

Before refitting the brush box assembly, inspect the slip rings for any signs of damage or contamination. The surface of the rings should be smooth and free from oil or other matter. The easiest way of removing surface dirt from the slip rings is to press a petrol-moistened cloth through the hole in the end bracket and hold it in contact with the slip ring surface while rotating the pulley.

If more serious contamination or damage is evident on the ring surface, the alternator must be partially dismantled to gain access. In this case the drive pulley and fan must first be removed to allow the three through-bolts to be unscrewed. The alignment of the end brackets and stator should be marked so that they may be reassembled in the correct angular relation to each other. The drive end bracket and rotor can then be separated from the stator and slip ring end bracket to allow inspection of the slip rings.

The surface of the slip rings can be cleaned using very fine glass paper but on no account must emery cloth or similar abrasive be used. If badly scored, pitted or burned, the complete rotor assembly must be renewed.

When inspection is completed, refit the brush box assembly to the slip ring end bracket and secure with the two retaining screws. Assemble the insulating pieces,

washers and nuts on the output terminal.

Overhaul

If any repair work, other than replacing the brushes, is necessary it will probably be more economical and convenient to have the alternator repaired by an electrical specialist, or to exchange it for a replacement unit.

STARTER MOTOR . . . . [5]

Removal & Installation (Figs. D:6 and D:7)

First, disconnect the battery. Remove the nut from the terminal on the end of the starter motor and disconnect the starter cable. Remove the two bolts (lower one first) retaining the starter motor to the engine and withdraw the starter motor from its location.

Install the starter motor in the reverse order of removing.

The starter motor may be either a Lucas M35G or a M35J type, the latter being a later fitment. Although externally similar, apart from the brush cover band on the M35G type, they differ mainly in two respects. The M35G type has a peripheral contact commutator on which the brushes bear from the side, whereas the M35J has a face-type commutator where the brushes bear on the end face. In the M35J unit, the field windings are earthed to the starter yoke but the brush box assembly and the commutator end plate brushes are fully insulated. The end terminal post is connected directly to the end plate brushes. The M35G field windings are insulated from the yoke and incorporate the field terminal post, but the end plate brushes are earthed directly to the end plate.

Brushes - M35G Starter (Figs. D:8 and D:9)

A good indication of the brush condition can be obtained by inspecting the brushes through the apertures in the starter body, after sliding away the cover band. If the brushes are damaged or worn so that they no longer make good contact on the commutator, they should be renewed as a set.

The brushes can be further inspected by lifting the brush springs, using a piece of hooked wire, and withdrawing them from their holders on the commutator end plate.

If the brushes are to be replaced, remove the nuts, washers and insulation bush from the field terminal post at the end plate. Unscrew the two through-bolts and withdraw the end plate from the starter body.

Inspect the contact surface on the outside of the commutator for any signs of wear, burning or other damage. If the surface is blackened or dirty, it should be wiped clean with a petrol-moistened cloth. Slight imperfections can be removed with fine glass paper, but emery cloth or similar abrasive must not be used. If the commutator is grooved, scored or badly worn, it should be skimmed or replaced.

To renew the earthed brushes on the commutator end

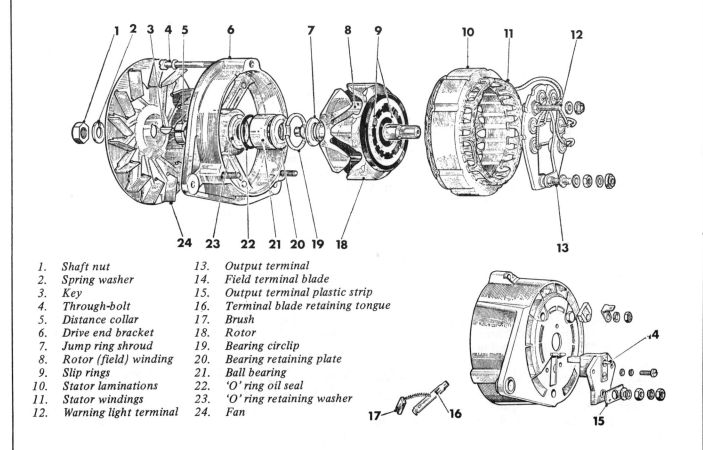

1.	Shaft nut	13.	Output terminal
2.	Spring washer	14.	Field terminal blade
3.	Key	15.	Output terminal plastic strip
4.	Through-bolt	16.	Terminal blade retaining tongue
5.	Distance collar	17.	Brush
6.	Drive end bracket	18.	Rotor
7.	Jump ring shroud	19.	Bearing circlip
8.	Rotor (field) winding	20.	Bearing retaining plate
9.	Slip rings	21.	Ball bearing
10.	Stator laminations	22.	'O' ring oil seal
11.	Stator windings	23.	'O' ring retaining washer
12.	Warning light terminal	24.	Fan

Fig. D:5 Exploded view of Lucas 11AC alternator

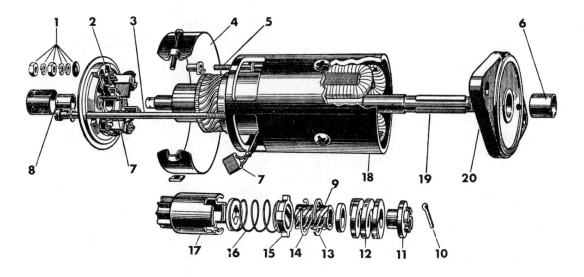

1.	Terminal nuts and washers	6.	Bearing bush	11.	Shaft nut	16.	Restraining spring
2.	Brush spring	7.	Brushes	12.	Main spring	17.	Pinion and barrel
3.	Through-bolt	8.	Bearing bush	13.	Retaining ring	18.	Yoke
4.	Band cover	9.	Sleeve	14.	Washer	19.	Armature shaft
5.	Terminal post	10.	Split pin	15.	Control nut	20.	Driving end bracket

Fig. D:6 Exploded view of Lucas M35G starter motor

plate, unsolder the flexible lead from the terminal eyelet adjacent to the brush holder. Open the eyelet, then insert the replacement brush lead, squeeze the eyelet closed and resolder the connection.

To renew the insulated brushes on the field coils, cut the existing brush leads approximately 0.25 in (6 mm) from the field coil connection. Clean the ends of the copper leads still attached to the field coils and solder the new brush leads to them. Note that the insulated brushes have longer leads than the earthed brushes, and also have a braided covering.

Check the new brushes for freedom of movement in their respective holders. Ease them if necessary by cleaning both the brushes and holders with a petrol-moistened cloth, or by polishing the sides of the brushes lightly with a fine file.

Check that the insulator band is fitted between the starter body and the end of the field coils, and that the insulating bush for the field terminal post is also fitted to the commutator end plate. Also check that the thrust washer is in place in the end of the armature shaft.

Pass the field brushes out through the apertures in the starter body. Fit the earthed brushes in their respective holders in the end plate and locate the brush springs on the side of each brush to hold them in the raised position. Assemble the end plate to the starter body, ensuring that the locating dowel on the plate correctly engages the notch in the yoke. Fit the through-bolts and tighten securely. Assemble the insulation bush, washers and nuts on the field terminal post.

Lift the brush springs and fit the field brushes into their respective holders. Press the brushes down into the commutator, then lift the brush springs into position on top of the brushes. Refit the brush cover band over the brush apertures and tighten the clamp screw to secure.

Brushes - M35J Starter

In this case the commutator end plate must be re-moved to allow inspection of the brushes as inspection apertures are not provided.

Remove the two retaining screws and withdraw the commutator end plate from the starter yoke. Withdraw the two field brushes from the brush box on the end plate and separate the end plate from the yoke.

Inspect the brushes for wear or damage. Brushes which are worn to, or are approaching the wear limit of 3/8 in (10 mm) must be renewed as a set.

Inspect the contact surface on the end of the commutator for any signs of scoring, burning or other damage. If the surface is grooved or badly scored, the commutator should be skimmed or replaced. If the surface is merely blackened or dirty it can be cleaned with a petrol-moistened cloth, or fine glass paper, but emery cloth or similar abrasive must not be used for this purpose.

If the brushes on the commutator end plate are to be renewed, these are supplied attached to a new terminal post. Withdraw both brushes from their holders, then remove the nuts, washers and insulation sleeve from the terminal post and withdraw the terminal post and remove the insulation piece. Install the new brushes and terminal post in the reverse order of removing. Ensure that the insulation piece and sleeve are correctly located. Retain the longer brush lead under the clip on the end plate.

If the field winding brushes are to be renewed, these are supplied attached to a common lead. Cut the old brush leads approximately 0.25 in (6 mm) from their joint on the field windings (Fig. D:10). Clean the leads still attached to the joint and solder the common lead of the new brushes to them. Do not attempt to solder directly to the field winding strip as this may be made of aluminium.

Check the brushes for freedom of movement in their respective holders. Any brushes which are stiff should be cleaned with a petrol-moistened cloth, or eased by lightly polishing the sides of the brush with a fine file.

Install the two commutator end brushes and the two field winding brushes in their respective holders on the brush box. Check that the thrust washer is in position on the end of the armature shaft, then assemble the commutator end plate to the starter yoke. Secure the end plate with the two retaining screws.

Drive Pinion

If difficulty is experienced with the starter motor pinion not meshing correctly with the flywheel ring gear, it may be that the drive assembly requires cleaning. The pinion and barrel assembly should move freely on the screwed sleeve. If there is dirt or other foreign matter on the sleeve it should be washed off with paraffin. Do not use grease or oil on the drive assembly as this would attract dirt.

To replace the drive pinion assembly, compress the main drive spring using a suitable clamping device (e.g. Bendix Spring Compressor Tool) and remove the jump ring from its groove at the end of the armature shaft (Fig. D:11). Release the clamping device and remove the spring cup, drive spring, thrust washer and drive pinion assembly from the shaft. It may be necessary to depress the pinion assembly and turn it slightly to disengage it from the shaft splines.

It should be noted that, if the screwed sleeve is worn or damaged, it is essential that it is renewed together with the barrel and pinion.

Fit the new pinion assembly on the armature shaft, with the pinion teeth towards the starter body. Assemble the thrust washer, drive spring and spring seat on the shaft, compress the drive spring and fit the jump ring. Ensure that the ring is correctly seated in the shaft groove once the spring is released.

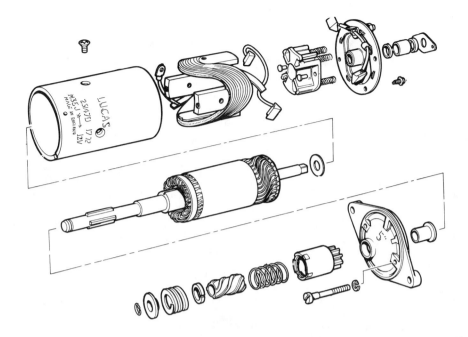

Fig. D:7 Exploded view of Lucas M35J starter motor

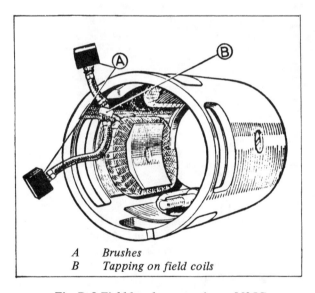

A   Brushes
B   Tapping on field coils

Fig. D:8 Field brush connections - M35G

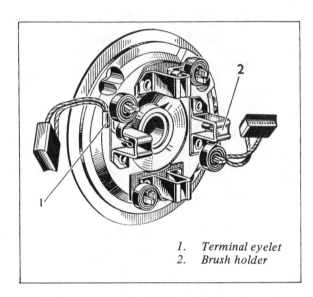

1.   Terminal eyelet
2.   Brush holder

Fig. D:9 Field brush assembly on commutator
end plate

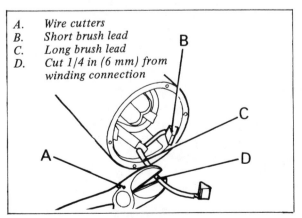

A.   Wire cutters
B.   Short brush lead
C.   Long brush lead
D.   Cut 1/4 in (6 mm) from
      winding connection

Fig. D:10 Cutting brush leads from field
winding connections

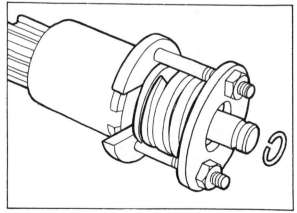

Fig. D:11 Using compressing tool to remove
drive pinion

Technical Data

DISTRIBUTOR

Make/type . . . . .Lucas 25D4
Contact points gap. . . . . .0.014-0.016 in (0.35-0.40 mm)
Dwell angle . . . .$60^{\circ} \pm 3^{\circ}$
Condenser capacity . . . . .0.18-0.24 mfd
Rotor rotation . . . . .Anti-clockwise
Ignition timing . . . . .See 'Tune-Up' data

IGNITION COIL

Make/type . . . . Lucas LA12
Resistance . . . . .3.2-3.4 ohms

DYNAMO

Make/type . . . . Lucas C40/1
Maximum output . . . . 22 amps
Cut-in speed . . . . 1450 rpm at 13.5 volts
Control box . . . . .Lucas RB 106/2
Regulating voltage . . . . .12.7-13.3 volts

ALTERNATOR

Make/type . . . . Lucas 11AC
Polarity . . . . .Positive earth
Maximum output . . . . 43 amps
Brush length wear limit. . . . . 0.16 in (4 mm)

STARTER MOTOR

Make/type . . . . .Lucas M35G or M35J, inertia type
Commutator min. diam. (M35G) . . . . .1.34 in (34 mm)
Commutator min. thickness (M35J) . . . . 0.08 in (2.03 mm)
Armature endfloat
   M35G . . . . 0.004-0.012 in (0.1-0.3 mm)
   M35J . . . . 0.010 in (0.25 mm)
Min. brush length (M35J) . . . . 0.31 in (8 mm)

SYSTEM POLARITY

All models . . . . .Positive earth

Cooling

DRAINING & REFILLING . . . . [1]

All models have a cooling system which incorporates a pressure cap (Fig. E:1) fitted to the radiator filler neck. There are two drain points in the system - one on the left-hand side of the cylinder block at the rear (Fig. E:2) and one at the bottom of the radiator (Fig. E:3). On early models, the points are fitted with taps. The later models are fitted with plugs.

To drain the system, first remove the pressure cap from the radiator (only when the engine is cold) and open the drain points.

If the system contains anti-freeze and it is to be used again, the coolant should be drained into a suitable clean container.

To refill the system, close the drain points, open the heater valve (if fitted) and add coolant through the filler neck until the level is just below the filler neck.

A funnel may be required for this operation. If necessary check that the heater unit is completely full by disconnecting the heater outlet pipe. Refit the filler cap.

Run the engine at a fast idle for about half a minute, then stop the engine and top up the system.

Refit the filler cap and run the engine up to normal operating temperature. Stop the engine, allow it to cool and then recheck the level.

THERMOSTAT. . . . . [2]

The thermostat is located under the water outlet housing on the cylinder head (Fig. E:4).

A defective thermostat will cause over-heating if jammed shut, or excessive warm-up time if jammed open. No attempt should be made to repair the thermostat. If defective, or even suspect, it should be replaced. Ensure that the replacement is of the correct specified rating. The nominal temperature in degrees Centigrade at which the thermostat opens is stamped on the base of the thermostat bulb.

Removal and Installation

A new water outlet housing gasket should be obtained before attempting to remove the water outlet housing.
1. Partially drain the cooling system, so that the coolant level is below the water outlet housing.
2. Disconnect the radiator top hose from the water outlet housing.
3. Remove the securing nuts and spring washers from the water outlet housing, and lift the housing off the studs.
4. Remove the paper gasket and lift the thermostat out of its housing.
5. If required, the thermostat can be tested as described under the heading below.
6. Clean all old gasket material from the mating faces of the water outlet housing and the thermostat housing.
7. Install the thermostat with the bulb downwards - it is most important that the thermostat be correctly positioned, otherwise over-heating will result.
8. Locate a new gasket on the thermostat housing and fit the water outlet on the studs. Secure with the nuts and washers.
9. Reconnect the radiator top hose to the water outlet housing and top up the cooling system.

Testing

Examine the thermostat valve. If stuck in the open position, the thermostat is faulty and must be renewed.

To test the operation of the thermostat, suspend it fully submerged along with a suitable thermometer in a container of water. Both the thermostat and the thermometer should be suspended in such a way that they do not touch the sides of the container.

Heat the water gradually and observe the function of the thermostat valve. Note the temperature at which the thermostat opens. The nominal temperature in degrees Centigrade is stamped on the base of the thermostat bulb. If the thermostat does not function correctly it must be renewed.

Fig. E:1 Removing the pressure filler cap

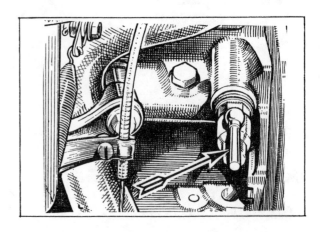

Fig. E:2 Position of the cylinder block drain tap

Fig. E:3 Position of the radiator drain tap

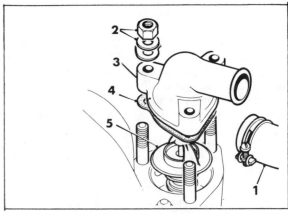

1. Top hose
2. Housing nut
3. Thermostat housing
4. Gasket
5. Thermostat

Fig. E:4 Thermostat location in cylinder head

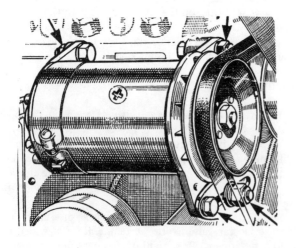

Fig. E:5 Dynamo mounting bolt

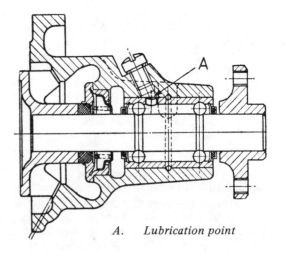

A. Lubrication point

Fig. E:6 Water pump cross-section

WATER PUMP . . . . [3]

Removal

1. Remove the radiator as described later in this section.
2. Slacken the dynamo/alternator mounting bolts (Fig. E:5) and remove the fan belt.
3. Remove the three dynamo/alternator mounting bolts and remove the dynamo/alternator.
4. Remove the cooling fan and detach the drive pulley from the water pump hub.
5. Disconnect the small by-pass hose from the water pump.
6. Disconnect the radiator bottom hose from the water pump inlet and the heater tube.
7. Remove the four bolts securing the water pump to the cylinder block face and detach the pump together with its gasket.

Dismantling (Fig. E:6)

1. Unscrew the four set bolts which attach the fan and belt pulley to the hub and remove the fan and pulley.
2. Remove the fan hub with a suitable extractor.
3. Pull out the bearing locating wire through the hole in the top of the pump body.
4. Gently tap the pump bearing assembly rearwards out of the pump body. This will release the combined bearing and spindle assembly together with the seal and vane.
5. Remove the vane from the bearing assembly with a suitable extractor and remove the pump seal assembly.
6. Reassembly is a reversal of the dismantling procedure, but care must be taken to see that the seal assembly is in good condition. If there is any sign of damage the seal should be replaced by a new component. When the bearing assembly is assembled into the pump the hole in the bearing must coincide with the lubricating hole in the water pump body.

Installation

Installation is a simple reversal of the removal procedure, with special attention to the following points:
a) Ensure that the mating faces on the pump and cylinder block are clean and free from old gasket material.
b) Use a new water pump gasket.
c) Tension the drive belt so that a total free-movement of approximately 0.5 in (13 mm) is present at a point midway along the longest run between the pulleys.
d) Refit the radiator and refill the cooling system as detailed under the respective headings in this section.
e) When installation is complete, run the engine up to normal operating temperature and check for leaks.

RADIATOR . . . . [4]

Removal

1. Drain the cooling system as detailed previously.
2. Disconnect the radiator top and bottom hoses.
3. Remove the four bolts which secure the radiator to the body and remove the radiator.

Installation

Installation is a simple reversal of the removal procedure. Renew any hose clips which are damaged or suspect, especially the clip on the expansion tank hose.

Finally, refill the cooling system.

Technical Data

COOLING SYSTEM

Type. . . . . Pressurised, thermo-siphon

CAPACITY

1098 without heater . . . . .8.75 pints
1098 with heater. . . . . .9.75 pints
948 without heater . . . . .9.75 pints
948 with heater. . . . . .10.75 pints

THERMOSTAT

Type. . . . . Bellows
Opening temperature
   cars without heater . . . . .72°C (162°F)
   cars with heater. . . . . 80-85°C (176-185°F)
Water pump drive belt tension . . . . 0.5 in (12 mm)
deflection on longest belt run

COOLING
Trouble Shooter

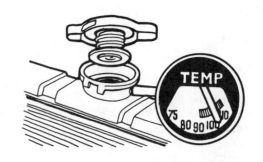

FAULT	CAUSE	CURE
Loss of coolant	1. Damaged radiator 2. Leak at heater connection or plug 3. Damaged cylinder head gasket 4. Cracked cylinder block. 5. Cracked cylinder head. 6. Loose cylinder head bolts	1. Repair or replace radiator. 2. Repair or replace. 3. Replace gasket. Check engine oil and refill as necessary. 4. Replace cylinder block. Check engine oil in crankcase for mixing with water. 5. Replace cylinder head. 6. Tighten cylinder head bolts.
Poor circulation	1. Restriction in system 2. Insufficient coolant 3. Inoperative water pump 4. Loose fan belt 5. Inoperative thermostat	1. Check hoses for crimping. Clear the system of rust and sludge. 2. Replenish. 3. Replace water pump. 4. Adjust for belt. 5. Replace thermostat.
Corrosion	1. Excessive impurity in water 2. Infrequent flushing and draining of system	1. Use soft, clean water. 2. Flush thoroughly at least twice a year.
Overheating	1. Inoperative thermostat 2. Radiator fin choked with mud, leaves etc. 3. Incorrect ignition and valve timing 4. Dirty oil and sludge in engine 5. Inoperative water pump 6. Loose fan belt 7. Restricted radiator 8. Inaccurate temperature gauge 9. Impurity in water	1. Replace thermostat. 2. Clean out air passage. 3. Tune engine. 4. Change engine oil and filter. 5. Replace (or check-electrical). 6. Adjust tension. 7. Flush radiator. 8. Replace temperature gauge. 9. Use soft, clean water.
Overcooling	1. Inoperative thermostat 2. Inaccurate temperature gauge	1. Replace thermostat. 2. Replace temperature gauge.

Fuel System

CARBURETTOR ....[1]

Adjustment

The procedure for setting the carburettor mixture and slow running adjustment is fully detailed in the Tune-Up chapter.

Float Chamber and Fuel Needle

If the engine cuts out, apparently through lack of fuel when there is plenty in the tank and the pump is working properly, this is probably due to a sticking float needle caused by foreign matter in the fuel.

The delivery at the carburettor should first be checked by disconnecting the fuel feed pipe from the carburettor and switching on the ignition, while the end of the pipe is directed into a pad of cloth or into a container. If the fuel delivery is satisfactory, the float chamber lid should be removed and the fuel needle valve and float chamber inspected.

Float chamber flooding is indicated by fuel flowing from the breather hole in the float chamber lid below the main fuel feed pipe, or by fuel leakage from the joint between the float chamber and the lid. It can also be caused by grit or dirt between the fuel needle and its seating.

The procedure for checking is as follows (Fig. F:1):
1. Disconnect the engine breather hose and adaptor from the carburettor (where applicable).
2. Disconnect the fuel hose from the float chamber.
3. Mark the position of the float chamber lid in relation to the float chamber to ensure correct alignment on reassembly.
4. Remove the three retaining screws and lift off the float chamber lid together with its gasket.
5. Clean any sediment from the float chamber - this is best done by soaking up the fuel in the chamber with a suitably absorbent lint-free cloth, then blowing the sediment out of the chamber with an air line.
6. Thoroughly clean the fuel needle and its seating and check that the needle operates freely in its guide without sticking. If necessary, the float hinge pin and fuel float

can be removed and the fuel needle withdrawn from its housing to check its condition. Hold the float pin at its serrated end when withdrawing it.
7. Examine the needle for wear, i.e. small ridges or grooves on the seat of the needle. If the needle is worn, it must be renewed.
8. Reassemble the components in the reverse order of removal. Inspect the lid gasket before refitting and renew if in unsatisfactory condition.
9. On models which have a metal float lever, the float level setting should be checked as follows (Figs. F:2 and F:3):-

With the float chamber lid held upside-down, insert a drill or gauge rod of suitable diameter between the hinged lever and the machined lip of the float chamber lid. The end of the lever should just rest on the rod when the needle is on its seating. If adjustment is necessary, this should be carried out at the point where the end of the lever meets the shank. Do NOT bend the shank, which must be perfectly flat and at right-angles to the needle when it is on its seating (Fig. F:4).

Piston and Suction Chamber Assembly

A sticking piston can be ascertained by removing the piston damper from the top of the suction chamber and lifting the piston with the lifting pin, or a finger inserted into the carburettor intake. The piston should move up quite freely when raised, and fall back smartly when released. If sticking does occur, the whole assembly should be removed and cleaned as described below (Fig. F:5):
1. Mark the position of the suction chamber in relation to the carburettor body to ensure correct alignment on reassembly.
2. Thoroughly clean the outside of the suction chamber and carburettor body.
3. Remove the damper from the top of the suction chamber.
4. Remove the three securing screws and lift off the suction chamber.
5. Remove the piston spring.
6. Carefully lift the piston assembly out of the carburettor body and empty the oil from the reservoir in the top

of the piston rod.

7. Carefully clean all fuel deposits, etc., from the inside of the suction chamber and the two diameters of the piston, using petrol, or preferably methylated spirits, then wipe the components dry.

8. Lubricate the piston rod lightly with a drop of thin oil - one of the non-oil lubricants such as WD 40 may be used instead for this purpose.

9. Reassemble the piston, spring and suction chamber to the carburettor body. Ensure that the assembly marks made previously are correctly aligned. Tighten the securing screws evenly.

10. Fill the piston damper with light engine oil until the level is approximately 0.5 in (13 mm) above the top of the hollow piston rod (Fig. F:6), then refit the piston damper.

Jet Centring

If the piston does not fall freely on the carburettor bridge with a distinct metallic click when the jet adjusting nut is screwed to its uppermost position, the carburettor jet must be centralised as follows (Fig. F:8):-

1. Remove the air cleaner.

2. Support the plastic moulded base of the jet and remove the screw retaining the jet pick-up link and link bracket to the jet head.

3. Unscrew the flexible jet tube sleeve nut from the base of the float chamber and withdraw the jet assembly.

4. Remove the jet adjusting nut and spring, then refit the adjusting nut without the spring. Screw the nut up as far as possible.

5. Refit the jet assembly.

6. Unscrew the jet locking screw until the jet bearing is just free to rotate under finger-pressure.

7. Remove the piston damper from the top of the suction chamber and, using a pencil or similar instrument, apply gentle pressure to the top of the piston rod.

8. Tighten the jet locking nut while holding the jet hard up against the jet bearing.

9. Ensure that the jet head is in its correct angular position during this operation.

10. With the jet in the fully raised position, lift the piston with the lifting pin then release it. Check that it falls freely on to the carburettor bridge with a soft metallic click.

11. Lower the jet and repeat the check.

12. An identical sound should be heard with the jet raised or lowered. If a sharper click is heard with the jet in the lowered position, repeat the centring procedure.

13. When the centring procedure is successfully completed, remove the jet assembly and refit the adjusting nut with its locking spring. Screw the nut up as far as possible.

14. Refit the jet in the bearing and connect the flexible jet tube to the float chamber. Ensure that the end of the tube projects a minimum of 0.188 in (5 mm) beyond the sealing gland before fitting the tube. Tighten the sleeve nut only until the gland is compressed; over-tightening can cause leakage.

15. Support the jet head and reconnect the jet pick-up link and link bracket with the securing screw.

16. Screw the jet adjusting nut down two complete turns (12 flats) to provide the initial setting.

17. Top up the piston damper with thin engine oil as necessary, and refit the air cleaner assemblies.

18. Finally, check the idling speed and mixture setting, adjusting as necessary.

Removal and Installation

1. Remove the air cleaner.

2. Disconnect the throttle and mixture (choke) control cables, the distributor vacuum pipe and the fuel hose from the carburettor.

3. Remove the nuts and spring washers securing the carburettor to the inlet manifold studs, and lift off the carburettor.

4. Install the carburettor in the reverse order of removal.

5. When reconnecting the mixture control cable, ensure that there is approximately 0.063 in (1.6 mm) free-movement before the cable starts to pull the lever.

6. When installation is complete, check the mixture and slow-running adjustment as detailed in the Tune-Up chapter.

FUEL PUMP . . . . [2]

Removal and Installation

The SU Type L electric fuel pump (Fig. F:7) fitted to all Minor 1000 models is situated on the left-hand front wing valance.

To remove the pump, first disconnect the battery earth lead. Detach the earth and supply leads from the terminals on the pump. Disconnect the fuel hoses from the pump inlet and outlet nozzles, and the vent pipe from the connection on the pump end cover. Remove the bolts securing the pump to the body and remove the pump.

When refitting the pump, ensure that the outlet is vertically above the inlet port with the inlet and outlet nozzles horizontal. Also ensure that a good earth connection is made.

Contact Points Replacement

1. Remove the insulated sleeve, nut and connector together with its shakeproof washer from the terminal at the pump end cover. Remove the tape seal (if fitted) and detach the end cover.

2. Remove the condenser (if fitted) from its clip.

3. Remove the 5 BA screw securing the contact blade to

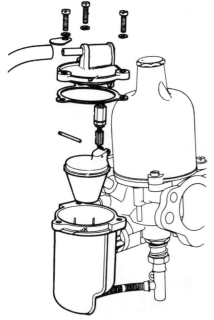

Fig. F:1 Components of float chamber assembly

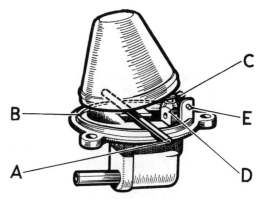

A. Gauge rod or drill
B. Machined lip
C. Adjustment point
D. Needle housing
E. Lever hinge pin

Fig. F:2 Checking float level setting on cars with metal float lever

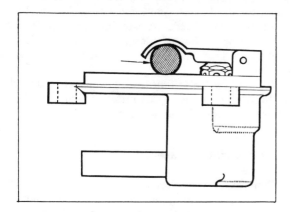

Fig. F:3 Float lever adjustment correctly set

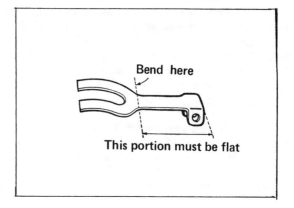

Bend here

This portion must be flat

Fig. F:4 Float lever arm

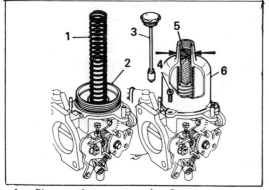

1. Piston spring   4. Securing screws
2. Piston assembly   5. Oil level
3. Damper assembly   6. Suction chamber

Fig. F:5 Piston and suction chamber assembly

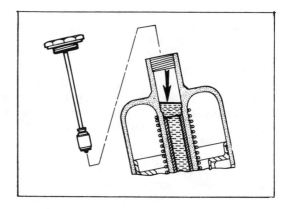

Fig. F:6 Piston damper oil level

the pedestal, and detach the contact blade. The long lead also secured by this screw will now be disconnected (Fig. F:9).

4. Examine the contact breaker points for signs of burning and pitting: if this is evident, the rocker assembly and spring blade must be renewed.

5. To remove the rocker assembly, remove the seal washer, nut and lead washer from the terminal stud. The lead washer will have flattened on the terminal tag and thread, and is best cut away with a knife. Unscrew the two screws securing the pedestal to the coil housing and remove the earth terminal tag together with the condenser clip (if fitted). Tip the pedestal and withdraw the terminal stud from the terminal tag. The pedestal may now be removed with the rocker mechanism attached.

6. To separate the rocker mechanism from the pedestal, push out the hardened steel pin and detach the rocker mechanism.

7. Invert the pedestal and fit the rocker assembly to it by pushing the steel pin through the small holes in the rockers and pedestal struts. It should be noted that the steel pin is specially hardened and must not be replaced by other than a genuine SU part.

8. Position the centre toggle so that, with the inner rocker spindle in tension against the rear of the contact point, the centre toggle spring is above the spindle on which the white rollers run (Fig. F:10). This is important to obtain the correct 'throw-over' action; it is also essential that the rockers are perfectly free to swing on the pivot pin and that the arms are not binding on the legs of the pedestal. If necessary, the rockers can be squared-up with a pair of long-nosed pliers.

9. Assemble the square-headed terminal stud to the pedestal, the back of which is recessed to take the square head. Fit the spring washer and electrical lead tag on to the terminal stud, then fit the lead washer and the coned nut with its coned face towards the lead washer. Tighten the nut and fit the end-cover seal washer.

10. Assemble the pedestal to the coil housing and secure with the two screws. Ensure that the spring washer on the left-hand screw is fitted between the pedestal and the earth lead tag. Do not over-tighten the screws otherwise the pedestal may be cracked.

11. Fit the contact blade and coil lead to the pedestal and secure lightly with the screw and washer. Adjust the position of the contact blade so that the contact points on it are a little above the contact points on the rocker arm when the points are closed (Fig. F:9). Also, when the contact points make or break, one pair of points wipe over the centre-line of the other in a symmetrical manner. Tighten the contact blade attachment screw when the correct setting is obtained.

12. Check that when the outer rocker is pressed on to the coil housing, the contact blade rests on the narrow rib which projects slightly above the main face of the pedestal (arrowed in Fig. F:11). If it does not, slacken the contact blade attachment screw, swing the blade clear of the pedestal, and bend it downwards a sufficient amount so that when repositioned it rests against the rib lightly; any over-tensioning of the blade will restrict the rocker travel.

Contact Gap Checking

1. Check the contact gap setting by carefully holding the contact blade against the rib on the pedestal without pressing the tip. Check that a 0.030 in (0.8 mm) feeler blade will pass between the fibre rollers and the face of the coil housing (Fig. F:11). If adjustment is necessary, the tip of the blade can be reset to obtain the correct gap.

2. Ensure that the end cover sealing washer is in place on the terminal stud, then fit the bakelite end cover. Secure in position with the brass nut, and fit the terminal tag or connector and the insulated sleeve.

CONTROL CABLES. . . . . [3]

Throttle Cable Replacement

Detach the throttle return spring from the throttle lever and its abutment bracket. Slacken the clamp nut to release the cable at the throttle lever then withdraw the cable from the bracket and its ferrule guide (Fig. F:12).

At the throttle pedal, release the nipple end from the slot in the top of the pedal lever, push the cable through the bulkhead into the engine compartment and withdraw the cable assembly.

Fit the new cable in the reverse sequence. Ensure that the throttle pedal has approximately 1/8 in (4 mm) free movement before it begins to open the throttle.

Choke Control Replacement

Remove the air cleaner assembly to allow access. Detach the clip securing the choke cable to the abutment bracket, then slacken the clamp screw at the cable trunnion and disconnect the cable from the carburettor (Fig. F:12).

Working inside the car, remove the locking nut and washer securing the choke outer cable to the switch panel. Pull the complete cable assembly through the bulkhead grommet and withdraw it from the switch panel.

Install the new cable in the reverse order of above. Ensure that the cable has 1/16 in (2 mm) free movement before it starts to pull on the fast idle cam lever.

FUEL TANK. . . . . [4]

Removal

1. From underneath the car, drain all petrol from the tank by removing the ½ in hexagon-headed drain plug underneath the tank. Replace the plug when the tank is empty.

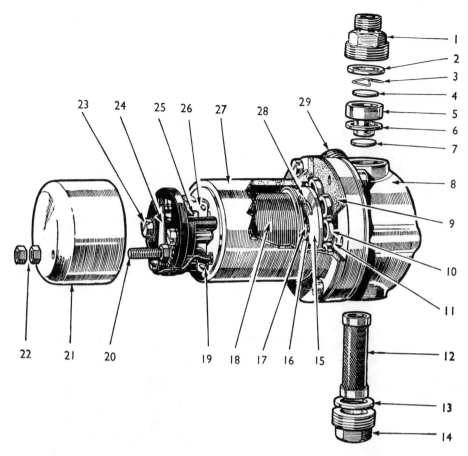

1.	Outlet union	8.	Pump body	15.	Steel armature
2.	Fibre washer (thick orange)	9.	Diaphragm assembly	16.	Pushrod
3.	Spring clip	10.	Armature guide rollers	17.	Magnet iron core
4.	Delivery valve disc	11.	Retaining plate	18.	Magnet coil
5.	Valve cage	12.	Filter	19.	Rocker hinge pin
6.	Fibre washer	13.	Fibre washer (thick orange)	20.	Terminal screw
7.	Suction valve disc	14.	Filter plug	21.	Cover

22.	Cover and terminal nuts
23.	Earth terminal screw
24.	Spring blade
25.	Inner rocker
26.	Outer rocker
27.	Magnet housing
28.	Armature spring
29.	Inlet union

Fig. F:7 Exploded view of S.U. fuel pump

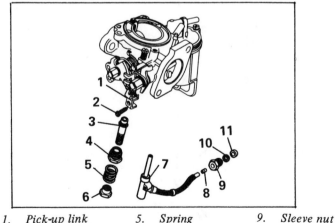

1.	Pick-up link	5.	Spring	9.	Sleeve nut
2.	Retaining screw	6.	Jet adjusting nut	10.	Washer
3.	Jet bearing	7.	Jet assembly	11.	Gland
4.	Bearing locking nut	8.	Ferrule		

Fig. F:8 Details of jet assembly

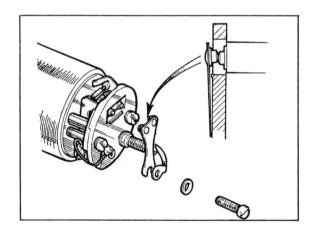

Fig. F:9 Correct setting of blade in relation to to rocker contact points

Fig. F:10 Fitting rocker assembly to pedestal.
Inset shows correct position of centre
toggle spring after assembly

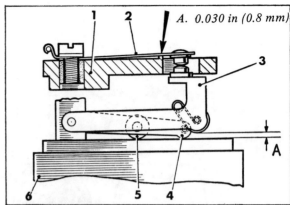

1.	Pedestal	4.	Inner rocker
2.	Contact blade	5.	Trunnion
3.	Outer rocker	6.	Coil housing

Fig. F:11 Contact gap setting on early type
rocker assembly

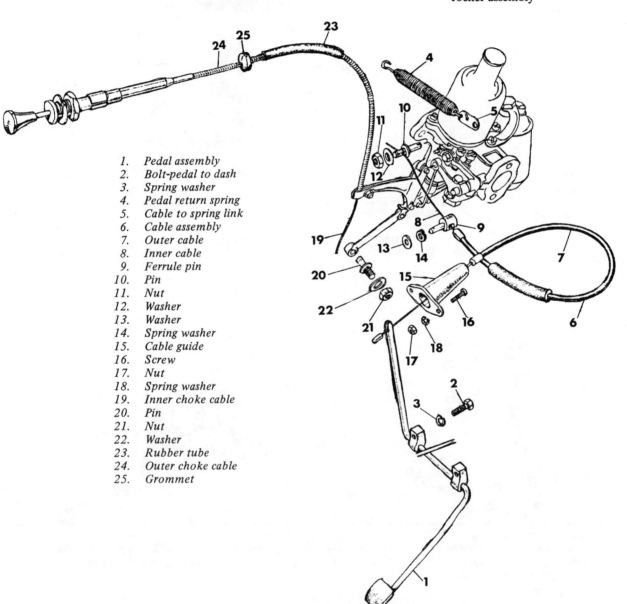

1. Pedal assembly
2. Bolt-pedal to dash
3. Spring washer
4. Pedal return spring
5. Cable to spring link
6. Cable assembly
7. Outer cable
8. Inner cable
9. Ferrule pin
10. Pin
11. Nut
12. Washer
13. Washer
14. Spring washer
15. Cable guide
16. Screw
17. Nut
18. Spring washer
19. Inner choke cable
20. Pin
21. Nut
22. Washer
23. Rubber tube
24. Outer choke cable
25. Grommet

Fig. F:12 Control cable linkages

Fuel System

2. Disconnect the petrol pipe from the tank by undoing the 5/16 in union nut.

3. Support the luggage boot lid in the open position or keep doors open (Traveller) and remove the spare wheel.

4. Extract the screws securing each half of the luggage compartment floor and lift the floor from its frame.

5. Slacken the filler neck hose clip and withdraw the filler and rubber ferrule.

6. Disconnect and insulate the flexible lead from the negative battery terminal and disconnect the petrol gauge wire from the tank attachment.

7. Withdraw the screws securing the petrol tank to the body and lift out the tank, taking care not to damage the packing strip beneath the flange.

Installation

Installation is a reverse of the removal procedure, but ensure that the filler neck rubber ferrule forms an effective joint with the body and that the drain plug and washer are fully tightened.

Technical Data

FUEL PUMP

Delivery . . . . SU Electric type L
Pressure . . . . 0.75 - 1 lb/in^2 (0.05-0.07 kg/cm^2)
Filter . . . . In pump body

CARBURETTOR

	948 cc	1098 cc
Type	SU H2 or HS2	SU HS2
Needle		
standard	M	AN
rich	AH2	H6
weak	EB	EB
Spring	Red	Red
Float setting	0.125-0.188 in (3.18-4.76 mm)	0.125-0.188 in (3.18-4.76 mm)
Float diameter	1.25 in (31.75 mm)	1.25 in (31.75 mm)
Jet	0.090 in (2.29 mm)	0.090 in (2.29 mm)

FUEL
Trouble Shooter

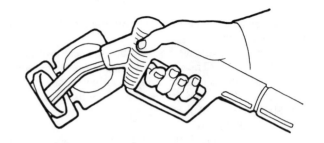

FAULT	CAUSE	CURE
Flooding	1. Improper seating or damaged float needle valve or seat 2. Incorrect float level 3. Fuel pump has excessive pressure	1. Check and replace parts as necessary. 2. Adjust float level. 3. Check fuel pump.
Excessive fuel consumption	1. Engine out of tune 2. Float level too high 3. Loose plug or jet 4. Defective gasket 5. Fuel leaks at pipes or connections 6. Choke valve operates improperly 7. Obstructed air bleed	1. Tune engine. 2. Adjust float level. 3. Tighten plug or jet. 4. Replace gaskets. 5. Trace leak and rectify. 6. Check choke valve. 7. Check and clear.
Stalling	1. Main jet obstructed 2. Incorrect throttle opening 3. Slow-running adjustment incorrect 4. Slow-running fuel jet blocked 5. Incorrect float level	1. Clean main jet. 2. Adjust throttle. 3. Adjust slow-running. 4. Clean jet. 5. Adjust float level.
Poor acceleration	1. Defective accelerator pump (if fitted) 2. Float level too low 3. Incorrect throttle opening 4. Defective accelerator linkage 5. Blocked pump jet	1. Overhaul pump. 2. Adjust float level. 3. Adjust throttle. 4. Adjust accelerator linkage. 5. Clean pump jet.
Spitting	1. Lean mixture 2. Dirty carburettor 3. Clogged fuel pipes 4. Manifold draws secondary air	1. Clean and adjust carburettor. 2. Clean carburettor. 3. Clean or replace pipes. 4. Tighten or replace gasket.
Insufficient fuel supply	1. Clogged carburettor 2. Clogged fuel pipe 3. Dirty fuel 4. Air in fuel system 5. Defective fuel pump 6. Clogged fuel filter	1. Dismantle and clean carburettor. 2. Clean fuel pipe. 3. Clean fuel tank. 4. Check connections and tighten. 5. Repair or replace fuel pump. 6. Clean or replace filter.
Loss of fuel delivery	1. Pump faulty (electric) 2. Slotted body screws loose 3. Diaphragm cracked 4. Loose fuel pipe connections 5. Defective valves 6. Cracked fuel pipes	1. Replace pump. 2. Tighten body screws. 3. Overhaul fuel pump. 4. Tighten fuel pipe connections. 5. Replace valves. 6. Replace fuel pipes.
Noisy pump	1. Loose pump mounting 2. Worn or defective rocker arm (if manual) 3. Broken rocker arm spring (if manual)	1. Tighten mounting bolts. 2. Replace rocker arm. 3. Replace spring.

Clutch & Gearbox

CLUTCH LINKAGE . . . . [1]

The clutch linkage on all Morris Minor models is mechanical. The clutch pedal, when depressed, turns a relay shaft at its base, (Fig. G:1) which in turn moves an adjustable connecting rod underneath the car. When the connecting rod moves, the attached clutch actuating lever operates the clutch mechanism.

Adjustments

The free pedal movement, measured at the pedal, should be between 1.375-1.5 in (35-38 mm). It is essential that this clearance be adhered to in order to allow the clutch to be completely released and at the same time prevent the possibility of damage to the clutch release bearing due to over-travel.

The clutch is adjusted by releasing the locknut on the clutch operating rod under the car (Fig. G:2). The spherical adjusting nut may then be screwed in the required direction. If the backlash is insufficient it will be increased by moving the adjusting nut towards the front of the car, and vice versa. Do not forget to retighten the locknut.

If any difficulty is experienced in freeing the clutch when the correct free pedal movement is provided, on no account should efforts be made to improve matters by attempting to increase the effective pedal travel. The actual cause must be found and rectified.

CLUTCH ASSEMBLY . . . . [2]

Removal

The gearbox must first be removed from the car as detailed later in this chapter.

From under the car, slacken the six clutch assembly retaining bolts on the flywheel evenly, working in diagonal sequence across the clutch. Hold the pressure plate cover, remove the bolts and detach the pressure plate assembly and clutch disc from the flywheel. Note that two dowels locate the pressure plate on the flywheel.

Inspection - Clutch Disc (Figs. G:3 and G:4)

Inspect the friction linings on the disc for wear, burning or contamination by oil or grease. The disc hub should be a free sliding fit on the gearbox input shaft without excessive side-play.

If the linings are worn down to near the rivet heads, or if any other of the above conditions are apparent, the disc must be renewed.

If oil or grease is present on the friction faces, the source must be determined and the fault rectified before fitting a new disc. This may be due to a defective gearbox input shaft bearing or crankshaft rear oil seal.

Pressure Plate Assembly

Inspect the machined face of the pressure plate for cracks, signs of burning and wear. Check the plate for distortion with a straight-edge.

Inspect the machined surface of the release lever thrust plate for wear or grooving.

Inspect the tips of the release levers, and the groove in the levers in which the fulcrum pin bears. If the metal has worn at all thin at any of these points, there is a danger of it breaking under load.

Inspect the thrust springs and release lever retaining clips for signs of wear or breakage.

If any adverse conditions are apparent, the pressure plate assembly must be exchanged.

Flywheel

Inspect the friction surface on the flywheel. Blueing or small cracks are of no particular importance, but if any deep scratches, scores, cracks or heat marks are present, the flywheel should be machined down or preferably replaced.

Release Bearing

All models are fitted with a carbon release bearing. Examine the bearing for cracks, bad pitting and wear. If there is less than 0.063 in (1.6 mm) of the bearing standing proud of the bearing cup, it must be renewed together with its cup. The bearing assembly is held in position on the withdrawal lever by two spring clips. Rotate the clips through 90° to release the bearing. Ensure the spring clips are correctly located when refitting the bearing.

Installation

A clutch centraliser tool is almost essential to ensure correct alignment of the clutch disc and flywheel during reassembly, see Fig. G:5. However, if great care is taken, it is possible to align the clutch by eye before finally tightening the pressure plate retaining bolts. If the disc is misaligned, difficulty will be encountered when attempting to refit the engine to the transmission assembly.

Ensure that the friction surfaces on the flywheel and pressure plate are perfectly clean and free from oil or grease.

Place the clutch disc in position on the flywheel. The flywheel side is normally marked on the hub of the disc. Align the disc with the centring tool, and locate the pressure plate assembly on the flywheel face.

Fit the pressure plate retaining bolts and tighten evenly, working diagonally to their specified torque. Remove the centring tool.

Finally, refit the gearbox to the engine, as detailed in the GEARBOX section of this chapter.

REAR COVER OIL SEAL . . . . [3]

Replacement (Figs. G:6 and G:7)

The procedure for replacing the rear gearbox oil seal is as follows:
1. Remove the propshaft as described in the Rear Axle and Propshaft chapter.
2. Using a suitable sharp drift drive off the old seal, by striking each side of the seal outer casing alternately.
3. Soak the new seal in oil and drive it on to the rear end of the cover using a suitable drift.
4. Replace the propshaft.
5. Run the engine to circulate the oil and top up if necessary.

GEARBOX . . . . [4]

Removal

1. To remove the gearbox, first chock the rear wheel and support the front of the car on axle stands. Remove the front floor carpet and disconnect the battery. Remove the battery if a heater is fitted to the vehicle.
2. Remove the screws which retain the gearbox cover - note that two of the inner row of screws, on each side of the gear lever, are longer than the remainder and that

these secure the gearbox crossmember to the chassis and remove the cover, the gear lever and the lever seating brackets.
3. Disconnect the exhaust pipe, at the flange, from the inlet manifold, and the cable from the starter motor. Drain the oil from the gearbox (Fig. G:8).
4. Remove the air cleaner assembly - see Tune-up chapter.
5. Support the engine with a jack.
6. Mark the flange of the propeller shaft rear joint and the input flange of the rear axle, to aid replacement.
7. Support the propeller shaft, remove the locknuts and bolts from the flanges, push the shaft forward, lower the rear end and withdraw the shaft from the vehicle. See Rear Axle & Propshaft chapter.
8. Disconnect the speedometer cable from the housing, see General Electrics chapter, and the earth cable from the gearbox. Detach the clutch pedal return spring, and extract the split pins and the anti-rattle washers which connect the operating rods to the clutch relay levers. See CLUTCH LINKAGE section previously.
9. Remove the bolts and washers which secure the relay shaft bracket to the chassis, remove the packing plate, the bracket and the bushes - do not misplace the washer which is between the inner bush and the lever - and withdraw the shaft from the spherical bush; remove the spring, and without disturbing the adjustment, the operating rod from the clutch withdrawal lever (Fig. G:1).
10. Remove the engine steady cable, Fig. G:9, (by removing the nut and the locknut from the rear end and unscrewing the cable from the bracket on the rear gearbox cover).
11. Remove the nut, the spring washer and the plain washer from each of the crossmember rear rubber mountings, the bolts which secure the crossmember to the chassis (note that the front, left-hand side bolt is longer than the remainder, and that it secures the earth cable) and remove the crossmember (Fig. G:10).
12. Fully lower the engine, remove the bolts which secure the gearbox and the starter motor to the engine rear mounting plate, withdraw the gearbox from the flange dowel pins and rotate it in a clockwise direction (when viewed from the rear), ensuring that the gearbox is not supported by the hub of the driven plate, and lower the gearbox from the vehicle (Fig. G:11).

Installation

Installation is a reversal of the removal procedure, but note the following.
a) When aligning the drive shaft with the clutch and the flywheel wheel, ensure that the gearbox is not supported by the hub of the driven plate, or the plate may be damaged.
b) With the drive shaft splines matched with those of the clutch, align the dowel pins with the holes by carefully rotating the gearbox. Check that the speedometer cable, when re-connected, is not tightly curved.

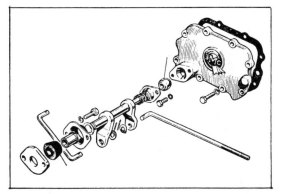

Fig. G:1 Exploded view of the clutch relay shaft

Fig. G:2 Clutch adjusting point

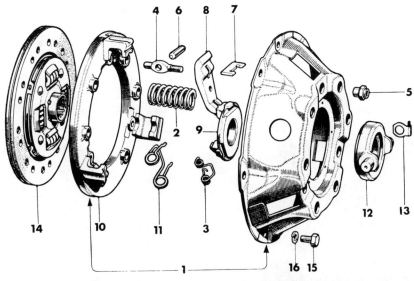

1.	Clutch assembly	5. Eyebolt nut	9. Bearing thrust plate	13. Retainer

1.   Clutch assembly
2.   Thrust spring
3.   Release lever retainer
4.   Eyebolt
5.   Eyebolt nut
6.   Release lever pin
7.   Strut
8.   Release lever
9.   Bearing thrust plate
10. Pressure plate
11. Anti-rattle spring
12. Release bearing
13. Retainer
14. Driven plate assembly
15. Clutch to flywheel screw
16. Spring washer

Fig. G:3 Exploded view of clutch assembly

A.   Flywheel
B.   Holding screw
C.   Driven plate
D.   Cover
E.   Thrust spring
F.   Clearance
G.   Graphite release bearing
H.   Release bearing cup
J.   Release bearing retainer
K.   Release lever plate
M.   Lever retainer and
       anti-rattle spring
N.   Release lever
O.   Knife-edge fulcrum
P.   Tag lock washer
Q.   Stud
R.   Adjusting nut
S.   Bearing plate
T.   Pressure plate

Fig. G:4 Cross section through clutch assembly

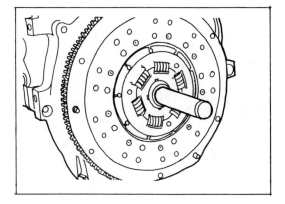

Fig. G:5 Using an aligning tool to centre the clutch disc

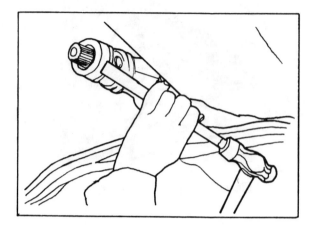

Fig. G:6 Removing a typical rear cover oil seal

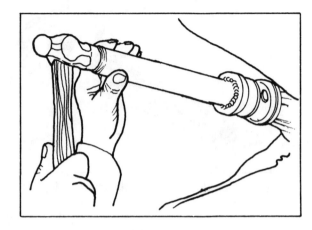

Fig. G:7 Installing a typical rear cover oil seal

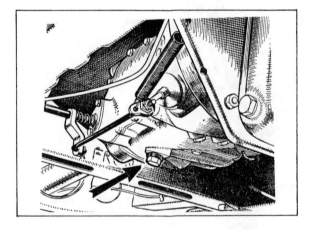

Fig. G:8 Location of the gearbox drain plug

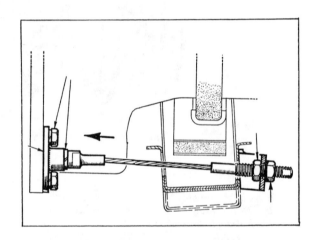

Fig. G:9 Engine steady cable assembly

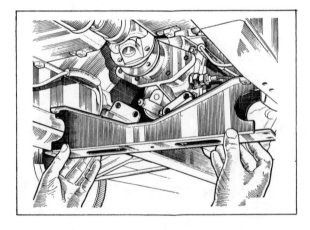

Fig. G:10 Removing the body crossmember

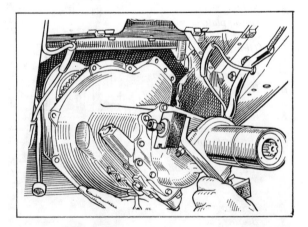

Fig. G:11 Withdrawing the gearbox from the engine

Technical Data

CLUTCH

Type. . . . . Single dry plate
Spring identification colour
    Early 948 models . . . . .3 dark blue, 3 yellow and green
    Later 948 models . . . . 6 yellow and green
    1098 models. . . . . .6 yellow
Plate. . . . . .Light grey
Diameter (1098 models) . . . . .7.25 in (184 mm)
Pedal free movement . . . . 1.375-1.5 in (35-38 mm)

GEARBOX - 948 cc

Ratios
    Reverse 4.664:1
    First 3.628:1
    Second 2.374:1
    Third 1.412:1
    Top 1:1
Overall Ratios
    Reverse 21.221:1
    First 16.507:1
    Second 10.802:1
    Third 6.425:1
    Top 4.555:1
Speedometer drive gear/pinion ratio 5/13

GEARBOX - 1098 cc

Synchromesh . . . . Second, third and top gears
Ratios
    Reverse 4.664:1
    First 3.628:1
    Second 2.172:1
    Third 1.412:1
    Top 1:1
Overall Ratios
    Reverse 19.665:1
    First 15.276:1
    Second 9.169:1
    Third 5.950:1
    Top 4.220:1

CLUTCH
Trouble Shooter

FAULT	CAUSE	CURE
Clutch slips	1. Clutch facing worn. 2. Clutch facing contaminated. 3. Warped clutch cover or pressure plate. 4. Incorrect adjustment (if adjustable).	1. Replace clutch assy. 2. Replace clutch assy. 3. Replace clutch assy. 4. Adjust clutch.
Clutch drags	1. Faulty clutch hydraulics (if hydraulic). 2. Faulty clutch adjustment (if adjustable). 3. Clutch disc warped. 4. Clutch hub splines worn or rusty. 5. Diaphragm worn or mal-adjusted.	1. Overhaul or replace clutch hydraulics. 2. Adjust clutch. 3. Replace clutch disc. 4. Replace or lubricate clutch. 5. Replace pressure plate.
Clutch chatter	1. Faulty pressure plate. 2. Faulty clutch disc. 3. Loose or worn engine mounting.	1. Replace pressure plate. 2. Replace clutch disc. 3. Replace mounting.
Clutch noise	1. Insufficient grease on bearing sleeve. 2. Clutch installed incorrectly.	1. Lubricate. 2. Check installation.
Clutch noise (pedal down)	1. Faulty release bearing.	1. Replace bearing.
Clutch noise (pedal on the way up)	1. Damaged or worn pilot bearing.	1. Fit new bearing.
Clutch grabs	1. Contaminated clutch lining. 2. Clutch worn or loose rivets. 3. Clutch splines worn or rusted. 4. Warped flywheel or pressure plate. 5. Loose mountings on engine or power unit	1. Replace clutch. 2. Replace clutch. 3. Clean or replace. 4. Repair or replace. 5. Tighten or replace.

Rear Axle/Propshaft

PROPSHAFT . . . .[1]

The propeller shaft and universal joints are of the Hardy Spicer type with needle-roller bearings.

A single shaft connects the rear axle and the gearbox. To accommodate fore and aft movement of the axle the shaft is provided with a splined sliding joint (Fig. H:1) at the front end. Each joint consists of a centre spider, four needle-roller bearing assemblies, and two yokes.

Inspection

Wear on shaft is ascertained by testing the lift in the joints either by hand or with a length of wood suitably pivoted.

Any circumferential movement of the shaft relative to the flange yokes indicates wear in the needle-roller bearings or in the splined shaft.

Removal

1. Mark the relative positions of the propeller shaft rear flange and the axle input flange.
2. Support the propshaft, detach it from the marked flanges by removing the flange bolts.
3. Withdraw the propshaft by lowering it and drawing it towards the rear of the car.

Installation

Installation is a reverse of the removal sequence, but make sure the marks are correctly aligned.

Universal Joint Replacement (Fig. H:2)

1. Mark the two yokes of the joint in relation to each other to ensure reassembly in the original position.
2. Remove the two circlips or snap rings from the two fixed yoke bearings. If the ring does not come out easily, tap the bearing face lightly to relieve the pressure against the ring.
3. Using a soft hammer, gently drive one housing towards the centre of the joint so that the opposite bearing housing is partially exposed.
4. Grip the exposed bearing in a vice or with Mole grips and pull it out of the yoke.
5. Drive the opposite housing out of the other side of the yoke, by tapping on the exposed trunnion of the joint spider, and remove the housing from the yoke.
6. Take great care to avoid damaging the inner edge of the bearing bores in the yoke during this operation. If the yoke is damaged by the joint spider during removal, any metal turned over the edge of the bore must be carefully relieved with a needle file, otherwise difficulty will be encountered when attempting to install the new bearing housings.
7. Disengage the joint spider from the yoke.
8. Repeat the operation to separate the spider from the other yoke.
9. Discard the complete joint assembly (spider, bearing housings etc.).
10. Fill the reservoir holes in the ends of the spider journals with grease, taking great care to exclude all air pockets. Fill each bearing assembly with grease to a depth of about 0.125 in (3 mm).
11. Fit the new spider into one of the yokes.
12. Fit one of the bearing assemblies into one of the yoke bores and tap it squarely into place, using a soft-nosed drift slightly smaller in diameter than the bearing housing. Ensure that the bearing does not tilt as it is installed.
13. Engage the spider journal in the bearing housing, and fit the second bearing to the opposite yoke bore.
14. Tap each bearing in turn into the yoke bore until it is possible to fit the circlip. Ensure the circlip seats correctly in its groove.
15. Repeat for the other yoke.
16. After assembly, if the bearing appears to bind, tap the ear of each yoke lightly in turn with a soft-faced hammer; this will relieve any pressure of the bearing on the ends of the journals.

REAR AXLE ASSEMBLY . . . .[2]

Removal (Figs. H:3 and H:4)

1. Chock the front wheels and raise the rear of the car, supporting it with axle stands on the body side members in front of the rear wheels.
2. Feed a trolley jack under the car from the rear and

use it to support the differential casing. Make sure the jack is only supporting the differential, not lifting it.

3. Remove both rear wheels and release the handbrake.

4. If the exhaust pipe runs underneath the axle assembly, remove it by undoing its support clamps and its flange at the exhaust manifold on side of the engine.

5. If check straps are fitted, remove the nuts and bolts which attach them to the car body (Fig. H:4).

6. Remove the nuts and bolts securing the dampers to the attachment points on the rear axle casing (see the Rear Suspension chapter).

7. Disconnect the handbrake cable from the brake drums (see the Brakes chapter).

8. Undo the hydraulic brake pipe union at the point in front of the differential housing.

9. Remove the propshaft assembly as described previously.

10. Check that the trolley jack is still in position under the differential housing.

11. Remove the nuts (eight in all) from the inverted U bolts which hold the axle to the rear springs at either end of the assembly (Fig. H:4).

12. Lower the trolley jack and remove the axle from the car.

Installation

Installation is a straightforward reverse of the removal procedure, but pay attention to the following points:

a) Make sure any damaged nuts and bolts are replaced.

b) Remember to bleed the brake system as described in the Brakes chapter before attempting to road test the vehicle.

AXLE SHAFTS . . . . [3]

Removal (Fig. H:5)

1. Chock the front wheels and raise the rear of the car, supporting the side of the car to be worked on with an axle stand on the body side member in front of the rear wheel. If the car is raised on both sides, oil will run out of the axle shaft and probably contaminate the brake linings.

2. Feed a trolley jack under the car from the rear and use it to support the differential casing. Make sure the jack is only supporting the differential, not lifting it.

3. Remove the rear wheel, release the handbrake and slacken off the brake adjusters.

4. Unscrew the two cross-head brake drum retaining screws and withdraw the brake drum.

5. Remove the single shaft flange locating screw and pull the half shaft by its flange out of the axle casing.

NOTE: If both axle shafts are being removed at the same time, support the car as described for removal of the REAR AXLE ASSEMBLY, remove the drain plug from

the bottom of the differential (Fig. H:7) and drain the oil before removing the brake drums.

Installation

Installation is a straightforward reverse of the removal procedure, but make sure the brakes are readjusted and that the differential is topped up with the appropriate grade of oil.

DIFFERENTIAL ASSEMBLY . . . . [4]

Overhaul of the differential assembly is not a practical proposition for the home-mechanic as a variety of special tools is required to strip and rebuild the unit. A more satisfactory solution would be to remove it from the axle casing and deliver it to a specialist for attention.

Removal (Figs. H:3 and H:7)

1. Remove both axle shafts as detailed above.

2. Disconnect the propshaft from the differential pinion flange.

3. Remove the drain plug from the underside of the axle casing and drain the oil from the axle (Fig. H:6).

4. Remove the eight nuts securing the differential casing to the axle banjo and withdraw the differential assembly.

Installation

5. Ensure that the mating faces on the axle casing and differential housing are perfectly clean and free from old gasket material.

6. Refit the differential assembly, using a new paper gasket.

7. Reconnect the propshaft, and refit the axle shaft as detailed previously.

8. Refit the axle with the recommended grade of oil.

PINION OIL SEAL . . . . [5]

Replacement

1. Jack up and support the rear of the car.

2. Disconnect the propshaft from the differential drive flange (Fig. H:8). Mark the flanges before removal to ensure correct alignment on reassembly.

3. Unscrew the nut from the centre of the drive flange using a suitable socket. It will be necessary to fabricate a locking tool, such as that shown in Fig. H:8, to prevent the flange from turning while releasing the nut.

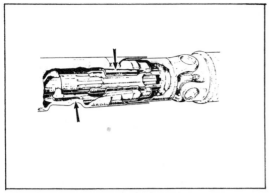

Fig. H:1 Section through sliding joint, showing oilways

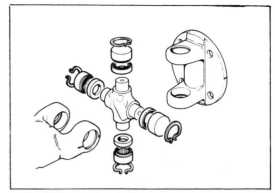

Fig. H:2 Overhauling propshaft universal joint

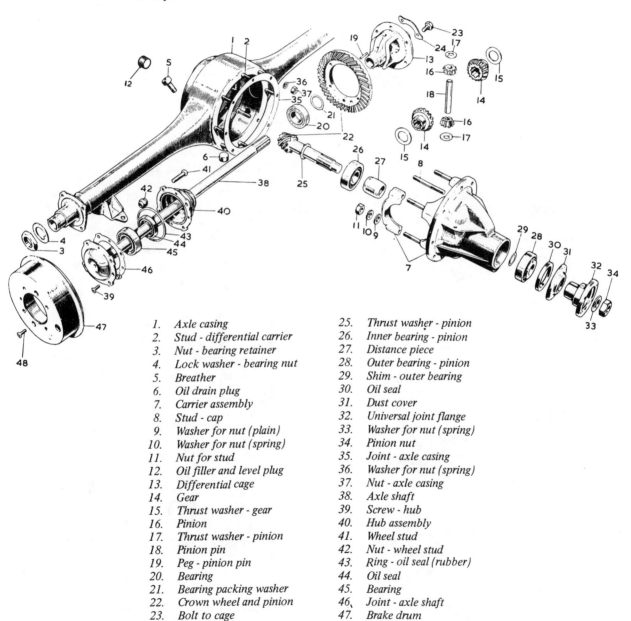

1.	Axle casing	25.	Thrust washer - pinion
2.	Stud - differential carrier	26.	Inner bearing - pinion
3.	Nut - bearing retainer	27.	Distance piece
4.	Lock washer - bearing nut	28.	Outer bearing - pinion
5.	Breather	29.	Shim - outer bearing
6.	Oil drain plug	30.	Oil seal
7.	Carrier assembly	31.	Dust cover
8.	Stud - cap	32.	Universal joint flange
9.	Washer for nut (plain)	33.	Washer for nut (spring)
10.	Washer for nut (spring)	34.	Pinion nut
11.	Nut for stud	35.	Joint - axle casing
12.	Oil filler and level plug	36.	Washer for nut (spring)
13.	Differential cage	37.	Nut - axle casing
14.	Gear	38.	Axle shaft
15.	Thrust washer - gear	39.	Screw - hub
16.	Pinion	40.	Hub assembly
17.	Thrust washer - pinion	41.	Wheel stud
18.	Pinion pin	42.	Nut - wheel stud
19.	Peg - pinion pin	43.	Ring - oil seal (rubber)
20.	Bearing	44.	Oil seal
21.	Bearing packing washer	45.	Bearing
22.	Crown wheel and pinion	46.	Joint - axle shaft
23.	Bolt to cage	47.	Brake drum
24.	Locking washer for bolt	48.	Locating screw - brake drum

Fig. H:3 Exploded view of rear axle assembly

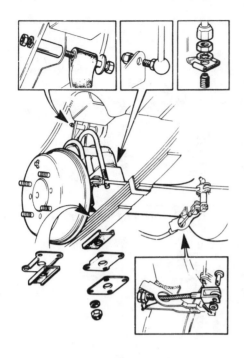

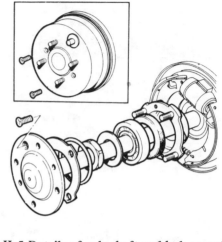

Fig. H:5 Details of axle shaft and hub assembly

Fig. H:4 Rear axle attachments

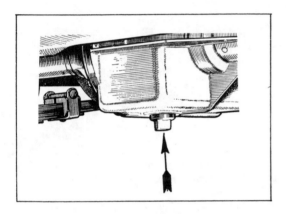

Fig. H:6 The rear axle drain plug

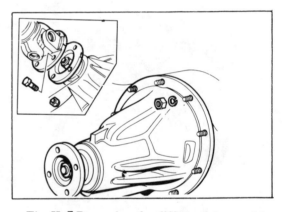

Fig. H:7 Removing the differential assembly

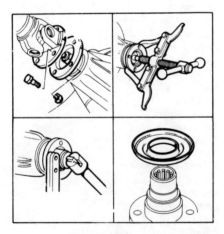

Fig. H:8 Differential drive flange removal

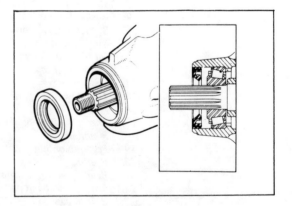

Fig. H:9 Replacing pinion oil seal

4. Withdraw the drive flange using a suitable puller, and remove the stone guard located behind the flange.

5. Extract the oil seal from the differential casing (Fig. H: 9). This can be done with a screwdriver or other suitable lever.

6. Press the new oil seal into position with the lip of the seal facing inwards. It will facilitate installation if the outer circumference of the seal is lubricated with oil.

7. Refit the stone guard and replace the drive flange, taking care not to damage the edge of the oil seal. Fit the flange retaining nut and washer and tighten to 140 lb ft (19.34 kg m) with a torque wrench while preventing the flange from turning.

8. Reconnect the propshaft, with the marks on the flange aligned.

9. Check the rear axle oil level and top up if necessary.

Technical Data

REAR AXLE

Type of axle . . . . Three-quarter-floating
Ratio . . . . 4.55:1, or 4.22:1

SPRINGS - EARLY TYPE

Type . . . . Semi-elliptic
Working load . . . . .440 lb (199.6 kg)
Length . . . . .43.5 in (110.5 cm)
Width . . . . 1.5 in (38.1 mm)
Number of leaves - rear 7
Thickness of leaves - rear . . . . .0.21875 in (5.56 mm)
Free camber - rear . . . . .3.5 in (88.9 mm), models with second-type axle 4.125 in (10.5 cm)
Working camber - rear . . . . 0.28 in (7.1 mm) negative, models with second-type axle 0.34 in (8.6 mm) positive

SPRINGS - LATER TYPE

Number of leaves 5
Thickness of leaves . . . . 0.25 in (6.35 mm)
Free camber . . . . .4.22 in (10.72 cm)
Working camber . . . . .0.78 in (19.84 mm) positive

Rear Suspension

GENERAL DESCRIPTION. . . . .[1]

The semi-elliptic leaf springs provided for rear suspension are secured beneath the rear axle by 'U' bolts as shown in Fig. I:1.

The front ends of the springs are anchored in flexing rubber bushes, while the rear ends are mounted in similar bushes in swinging shackles.

Moulded rubber packing pads are inserted between the leaves and the spring clips. It is essential that no lubricant be used on the spring leaves or shackles.

The spring action is controlled by shock absorbers of the piston type.

All the working parts of the shock absorbers are submerged in oil.

The shock absorbers are carefully set before dispatch and cannot be adjusted without special equipment. Their design is such that they are capable of giving long service without attention other than the periodical replenishment of the fluid.

REAR SPRINGS. . . . .[2]

Removal (Figs. I:2 and I:3)

1. Jack the rear of the car and place a suitable support beneath the axle casing.
2. Slacken off the 'U' bolt locknuts and remove the nuts. Raise the 'U' bolts until the shock absorbers and brackets can be pivoted clear of the springs. Remove the plate and rubber pad.
3. Remove the rear shackle nuts and plates.
4. Undo the 5/16 in nut from the spring front anchorage bolt. The bolt has pin spanner holes in its head to permit it to be held against rotation while loosening or tightening up the nut.
5. The spring is now free to be removed.

Installation

Installation of the spring is a reversal of the above procedure, but before replacing the shackle bolts, bushes, and plates they must be inspected for wear and, if necessary, replaced by new components.

Ensure that the rubber pads are positioned correctly and that the head of the spring centre bolt registers with the spring bracket on the axle case.

The spring must be replaced with two spring clips forward of the axle, and the front anchorage bolt has to be inserted from the inner side of the bracket.

NOTE: Before tightening the spring bolts it is essential that the normal working load be applied to the springs so that the flexing rubber bushes are deflected to an equal extent in both directions during service. Failure to take this precaution will inevitably lead to early deterioration of the bushes.

Dismantling

1. Slacken off and remove the three spring clip bolts, distance pieces, and rubber packings.
2. Release the locknut and nut from the spring centre bolt and remove the distance piece and bolt.

The leaves may now be separated.

Inspection

Clean each leaf thoroughly and examine for cracks or breakages. Check the centre bolt for wear or distortion (this bolt forms the location for the spring on its axle pad and should be in good condition).

NOTE: When fitting new leaves it is important that they are of the correct length and thickness and have the same curvature as the remaining leaves.

It is advisable, even when no leaves are broken, to fit replacement springs when the originals have lost their camber due to settling.

Reassembly

1. Place the leaves together in their correct order, locating them with the centre bolt.
2. The dowel head of the bolt must be on top of the spring.
3. Fit No. 5 leaf with its clip on the forward side of the centre dowel bolt.
4. Replace the spring clip rubber packings, clip distance

Fig. I:1 Positioning of the rear springs

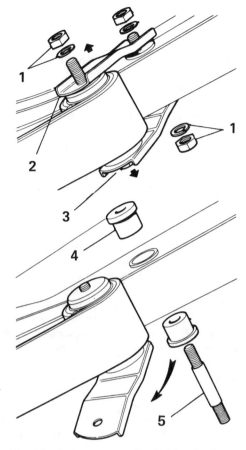

1. Shackle plate nuts
2. Loose shackle plate
3. Spring bolt
4. Rubber bushes
5. Pin through body

Fig. I:2 Shackle plate fixing on rear spring

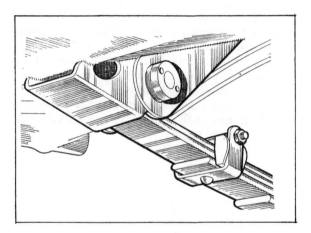

Fig. I:3 Rear spring anchorage pin

Fig. I:4 Location of rear shock absorber, showing filler cap

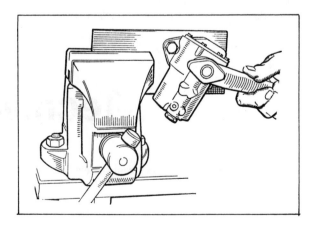

Fig. I:5 A shock absorber being tested in a vice

©BLUK

pieces, and bolts.

NOTE: On later models the rear spring front brackets are fitted with detachable and renewable bush plates.

SHOCK ABSORBERS. . . . . [3]

The maintenance of the shock absorbers (Fig. I:4) should include a periodical examination of their anchorage to the chassis and axle and tightening the fixing bolts up as required.

For replenishing the fluid, the rear shock absorbers must be removed from the car.

The cheese-headed screws securing the cover-plate must be kept fully tightened to prevent leakage of the fluid.

No adjustment of the dampers is required or provided. Any attempt to dismantle them will seriously affect their operation and performance. Should this be necessary, they must be replaced.

When handling dampers that have been removed from the car for any purpose it is important to keep the assemblies upright as far as possible, otherwise air may enter the operating chamber, resulting in free movement.

NOTE: Before fitting the link to the attachment on the axle or swivel pin it is advisable to work the lever arm a few times through its full range of movement to expel any air which has found its way into the operating chamber.

Removal

To remove the shock absorbers from their anchorage brackets, remove the split pin and the 5/16 in nut securing the damper arm link to the frame and extract the rubber bushes.

Remove the link from its pivot bolt and the two 5/16 in nuts, bolts, and spring washers securing the damper body to the spring bracket.

Installation

Installation of the dampers is carried out in the reverse order to the removal procedure, but if the rubber bushes on the damper links are worn, new ones must be fitted.

NOTE: When handling dampers that have been removed from the car for any purpose it is important to keep the assemblies upright as far as possible, otherwise air may enter the operating chamber, resulting in free movement. Before fitting the link to the attachment on the axle or swivel pin it is advisable to work the lever arm a few times through its full range of movement to expel any air which has found its way into the operating chamber.

Testing

If there is any doubt that the road springs are adequately damped the condition of the springs and the tyre pressures should also be considered as these have an appreciable bearing on the results obtained.

If the shock absorbers do not appear to function satisfactorily an indication of their resistance can be obtained by carrying out the following check:

1. Remove the shock absorbers from the car.
2. Hold them in a vice and move the lever arm up and down through its complete stroke (Fig. I:5). A moderate resistance throughout the full stroke should be felt; if, however, the resistance is erratic, or free movement in the lever is noted, lack of fluid is indicated or there may be air in front of the piston.
3. The free movement should not exceed 1/8 in (3 mm) at the outer end of the arm.
4. If the addition of fluid and working the arm over its full range of travel a number of times give no improvement a new shock absorber should be fitted.

Too much resistance, i.e. when it is not possible to move the lever arm slowly by hand, indicates a broken internal part or a seized piston.

Topping-Up

The shock absorbers must be removed from the car before they are given replenishment attention.

The use of good-quality mineral oil to Specification S.A.E. 20/20W should be used, but this alternative is not suitable for low-temperature operation.

When fluid has been added, the lever arm should be worked throughout its full stroke to expel any air that might be present in the operating chamber before the filler plug is replaced.

The interior of the body should be filled with fluid to within 3/8 in (10 mm) from the top of the cover.

Technical Data

REAR SPRINGS (from vehicle No. 680464)

Number of leaves. 5
Thickness of leaves . . . . 0.25 in (6.35 mm)
Free camber. . . . . 4.22 in (10.72 cm)
Working camber . . . . .0.78 in (19.84 mm) positive

Front Suspension

GENERAL DESCRIPTION .... [1]

The independent front suspension is made up of torsion bars disposed longitudinally and splined into arms attached to the lower ends of each swivel pin. At their upper ends, the swivel pins (see Steering chapter) are linked to the lever type shock absorbers.

The grease nipples provided at the swivel pin links are the only points requiring lubrication attention (see Routine Maintenance), the inner ends of the lower arms being anchored to the frame members in flexible rubber bushes.

Tie-rods between the forward side of the lower suspension arms and the frame members maintain rigidity of the assembly during acceleration and braking and abnormally rough road conditions.

The trim of the suspension is adjusted at the rear end of each torsion bar by means of an adjuster plate in conjunction with the torsion bar rear end lever. (See Fig. J: 2). *NOTE: Rubber bushes are used in the suspension and the rear springs are rubber-mounted. It is therefore most important not to lubricate these components with oil. If squeaks develop the springs should be sprayed with WD 40 or a similar lubricating compound.*

Normal maintenance is confined to lubrication of the linkage and grease nipples as described in the Routine Maintenance chapter.

TORSION BARS .... [2]

Adjustment

The adjuster plate, provided at the rear end of each torsion bar (See Fig. J:3) should be used to correct any list on the car which develops if the torsion bars do not settle evenly.

To carry out this adjustment, raise the front of the car until the road wheels are clear of the ground and remove the hub disc and wheel.

Place a jack beneath the outer end of the lower suspension arm (See Fig. J:4) and raise it until the hydraulic damper arm at the top of the swivel pin is just clear of the rubber rebound pad. Care must be taken to see that the jack is not liable to slip while it is taking the torsion bar load.

Remove the nut and bolt securing the tie-rod to the fork on the suspension arm and remove the nuts and bolts retaining the forward half of the arm.

Disengage the lower swivel pin link from the suspension arm and lower the jack until the load is taken off the torsion bar.

Slacken the nut and washer on the rear end of the torsion bar.

Withdraw the nut and bolt securing the torsion bar rear end lever to the frame crossmember and slide the adjuster plate in the required direction. Take care not to lose the flat washer which is between the lever and the plate.

To set the car upwards select a lower hole in the adjuster plate. Each successive hole raises the car approximately 0.25 in (6.3 mm). If the plate is moved in the reverse direction the car is, of course, lowered.

If the lever is rotated one spline on the torsion bar the car will be raised approximately 1.5 in (3.8 cm).

Replace the nut and bolt in the rear end lever and fully tighten it. The remainder of the assembly procedure is a reversal of the order of dismantling.

1. Raise the front of the car until the road wheels are clear of the ground.
2. Remove the hub cover and wheel.
3. Place a jack beneath the outer end of the rear portion of the lower suspension arm and raise it until the hydraulic damper arm at the top of the swivel pin is just clear of the rubber rebound pad. Care must be taken to see that the jack is not liable to slip while it is taking the torsion bar load.
4. Withdraw the securing bolt and disengage the tie-rod end from the fork on the suspension arm.
5. Remove the nuts and bolts securing the halves of the lower suspension arm and remove the front half of the arm (see Fig. J:5).
6. Disengage the swivel pin link from the suspension arm and lower the jack until the load is off the torsion bar.
7. Remove the nut from the rear end of the torsion bar

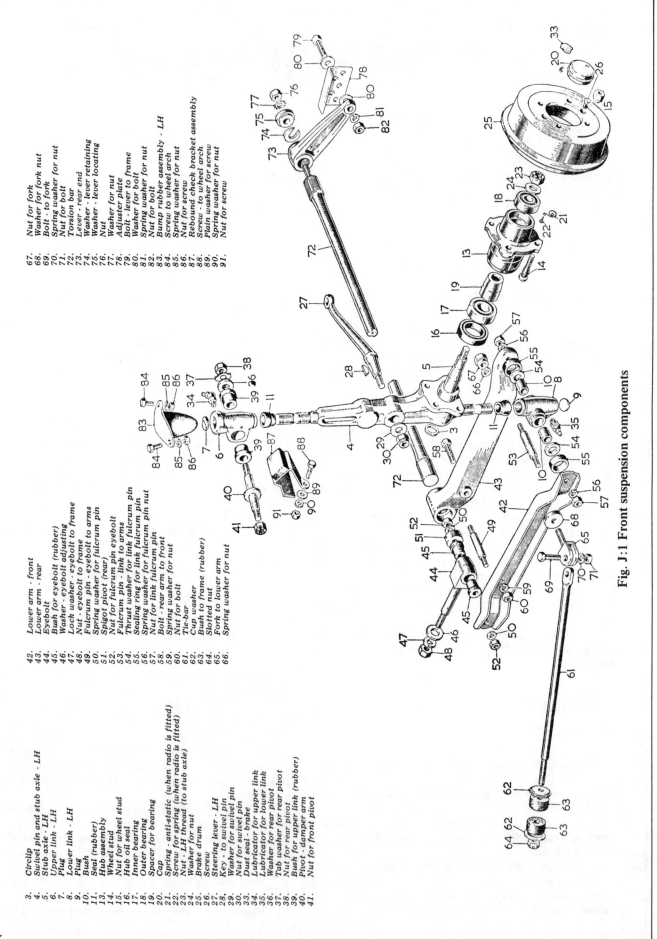

Fig. J:1 Front suspension components

3.   Circlip
4.   Swivel pin and stub axle - LH
5.   Stub axle - LH
6.   Upper link - LH
7.   Plug
8.   Lower link - LH
9.   Plug
10. Bush
11. Seal (rubber)
13. Hub assembly
14. Wheel stud
15. Nut for wheel stud
16. Hub oil seal
17. Inner bearing
18. Outer bearing
19. Spacer for bearing
20. Cap
21. Spring - anti-static (when radio is fitted)
22. Screw for spring (when radio is fitted)
23. Nut - LH thread (to stub axle)
24. Washer for nut
25. Brake drum
26. Screw
27. Steering lever - LH
28. Key - to swivel pin
29. Washer for swivel pin
30. Dust seal - brake
34. Lubricator for upper link
35. Lubricator for lower link
36. Washer for rear pivot
37. Tab washer for rear pivot
38. Nut for rear pivot
39. Bush for upper link (rubber)
40. Pivot - damper arm
41. Nut for front pivot

42. Lower arm - front
43. Lower arm - rear
44. Eyebolt
45. Bush for eyebolt (rubber)
46. Washer - eyebolt adjusting
47. Lock washer - eyebolt to frame
48. Nut - eyebolt to frame
49. Fulcrum pin - eyebolt to arms
50. Spring washer for fulcrum pin
51. Spigot pivot (rear)
52. Nut for fulcrum pin eyebolt
53. Fulcrum pin - link to arms
54. Thrust washer for link fulcrum pin
55. Sealing ring for link fulcrum pin
56. Spring washer for fulcrum pin
57. Nut for link fulcrum pin
58. Bolt - rear arm to front
59. Spring washer for nut
60. Nut for bolt
61. Tie-bar
62. Cup washer
63. Bush to frame (rubber)
64. Slotted nut
65. Fork to lower arm
66. Spring washer for nut

67. Nut for fork
68. Washer for fork nut
69. Bolt - to fork
70. Spring washer for nut
71. Nut for bolt
72. Torsion bar
73. Lever - rear end
74. Washer - lever retaining
75. Washer - lever locating
76. Nut
77. Washer for nut
78. Adjuster plate
79. Bolt - lever to frame
80. Washer for bolt
81. Spring washer for nut
82. Nut for bolt
83. Bump rubber assembly - LH
84. Screw to wheel arch
85. Spring washer for nut
86. Nut for screw
87. Rebound check bracket assembly
88. Screw - to wheel arch
89. Plain washer for screw
90. Spring washer for screw
91. Nut for screw

Fig. J:2 Layout of Morris Minor front suspension

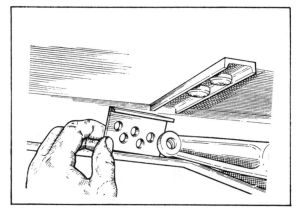

Fig. J:3 The vernier plate for adjusting the torsion bars

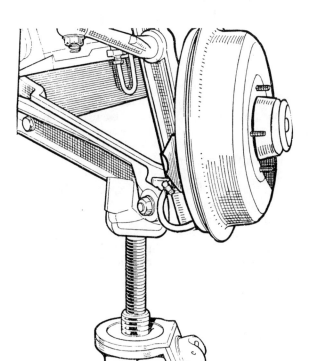

Fig. J:4 Supporting suspension arm with a jack

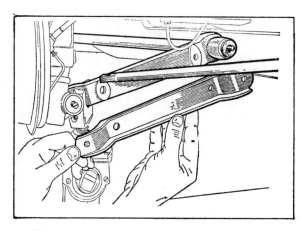

Fig. J:5 Removing part of the suspension arm to release the torsion bar

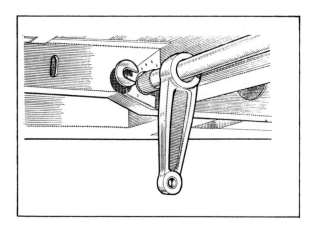

Fig. J:6 Inserting the slotted retaining washer at the end of the torsion bar

Fig. J:7 Replacing the shouldered washer to the torsion bar

©BLUK

and the nut and bolt securing the torsion bar lever to the frame.

8. Slide the lever forward along the torsion bar until it is clear of the splines and remove the lever locating and retaining washers.

9. Withdraw the torsion bar from the suspension arm splines and lift it clear.

Installation

A torsion bar which has been fitted and used on one side of the car must on no account be transferred for use on the other side. The torsion bars are only interchangeable when new. They become 'handed' once they have been in service and must from then on always be used on the same side of the car.

There are 48 splines on each end of the torsion bars, and for each consecutive spline position of the rear end lever a radial movement of the swivel pin of approximately 1.5 in. (3.8 cm.) is provided.

1. To fit the torsion bar support the front end of the car and adjust the jack beneath the lower suspension arm until there is a difference in height of 5.625 in. (14.3 cm.) between the inner and outer suspension arm fulcrum pins. *NOTE: The car must be standing on a level floor and measurements taken from a horizontal flat plate.*

2. When a new torsion bar is to be fitted this difference in height must be increased to 6 in. (15.2 cm.) to allow for the small permanent set which takes place when the bar is loaded for the first time.

3. Thread the rear end of the torsion bar through the rear end lever and the frame crossmember. The lever is offset and must be fitted with the recessed side to the rear.

4. Engage the front end of the torsion bar in the suspension arm and slide the lever over the rear end splines, bringing the eye of the arm into line with the slot in the frame crossmember.

5. Insert the slotted retaining washer (see Fig. J:6) between the lever and the crossmember with the countersunk side towards the torsion bar splines. Ensure that the washer fits into the register in the lever and refit the shouldered locating washer on the end of the torsion bar threaded attachment spigot (see Fig. J:7). The small diameter of this washer MUST register with the hole in the frame. Replace the torsion bar retaining nut and washer.

6. Insert the adjuster plate and flat washer between the rear end lever and the frame. Align a hole in the adjuster plate with the lever eye and insert the locking bolt and flat washer from the rear. Replace and tighten the nut and spring washer.

7. Raise the jack until the lower swivel pin link engages the suspension arm. Ensure that the rubber seals and thrust washers are in position and replace the foward half of the suspension arm.

8. Replace and tighten the suspension arm, swivel link, and tie-rod nuts and bolts.

Lower the car on to level ground and check the difference in vertical height of the inner and outer suspension arm fulcrum pins. This measurement should be 1.625 in. (4.1 cm.) and be the same on both right-hand and left-hand suspension assemblies.

SHOCK ABSORBERS .... [3]

Hydraulic shock absorbers are fitted to the front of all Minor suspensions. All the working parts are submerged in oil.

The shock absorbers are set during manufacture and cannot be adjusted without special equipment. Their design is such that they are capable of giving long service without attention other than the periodical replenishment of the fluid.

The maintenance of the shock absorbers (see Fig. J:8) should include a periodical examination of their anchorage to the chassis and axle and tightening the fixing bolts up as required. For replenishing the fluid the tops must be thoroughly cleaned before the filler plug is unscrewed.

The cheese-head screws securing the cover-plate must be kept fully tightened to prevent leakage of the fluid.

Removal

1. To disconnect the front shock absorbers, raise the front of the car and remove the hub cap and road wheel.

2. Place a jack beneath the outer end of the lower suspension arm (see Fig. J:4) and raise it until the shock absorber lever arm at the top of the swivel pin is just clear of the rebound pad.

3. Extract the split pin and slacken the 7/16 in. slotted nut securing the swivel pin bolt to the lever arm.

4. Tap the circumference of the eye and, placing a support behind the arm, use a copper hammer to drive the bolt from its tapered seat.

5. The shock absorber may be withdrawn after removal of the nuts and bolts securing it to the bulkhead crossmember. Note that a protector shield between the exhaust pipe and the left-hand shock absorber is attached to the shock absorber securing bolts.

Installation

Installation is carried out in the reverse order to the removal procedure. After replacing and tightening the swivel pin bolt in the eye of the front lever arm, check the clearance between the arm and swivel pin link. There must be a clearance of 0.002 in. (0.05 mm.).

If the clearance is not correct it must be adjusted as described in the Steering chapter. Also refer to Fig. J:1.

When handling dampers that have been removed from the car for any purpose it is important to keep the assemblies upright as far as possible, otherwise air may enter the operating chamber, resulting in free movement. *NOTE: Before fitting the link to the attachment on the axle or swivel pin it is advisable to work the lever arm a few times through its full range of movement to expel any air which has found its way into the operating chamber.*

Checking

If the shock absorbers do not appear to function satisfactorily, an indication of their resistance can be obtained by carrying out the following check:

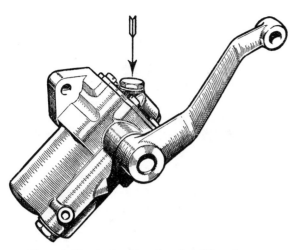

Fig. J:8 Shock absorber showing filler plug
(arrowed)

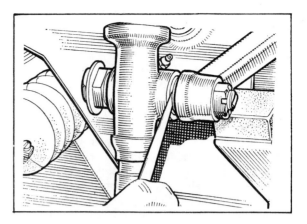

Fig. J:9 Measuring the clearance between arm
and swivel pin link

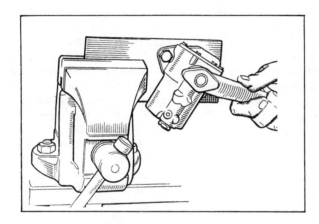

Fig. J:10 Using a vice to test a shock absorber

Fig. J:11 Replenishing the shock absorbers

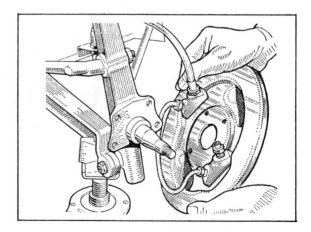

Fig. J:12 Removing the backplate assembly

1. Remove the shock absorbers from the car, as already described.

2. Hold them in a vice and move the lever arm up and down through its complete stroke. A moderate resistance throughout the full stroke should be felt; if, however, the resistance is erratic, or free movement in the lever is noted, lack of fluid is indicated or there may be air in front of the piston. The free movement should not exceed 0.12 in. (3 mm.) at the outer end of the arm.

If the addition of fluid, see Topping Up, and working the arm over its full range of travel a number of times give no improvement a new shock absorber should be fitted.

Too much resistance, i.e. when it is not possible to move the lever arm slowly by hand, indicates a broken internal part or a seized piston. In such cases the shock absorber should be changed for a new or reconditioned one. *NOTE: Shock absorbers should always be replaced in pairs on the same axle, otherwise the suspension and the vehicle handling could be unbalanced and possibly even dangerous.*

Topping Up (Fig. J:11)

The shock absorbers may be topped up in position, once the tops have been thoroughly cleaned to ensure that when the filler plug is extracted no dirt falls into the filler orifice.

NOTE: This is most important as it is absolutely vital that no dirt or foreign matter should enter the operating chamber. Use the fluid recommended in the Technical Data section at the end of this chapter, and fill up each shock absorber to within 0.39 in. (10 mm.) of the filler orifice.

SUSPENSION ARMS .... [4]

Removal — Front Arm (Fig. J:1)

1. Remove the hub cap, slacken the wheel nuts, jack the car and remove the road wheel.
2. Place a support under the body, remove the jack and put it under the outer end of the rear suspension arm.
3. Raise the jack until the underside of the shock absorber arm is 0.25 in. (6 mm.) clear of the rubber rebound stop.
4. Unscrew the nut bolt and washer which hold the end of the wishbone tie-bar to the wishbone fork and pull the tie-bar clear.
5. Remove the nuts and washers holding the front suspension arm to the rear suspension arm and remove the front suspension arm.

Installation

Installation is a reverse of the removal procedure.

Removal — Rear Arm (Fig. J:1)

1. Remove the front suspension arm as just described.
2. Remove the torsion bar as detailed previously.
3. Remove the nut, washer and fulcrum pin securing the arm to the eyebolt. This will make it possible to remove the arm.

Installation

Installation is a reverse of the removal procedure, but make sure the fulcrum pin and eyebolt rubber bushes are in good condition. If not, they should be replaced.

BACKPLATE ASSEMBLIES .... [5]

Removal (Fig. J:12)

Remove the brake-drum and hub as detailed in the Steering chapter.

If it is required to remove the brake backplate to the bench for attention, then the flexible hydraulic brake hose must be disconnected from its union at the wing valance, but this is not advisable unless absolutely necessary.

On later models the metal interconnecting pipe between the two wheel cylinders must be removed before the brake backplate can be detached from the stub axle owing to the pipe passing behind the swivel pin.

If the desired attention can be given without disconnecting the flexible brake pipe the brake backplate assembly can be hung on a suitable portion of the frame to take the load off the flexible pipe.

Unscrew the small union nut securing the metal feed pipe to the flexible pipe. Use a 3/8 in. spanner on the hexagon provided above the bracket to prevent the hose from turning while unscrewing the large hexagon nut to detach the flexible pipe.

Unscrew the four 1/4 in. bolts and nuts securing the brake backplate to the stub axle flange and remove the brake backplate complete with brake-shoes and wheel cylinders.

Installation

Reassembly takes place in the reverse order of dismantling, but do not forget to bleed the brakes if the flexible pipe has been disconnected.

Technical Data

Camber	Nil (1° on models with rubber top link bushes)
Castor angle	3°
Toe-in	0.09375 in (2.5 mm)
King pin inclination	8.5° (7.5° on models with rubber top link bushes)
Angle of inner wheel with outer wheel at 20°	18°15'
Turns of steering-wheel (lock to lock)	2.6
Track	50.625 in (1.284 m)

Steering

GENERAL DESCRIPTION. . . . .[1]

The rack and pinion steering gear (Fig. K:1) is linked to swivel pin assemblies by tie-rods which incorporate ball joints. The steering column is splined to a helical-toothed pinion; the pinion is adjustable by shims, and backlash is controlled by a damper pad.

STEERING WHEEL . . . .[2]

Removal - Three Spoke Type

1. Disconnect the positive battery terminal.
2. Refer to Fig. K:2 and remove the horn-push from the centre of the steering wheel by taking out the chromed countersunk screw from the hub of the wheel (Fig. K:3).
3. Remove the small circlip and plain washer from the terminal on the horn wire and then take away the rubber ferrule with its spring and washer.
4. Remove the steering wheel retaining nut, using a suitable box spanner.
5. Carefully push the horn wire and terminal inside the steering column to prevent them being damaged.
6. Withdraw the steering wheel, using a suitable extractor (Fig. K:4).

Removal - Two Spoke Type

1. Disconnect the positive battery terminal.
2. Remove the horn-push from the centre of the steering wheel by carefully levering it out.
3. Remove the steering wheel retaining nut, using a suitable box spanner and then tap the steering wheel off the column serrations with a mallet.

Installation

Replacement of both types is a reversal of the above procedure, although the puller is not required. Ensure that the steering wheel retaining nut is tight.

STEERING COLUMN. . . . .[3]

Removal - Early Type

1. Disconnect the positive battery terminal.
2. Remove the steering wheel as described previously.
3. Disconnect the five trafficator and horn control wires from the snap connectors beneath the fascia. Remove the screw from the end of the trafficator and horn control assembly and the nut, spring washer, flat washer, and earth wire terminal from the bottom cover bolt and withdraw the bolt, thus releasing the control assembly from the steering column.
4. Release the control cable from the steering column bracket clamp.
5. Remove the clamp nut and bolt from the bottom of the steering column and the two cap nuts and screws from the column support bracket and clamp beneath the fascia, and remove the clamp.
6. Disengage the column assembly from the pinion splines and lift from the car (Fig. K:5).

Installation

The method of replacing the steering assembly is a reversal of the above instructions, but the slot in the steering column clamp MUST coincide with the mark on the end of the pinion. The mark is at bottom dead centre when the wheels are in their straight-ahead position.

Removal - Later Type

Later cars are fitted with a modified steering column assembly having the horn-push mounted in the centre of the steering wheel (Fig. K:1 or K:2). The manually returned direction indicator switch and combined horn-push is replaced by a direction indicator switch of self-cancelling type with a warning lamp in the end of the operating lever.

The steering column and wheel may be interchanged as a complete assembly with the earlier column and wheel.

The new horn-push and self-cancelling direction indicator switch (Fig. K:2) cannot readily be fitted to earlier assemblies.

The procedure for removing this type of column is given as follows:-

1. Disconnect the positive battery terminal.
2. Disconnect the horn and direction indicator wires at the snap connectors beneath the fascia and draw them through the grommeted hole in the fascia.
3. In order to preclude the possibility of disrupting the spring contact blade in the direction indicator switch by relative movement between the column and outer tube it is advisable to remove the switch (as described in the General Electrics chapter), before freeing either the column or the outer tube.
4. Remove the clamp nut and bolt from the splined lower end of the column.
5. Remove the two domed nuts and screws from the column support bracket and clamp below the fascia, and remove the clamp.
6. Disengage the column assembly from the pinion splines and lift it from the car (Fig. K:5).

Installation

Installation is a reverse of the removal sequence but remember that the slot in the steering column clamp MUST coincide with the mark on the end of the pinion.

IGNITION STEERING LOCK . . . . [4]

Operation

Turn the key in a clockwise direction to the position marked 'IGN' ('FAHRT') to switch on the ignition, and further in the same direction to 'START' to operate the starter. If the engine fails to start the key must be returned to the 'GARAGE' position before the starter can be operated again.

To lock the steering, turn the key anti-clockwise to the 'LOCK' ('HALT') position and withdraw it, then turn the steering wheel until the lock is heard to click into engagement. With the switch in the 'GARAGE' position the ignition is switched off and the steering lock is disengaged. The key must be removed when the switch is in the 'GARAGE' position.

Removal

To remove the lock disconnect the battery and the ignition/starter switch connections and turn the lock setting to 'GARAGE' to unlock the steering.

Free the steering column assembly as described previously and remove the lock securing bolts.

NOTE: The steering lock/ignition/starter switch and its electrical circuits are designed to prevent the ignition system and starter from being energized while the steering lock is engaged. Serious consequences could result from alteration or substitution of the steering lock/ignition switch or its wiring.

RACK ASSEMBLY . . . . [5]

Removal

1. Remove the steering column assembly as detailed previously.
2. Remove the split pins and slacken the slotted nut on each tie-rod ball joint. DO NOT REMOVE THE NUT.
3. Tap the circumference of the steering arm eye sharply and then place a support above the arm and drive the taper pin from its seating.
4. The securing nut may now be removed and the tie-rod lifted from the arm. Note the position of the rubber washer.
5. Remove the front carpet and floorboard. Extract the four bolts and spring washers and nuts securing the rack housing to the engine bulkhead and remove the brackets. The housing may now be withdrawn.

Installation

Installation is a reverse of the removal procedure.

Rack Overhaul

1. To dismantle the steering gear, first remove the ball-end retaining nuts on the tie-rods, remove the ball-ends, release the clips and remove the gaiters. Refer to Fig. K:1. Exercising care, unscrew the damper pad housing and withdraw the pad, the spring and the shims; do not misplace the shims.
2. Extract the bolts which secure the pinion shaft tail bearing, and remove the bearing and the shims. Withdraw the pinion with the top thrust washer, and secure the steering gear housing in a vice.
3. Release the lock washers of the tie-rod ball housings, unscrew the caps and remove these, and the lock washers. Withdraw the rack assembly.
4. Unscrew the ball seat housing from the ball joint caps, and remove the shims and the seats.
5. Thoroughly clean and dry all components and inspect them for wear. Check the teeth of the rack or pinion for fractures, hollows or roughness of teeth faces, the rubber gaiters for splits or indications of perishing, the grease nipples for blockages and the ball joint housings and seats for wear.
6. Renew all faulty or excessively worn components. If the rack is badly worn, an exchange unit will be more economical.
7. Fit a new lock washer to one end of the steering rack, replace and tighten the ball seat housing, fit the shims and the seat, insert the ball end of the tie-rod and tighten the housing.
8. If necessary alter the total thickness of the shims which are fitted beneath the seating, to obtain a reasonably tight, sliding fit, without looseness; shims are available in 0.002 in, 0.003 in, and 0.005 in (0.05, 0.08, and 0.13 mm) thicknesses. When correctly adjusted, lock the ball housing in position with the lock washer.

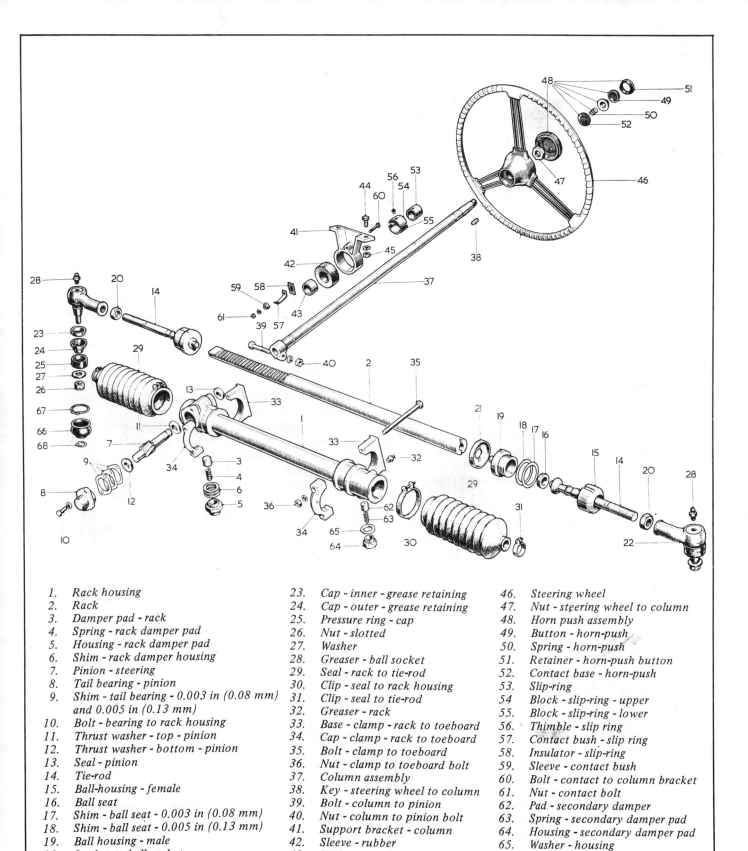

1.	Rack housing	23.
2.	Rack	24.

1. Rack housing
2. Rack
3. Damper pad - rack
4. Spring - rack damper pad
5. Housing - rack damper pad
6. Shim - rack damper housing
7. Pinion - steering
8. Tail bearing - pinion
9. Shim - tail bearing - 0.003 in (0.08 mm) and 0.005 in (0.13 mm)
10. Bolt - bearing to rack housing
11. Thrust washer - top - pinion
12. Thrust washer - bottom - pinion
13. Seal - pinion
14. Tie-rod
15. Ball-housing - female
16. Ball seat
17. Shim - ball seat - 0.003 in (0.08 mm)
18. Shim - ball seat - 0.005 in (0.13 mm)
19. Ball housing - male
20. Locknut - ball socket
21. Lock washer - ball housing - male
22. Ball socket assembly

23. Cap - inner - grease retaining
24. Cap - outer - grease retaining
25. Pressure ring - cap
26. Nut - slotted
27. Washer
28. Greaser - ball socket
29. Seal - rack to tie-rod
30. Clip - seal to rack housing
31. Clip - seal to tie-rod
32. Greaser - rack
33. Base - clamp - rack to toeboard
34. Cap - clamp - rack to toeboard
35. Bolt - clamp to toeboard
36. Nut - clamp to toeboard bolt
37. Column assembly
38. Key - steering wheel to column
39. Bolt - column to pinion
40. Nut - column to pinion bolt
41. Support bracket - column
42. Sleeve - rubber
43. Bush
44. Bolt - support bracket to fascia
45. Nut - support bracket bolt

46. Steering wheel
47. Nut - steering wheel to column
48. Horn push assembly
49. Button - horn-push
50. Spring - horn-push
51. Retainer - horn-push button
52. Contact base - horn-push
53. Slip-ring
54. Block - slip-ring - upper
55. Block - slip-ring - lower
56. Thimble - slip ring
57. Contact bush - slip ring
58. Insulator - slip-ring
59. Sleeve - contact bush
60. Bolt - contact to column bracket
61. Nut - contact bolt
62. Pad - secondary damper
63. Spring - secondary damper pad
64. Housing - secondary damper pad
65. Washer - housing
66. Boot - rubber
67. Clip - boot
68. Clip ring - boot

Fig. K:1 Exploded view of the steering gear

©BLUK

Steering

9. Insert the rack in the housing and fit and adjust the other ball seat. Position the rack, within the housing, with tooth number 12 (from either end) in the centre, place the thicker of the pinion thrust washers in position in the rack housing (with the chamfered edge towards the rack) and fit the thinner thrust washer to the plain end of the pinion shaft (with the chamfered edge towards the pinion teeth).

10. Replace the pinion, engaging the trough between the two teeth (which is in line with the mark on the splined end of the pinion shaft) with the centre tooth of the rack. Replace the shims and the pinion tail bearing, locate them in position and check the pinion shaft endfloat; this must be 0.002 - 0.005 in (0.05 - 0.13 mm); alter the total shim thickness if necessary.

11. Check that both tie-rods are of identical assembled lengths (measure the distance between the spanner flattened sections and the ball joint locknuts), fit the gaiters and clips and replace the ball end locknuts and joint assemblies.

12. Insert the damper pad plunger in the housing and fit this without the shims or the spring (Fig. K:6). Tighten it until the pinion shaft can just be rotated by moving the rack through the housing. Measure the clearance between the hexagon of the damper pad housing and its seating on the rack housing. To this measurement ADD 0.002 - 0.005 in (0.05 - 0.13 mm) to determine the required shim thickness. Shims are 0.003 in (0.08 mm) thick.

13. Remove the damper pad housing and plunger, insert the spring and re-fit the housing with the appropriate shims. Fit a new felt seal to the pinion shaft and pump approximately 0.5 pints (0.28 litre) (0.6 US pints) of hypoid oil (SAE 90 grade) into the rack housing via the nipple (Fig. K:8).

SWIVEL PIN ASSEMBLY . . . . [6]

Removal (Fig. K:7)

1. To remove a swivel pin assembly, first slacken the road wheel nuts or bolts, raise the front of the vehicle with a jack and remove the wheel; place a jack beneath the suspension arm and lower the vehicle until the shock absorber lever is clear of the bump rubber.

2. Disconnect the hydraulic brake connection at the bracket on the wing; drain any fluid into a container and blank off the opened connections. Remove the split pin and the slotted nut from the pin to the tie-rod ball joint, and drive the pin from the tapered seating.

3. Remove the nut and bolt which secure the tie-rod to the front suspension arm, and the nuts and bolts which retain the front suspension arm, and withdraw this. Disengage the lower swivel pin link from the suspension arm, and lower the jack until the torsion bar is no longer supported.

4. On swivel pins with plain pivot nuts, release the lock washer, slacken the two nuts on the pivot bolt which secures the swivel pin to the shock absorber lever, and remove the split pin and nut from the other end of the

bolt. Free the eye in the shock absorber lever, place a support behind it and, with a soft drift, extract the bolt. Support the swivel pin assembly and withdraw the pin from the shock absorber lever.

5. On swivel pins with threaded pivot nuts, remove the split pin and the nut from the pivot pin of the shock absorber lever. Free the eye in the lever, place a support behind it and, with a soft drift, extract the pivot pin.

Servicing

1. Remove the rubber seals and the thrust washers and unscrew the upper and lower links from the swivel pin; thoroughly clean and dry all items.

2. Check the links for wear of the thrust faces and of the threaded bores, and the top pivot pin and the seating. Renew the thrust washers and the rubber seals and any faulty or excessively worn components.

Installation

1. To install a swivel pin assembly, reverse the removal procedure, noting the following:-

a) The positioning of the pivot bolt is important. Screw the link on to the swivel pin until the waisted portion of the pin is aligned with the pivot bolt hole; place the pivot bolt in position, fully screw the link inward and then reverse this by screwing it outward approximately one and a half turns, to obtain the maximum clearance.

b) On swivel pins with plain pivots, ensure that the upper swivel pin link has a maximum endfloat of 0.002 in (0.05 mm). After adjustment, utilize the lock washer and the nut, and recheck the clearance. Plain-type bottom pivot bolts must have the same maximum endfloat.

c) On swivel pins with threaded pivots, fit the rubber seal between the link and the eye of the shock absorber lever (with the smaller diameter outward gripping the lever) and partially tighten the castellated nut. The pivot pin must be free to rotate. Rotate the pivot pin, by the square-section end, to obtain an outer dimension of 3.09375 - 3.125 in (78.6 - 79.4 mm).

HUB ASSEMBLY . . . . [7]

Removal (Fig. K:7)

1. To remove a hub, first slacken the road wheel nuts or bolts, raise the front of the vehicle and securely support it, and remove the wheel.

2. On models incorporating a brake drum which separates from the hub, remove the countersunk screws and withdraw the brake drum.

3. Remove the grease cap from the centre of the hub, extract the split pin and remove the nut and the flat washer from the stub axle.

4. Withdraw the hub, using a suitable extractor, withdraw the inner bearing, the spacer and the oil seal, from the interior of the hub or from the stub axle.

Steering

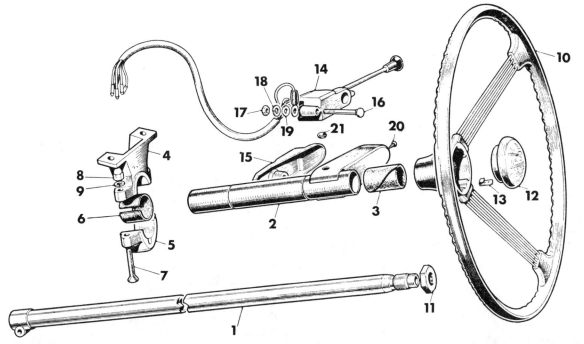

1. Column - steering
2. Tube assembly - outer
3. Bush - felt
4. Bracket - column support
5. Clamp - bracket
6. Packing strip - clamp
7. Screw - clamp
8. Nut - clamp screw
9. Spring washer - screw
10. Wheel - steering
11. Nut - wheel·
12. Motif - steering wheel
13. Spring clip - motif
14. Control assembly - horn and indicator
15. Cover - bottom
16. Screw - bottom cover
17. Nut - bottom cover
18. Spring washer - bottom cover
19. Plain washer - bottom cover
20. Screw - control assembly
21. Grommet - top cover

Fig. K:2 Exploded view of latest type steering column

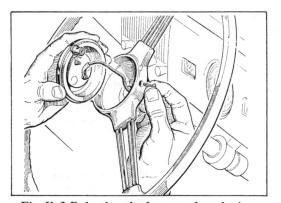

Fig. K:3 Releasing the horn push and wire

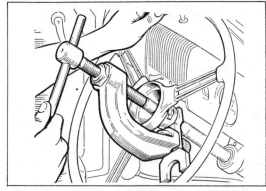

Fig. K:4 Removing the steering wheel with an extractor

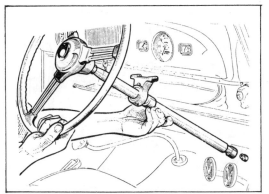

Fig. K:5 Withdrawing the steering column assembly

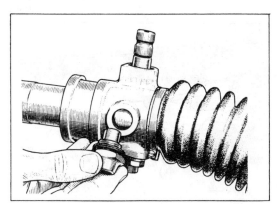

Fig. K:6 Steering rack damper and shims

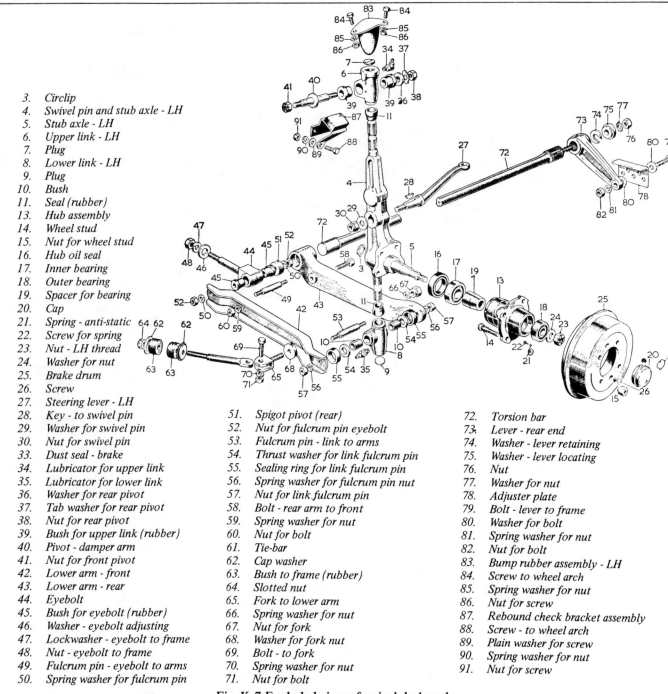

3. Circlip
4. Swivel pin and stub axle - LH
5. Stub axle - LH
6. Upper link - LH
7. Plug
8. Lower link - LH
9. Plug
10. Bush
11. Seal (rubber)
13. Hub assembly
14. Wheel stud
15. Nut for wheel stud
16. Hub oil seal
17. Inner bearing
18. Outer bearing
19. Spacer for bearing
20. Cap
21. Spring - anti-static
22. Screw for spring
23. Nut - LH thread
24. Washer for nut
25. Brake drum
26. Screw
27. Steering lever - LH
28. Key - to swivel pin
29. Washer for swivel pin
30. Nut for swivel pin
33. Dust seal - brake
34. Lubricator for upper link
35. Lubricator for lower link
36. Washer for rear pivot
37. Tab washer for rear pivot
38. Nut for rear pivot
39. Bush for upper link (rubber)
40. Pivot - damper arm
41. Nut for front pivot
42. Lower arm - front
43. Lower arm - rear
44. Eyebolt
45. Bush for eyebolt (rubber)
46. Washer - eyebolt adjusting
47. Lockwasher - eyebolt to frame
48. Nut - eyebolt to frame
49. Fulcrum pin - eyebolt to arms
50. Spring washer for fulcrum pin

51. Spigot pivot (rear)
52. Nut for fulcrum pin eyebolt
53. Fulcrum pin - link to arms
54. Thrust washer for link fulcrum pin
55. Sealing ring for link fulcrum pin
56. Spring washer for fulcrum pin nut
57. Nut for link fulcrum pin
58. Bolt - rear arm to front
59. Spring washer for nut
60. Nut for bolt
61. Tie-bar
62. Cap washer
63. Bush to frame (rubber)
64. Slotted nut
65. Fork to lower arm
66. Spring washer for nut
67. Nut for fork
68. Washer for fork nut
69. Bolt - to fork
70. Spring washer for nut
71. Nut for bolt

72. Torsion bar
73. Lever - rear end
74. Washer - lever retaining
75. Washer - lever locating
76. Nut
77. Washer for nut
78. Adjuster plate
79. Bolt - lever to frame
80. Washer for bolt
81. Spring washer for nut
82. Nut for bolt
83. Bump rubber assembly - LH
84. Screw to wheel arch
85. Spring washer for nut
86. Nut for screw
87. Rebound check bracket assembly
88. Screw - to wheel arch
89. Plain washer for screw
90. Spring washer for nut
91. Nut for screw

**Fig. K:7 Exploded view of swivel, hub and
suspension assembly**

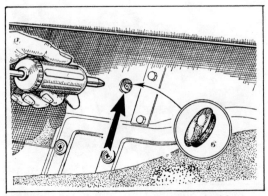

Fig. K:8 Lubrication nipple location inside car

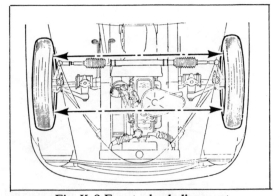

Fig. K:9 Front wheel alignment

Inspection

Clean all grease from the bearings and the hub interior, and inspect the bearings for wear. Renew the bearings if necessary. Pack or knead grease into the bearings that are to be used and grease the hub. Renew the seal.

Installation

1. Fit the smaller, outer bearing into position, replace the bearing spacer with the chamfered edge towards the outer bearing, and press the larger bearing into the hub. Fit the oil seal.
2. Note that on some vehicles, angular contact bearings and solid spacers are fitted. On such models, position each bearing with the thrust side (which is stamped with the bearing part number) facing the bearing spacer.
3. Replace the hub on the stub axle, fit the washer and the nut and tighten the latter to a torque of 35.0 - 40.0 lb.ft (4.8 - 5.5 kg m). Fit the split pin, grease the cap and replace it.
4. On models incorporating a brake drum which is separate from the hub, position the drum on the hub and retain it with the screws.
5. Fit the wheel, retain it with the wheel nuts or bolts, lower the vehicle to the ground and fully tighten the nuts or bolts.

WHEEL ALIGNMENT . . . . [8]

Toe Setting (Fig. K:9)

The following method of setting the toe-in should only be used as a temporary measure after the replacement of the steering components. It is essential that the toe-in be rechecked as soon as possible using proper wheel alignment equipment so that the toe-out on turns can also be checked. This should be entrusted to a local Leyland dealer or tyre service agent.

Before attempting to measure or adjust the toe-in, the following prechecks must be carried out first:
1. Ensure that the car is at its normal kerb weight and height.
2. The car should be standing on a level, horizontal surface.
3. Check that the tyre pressures are to specification.
4. Check the front wheel bearing adjustment and reset if necessary.
5. Check the steering and front suspension ball joints, bushes and mountings for excessive wear, looseness or tightness; rectify any faults before proceeding.
6. With steering in the straight-ahead position, roll the car forward about three feet (1 metre) and stop it without using the brakes.
7. Bounce the front corners of the car approximately 2 in (50 mm) a few times to settle the suspension.
8. Once the ride height has been established, it must not be disturbed by jacking up the vehicle or by someone sitting in the vehicle to centralise the wheels.

The toe setting can now be checked using a simple mechanical tracking bar, either home made or purchased inexpensively from local car accessory shops. Take an initial reading of the distance between the inside edges of the front wheel rims at a point level with, and in front of, the wheel centre. Mark the measurement points with chalk.

Roll the car forward until the chalk marks are level with, but behind, the wheel centre (i.e. a 180 degree revolution of the wheel). Take a second reading between the chalk marks. The toe-in setting is the difference by which the second reading is greater than the first.

If adjustment is necessary, slacken the locknuts and rubber gaiter clips on both tie-rod ball joints and turn each rod equally in the right direction, by small amounts, until the toe-in is correct.

Finally, retighten the locknuts and the rubber gaiter clips.

Technical Data

STEERING GEAR

Camber	Nil (1° on models with rubber top link bushes)
Caster angle	3°
Toe-in	0.094 in (2.5 mm)
King pin inclination	$8\frac{1}{2}^o$ ($7\frac{1}{2}^o$ on models with rubber top link bushes)
Angle of inner wheel with outer wheel at 20°	$18^o15'$
Turns of steering-wheel (lock to lock)	2.6
Track	50.625 in (1.284 m)
Turning circle	RH 33 ft 1 in (10.09 m)
	LH 32 ft 11 in (10.04 m)
Wheelbase	86 in (218.44 cm)
Ground clearance	6.75 in (17 cm)
Tyre size	5.00/5.20-14

STEERING

Trouble Shooter

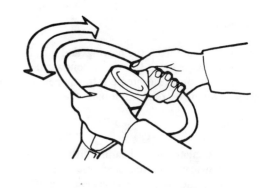

FAULT	CAUSE	CURE
Steering feels stiff	1. Low tyre pressures 2. Incorrect wheel alignment 3. Stiff track rod ends 4. Steering box/rack needs adjustment	1. Correct tyre pressures. 2. Correct wheel alignment. 3. Check and replace if necessary. 4. Adjust if necessary.
Steering wheel shake	1. Wheels and tyres need balancing 2. Tyre pressures incorrect 3. Incorrect wheel alignment 4. Wheel hub nut loose 5. Wheel bearings damaged 6. Front suspension distorted 7. Steering box/rack needs adjustment 8. Shock absorbers faulty	1. Balance as necessary. 2. Correct. 3. Correct alignment. 4. Adjust wheel bearings. 5. Replace wheel bearings. 6. Check, repair or replace. 7. Adjust as necessary. 8. Check and rectify.
Steering pulls to one side	1. Uneven tyre pressure 2. Wheel alignment incorrect 3. Wheel bearings worn or damaged 4. Brakes improperly adjusted 5. Shock absorbers faulty 6. Suspension distorted 7. Steering box/rack worn	1. Correct. 2. Correct. 3. Replace and adjust. 4. Adjust brakes. 5. Check and rectify. 6. Check and rectify. 7. Adjust or replace.
Wheel tramp	1. Over-inflated tyres 2. Unbalanced tyre and wheel 3. Defective shock absorber 4. Defective tyre	1. Correct pressure. 2. Check and balance if necessary. 3. Check and rectify. 4. Repair or replace.
Abnormal tyre wear	1. Incorrect tyre pressure 2. Incorrect wheel alignment 3. Excessive wheel bearing play 4. Improper driving	1. Check pressures. 2. Check wheel alignment. 3. Adjust wheel bearings. 4. Avoid sharp turning at high speeds, rapid starting and braking, etc.
Tyre noises	1. Improper tyre inflation 2. Incorrect wheel alignment	1. Correct tyre pressures. 2. Correct wheel alignment.

Brakes

DESCRIPTION . . . . [1]

The brake system is a single-line hydraulic system which operates on all road wheels; a cable handbrake operates on only the rear road wheels.

The hydraulic system (Figs. L:1 and L:2) comprises a fluid reservoir and integral master cylinder, which is mounted on the chassis below the driver's floor. A four-way junction on the master cylinder outlet incorporates a brake lights 'stop' switch and steel pipe connections to front and rear three-way junctions; from these, fluid is piped to the wheel cylinders.

Each front brake assembly, which incorporates two leading shoes, is fitted with a single-acting, rigidly mounted wheel cylinder for each shoe; each rear brake assembly, which incorporates one leading and one trailing shoe, is fitted with one single-acting, floating wheel cylinder for both shoes. Adjustment of each shoe (front brake assemblies) or pair of shoes (rear brake assemblies) is effected by slot-headed snail cams.

HYDRAULIC SYSTEM OVERHAUL. . . . . . [2]

Any components of the braking system which show signs of fluid leakage should be overhauled or replaced immediately. Only units which appear satisfactory after careful examination of the components should be reassembled using new seals. Any unit which has damaged bores or pistons must be discarded and replaced by a new unit. If in any doubt, replace the unit - your safety could depend on it!

When overhauling any components of the hydraulic system (Figs. L:1 and L:2), this must be carried out under conditions of scrupulous cleanliness. This cannot be over-emphasised. Clean all dirt and grease from the exterior of components before removal or dismantling.

Wash all components in methylated spirit or clean brake fluid only. Do not use any mineral-based oils, such as petrol, paraffin or carbon tetrachloride. All internal passages should be blown out with compressed air.

Inspect the piston and cylinder bore surfaces carefully for any signs of scores, ridges or corrosion pits. The unit must be discarded if any of these conditions are present.

Only new seals should be used when reassembling. These are generally available in the form of a repair kit containing all the necessary parts required for overhaul of a particular unit.

All seals, even when new, should be inspected carefully before fitting. Discard any seal which does not appear perfect, no matter how minute the blemish may appear to be.

BRAKE ADJUSTMENTS . . . . [3]

The procedure for adjusting the drum brakes and the handbrake is included in the Routine Maintenance section at the beginning of the manual. Refer to Fig. L:3 and the appropriate chapter.

BRAKE SHOES . . . . [4]

Removal - Front

1. To remove the front brake shoes, first remove the wheel covers, slacken the wheel nuts or bolts, and raise the front of the vehicle; support the vehicle, remove the front wheels and press the grease caps from the hub/drum centres.
2. At each assembly in turn, remove the countersunk screws from the drum, lightly tap it to free it and withdraw it from the hub.
3. Prise the end of one shoe from its location, slip the shoes from the wheel cylinders (Fig. L:4), and withdraw them from the backplate. If there is any tendency for the wheel cylinder pistons to 'creep' outward, due to residual pressure in the hydraulic system, restrain them with wire.

Removal - Rear

1. To remove the rear brake linings, first slacken the hand brake, remove the wheel covers, slacken the wheel nuts or bolts and raise the rear of the vehicle; support the vehicle and remove the rear wheels.
2. At each assembly in turn, remove the countersunk screws from the drum, lightly tap it to free it, and withdraw it from the hub.
3. Remove the steady springs from the shoes, prise the end of one shoe from its location, slip the shoes from the locations, and withdraw them from the backplate (Fig. L:5). If there is any tendency for the wheel cylinder pistons to 'creep' outward, due to residual pressure in the hydraulic system, restrain them with wire.

Inspection

1. If the linings are worn below the recommended minimum thickness, the whole set must be replaced.
2. Remove, with a brush or compressed air, all dust from the backplates and components, and inspect the drums (for excessive scoring - if necessary have the drums reground or renew them), the hubs (for lubricant leakage - action as necessary), and the wheel cylinders (for fluid leaks - service the cylinders if necessary).
3. Slacken the adjusters of each shoe or pair of shoes (fully rotate the adjusters in an anti-clockwise direction), and link the shoes with the springs; ensure that the springs are positioned correctly.

Installation

To replace the brake linings (Fig. L:6), reverse the removal procedure. At the appropriate stage, adjust the brake shoe positions as described in the Routine Maintenance chapter, and check the operation of the handbrake.

WHEEL CYLINDERS. . . . .[5]

Removal - Front

1. To remove the front wheel cylinders, first remove the brake shoes as already described.
2. Disconnect the flexible hydraulic connections to the wheel cylinders (Fig. L:7), drain any fluid into a container and blank the opened connections. Remove the nuts and washers from the studs of each cylinder, and remove the cylinders from the backplates.

Removal - Rear

1. To remove the rear wheel cylinders, first remove the brake shoes as already described.

2. Disconnect the hydraulic connections to the wheel cylinders and remove the bleed nipples; drain any fluid into a container and blank off the opened connections.
3. At each rear wheel cylinder, remove the split pin and clevis pin from the handbrake lever at the back of the cylinder, remove the rubber boot and the lower half of the piston, and remove the cylinder from the backplate.

Installation

To replace the wheel cylinders, reverse the removal procedure. Ensure that the shoe return springs are positioned correctly, and bleed the hydraulic system as described later in this chapter; check the operation of the handbrake linkage, after adjusting the footbrakes (see Routine Maintenance). Also make sure the flexible hoses are in good condition. If they are not, replace them.

Overhaul (Fig. L:8)

1. To dismantle a wheel cylinder, first drift out the pivot pin and remove the handbrake lever (rear wheel cylinders only) then remove the piston (rear cylinders) or the piston and dust cover (front cylinders), the piston cup, the cup filler and, if fitted, the spring.
2. Clean all components thoroughly, using brake fluid on the rubber components and methylated spirit on the metal components, remove all traces of cleaning fluid.
3. Inspect the cylinder bore for scoring or ridges, and the metal components for wear; renew the seals, and any faulty or worn components.
4. Lubricate the internal components and the bore of the cylinder with brake fluid, and reverse the dismantling procedure to reassemble the cylinders.

MASTER CYLINDER. . . . .[6]

Removal (Fig. L:9)

1. To remove the master cylinder, first remove the front floor carpet, then remove the mounting bolts and clips from the driver's seat and remove the seat. Slacken the locknut, remove the gear lever knob, and withdraw the rubber cowl from the base of the lever; remove the floor panel above the gearbox.
2. Remove the torsion bar from the driver's side of the vehicle (see the Front Suspension chapter), and the mounting bolts from the master cylinder.
3. From the rear end of the clutch operating rod remove the return spring, the split pin and the Belleville washer, slacken the nut of the cotter pin on the clutch pedal lever, unseat the cotter pin, remove the nut and withdraw the cotter pin.

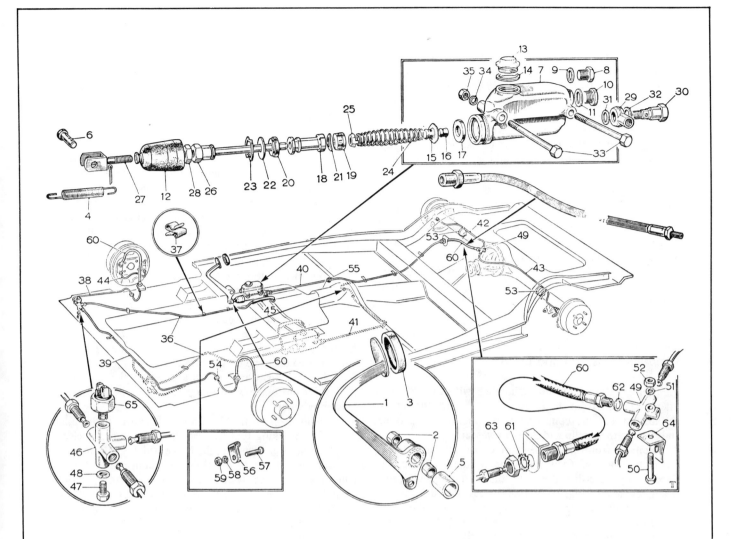

1. Brake pedal	22. Washer for retainer	44. Pipe - cylinder bridge
2. Bush for pedal shaft	23. Circlip for retainer	45. Sleeve - pipe protecting (rubber)
3. Rubber pad	24. Piston return spring	46. Three-way piece (front)
4. Return spring	25. Retainer	47. Screw for front three-way piece
5. Spacer	26. Push rod	48. Spring washer for screw
6. Clevis pin to master cylinder	27. Yoke push-rod	49. Three-way piece for rear axle
7. Master cylinder and tank	28. Locknut for yoke	50. Bolt for rear axle three-way piece
8. Drain plug (earlier)	29. Banjo connection	51. Spring washer for nut
9. Gasket (earlier)	30. Bolt for banjo connection	52. Nut for bolt
10. Drain plug (later)	31. Gasket for banjo bolt (small)	53. Strap - pipe to rear axle
11. Gasket (later)	32. Gasket for banjo bolt (large)	54. Grommet for front wheel arch
12. Rubber boot	33. Bolt - master cylinder to frame	55. Grommet for centre crossmember
13. Filler plug	34. Spring washer for nut	56. Clip - pipe to crossmember
14. Gasket	35. Nut for bolt	57. Screw for clip
15. Body - valve assembly	36. Pipe - master cylinder to three-way front	58. Spring washer for nut
16. Cup - valve assembly	37. Clip - pipe to longitudinal member	59. Nut for screw
17. Washer - valve assembly	38. Pipe - three-way to RH front	60. Hose
18. Piston	39. Pipe - three-way to LH front	61. Washer
19. Cup - main	40. Pipe - master cylinder to rear hose (LHD)	62. Gasket
20. Cup - secondary	42. Pipe - hose to RH rear	63. Locknut
21. Washer - dished	43. Pipe - hose to LH rear	64. Bracket for rear hose
		65. Switch for stop-light

Fig. L:1 Layout of braking system

4. Disconnect the speedometer cable from the gearbox, withdraw the pedal cross-shaft and the clutch pedal, and disconnect the hydraulic connections from the master cylinder outlet; drain any fluid into a container and blank off the opened connections.

5. Detach the brake pedal return spring, lift out the brake pedal and master cylinder as an assembly, and withdraw from the cylinder the pedal and push rod.

Installation

1. To replace the master cylinder, reverse the removal procedure. Bleed the hydraulic system as described later in this chapter, and check the system for leaks.

2. Check that the brake pedal free-play is 0.75 in (19 mm); if the free-play is incorrect, adjust the effective length of the push rod at the nut on the cylinder.

Overhaul (Figs. L:1 and L:10)

1. Remove the filler and drain plugs with the washers, drain the fluid from the cylinder, and remove the outlet connection and the copper washers. Depress the piston, and remove the circlip and the stop washer.

2. Remove from within the cylinder, the piston with the secondary cup seal (which may be withdrawn using the fingers only), the dished washer, the master cup seal, the spring seat and spring, and the valve body, cup and washer.

3. Clean all components thoroughly, using brake fluid on the rubber components, and methylated spirit on the metal components; remove all traces of cleaning fluid.

4. Inspect the cylinder bore for scoring or ridges, and the metal components for wear; renew the seals and any faulty or worn components.

5. Lubricate the internal components and the bores of the cylinder with brake fluid, and carefully fit the secondary cup seal to the piston. Assemble, in order, the valve washer, the valve cup and the valve body to one end of the spring and the spring seat to the other end, and insert the assembly into the cylinder.

6. Insert, taking care not to damage it, the master cup seal with the lip of the seal facing the spring; follow this with the dished washer, the concave side of which MUST face the cup seal. This washer MUST be fitted, even if it was not previously fitted (see Fig. L:10 & 11).

7. Insert the piston with the secondary cup seal (do not damage the seal lips), depress the piston sufficiently and fit the stop washer and the circlip. Fill the reservoir with fluid, to the correct level: this is 0.5 in (13.0 mm) below the bottom of the filler neck.

BLEEDING THE SYSTEM . . . . [7]

The fluid level in the master cylinder reservoir must be maintained at a reasonable level throughout the bleeding operation as, if the level is allowed to drop excessively, air may be drawn into the system through the master cylinder. Use only fresh brake fluid for topping up. Never re-use fluid which has already been passed through the system. To bleed the system, proceed as follows:-

1. Remove the filler cap from the master cylinder reservoir and top up the fluid level as required.

2. Attach one end of the bleed tube to the bleed valve at the left-hand rear brake and immerse the free end in a small quantity of hydraulic fluid in a glass jar (Fig. L:12).

3. Open the bleed valve about a half turn. Depress the brake pedal rapidly through its full travel and then allow it to return to the fully released position. Hydraulic fluid should have been pumped into the jar; if not, open the bleed valve further.

4. Continue depressing and releasing the pedal, pausing for a few seconds after each stroke, until the fluid coming from the bleed tube is completely free from air bubbles.

5. Finally, with the pedal held down to the floor, close the bleed valve. Take care not to over-tighten the valve; tighten it only sufficiently to seal. Remove the bleed tube and refit the dust cap on the bleed valve.

6. Bleed the right-hand rear brake next in the same way, then the front brakes, finishing at the brake nearest to the master cylinder.

7. Finally, top up the fluid reservoir and refit the filler cap, after checking that the vent hole in the cap is clear.

8. If even after bleeding, the brake pedal is still 'spongy' or goes right down to the floor, this indicates that air is still present in the system, and the bleeding operation should be repeated. If subsequent attempts at bleeding still fail to produce a satisfactory result, the system should be checked for leaks, as air is obviously being drawn into the system.

HANDBRAKE . . . . [8]

Cable Replacement

With this system, either of the two cables can be replaced separately without disturbing the other one.

With the handbrake lever fully released, screw the cable adjustment nuts off the front end of the cable (Fig. L:13), at the lever trunnion. Remove the cable guide plate (fairlead) located in the centre of the floor between the front seats.

Jack up the rear of the car and support on stands. Remove the appropriate rear wheel. Draw the cable through the floor pan from underneath the car and release it from the guide channel on the sub-frame front cross-member. Lever back the corners of the flange at the sector on the rear radius arm and release the cable from the sector. Draw the cable through the aperture in the sub-frame towards the outside.

Remove the split pin and clevis pin securing the rear

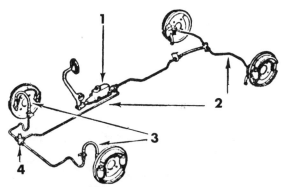

1. Master cylinder   3. Flexible connections
2. Pipe lines   4. Stop-lamp switch

Fig. L:2 Simplified layout of braking system

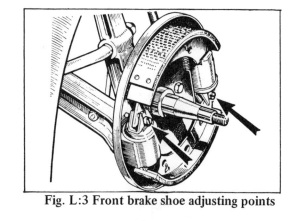

Fig. L:3 Front brake shoe adjusting points

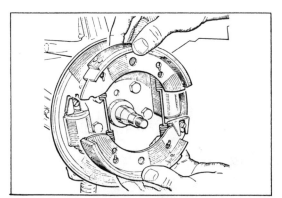

Fig. L:4 Front brake shoe removal

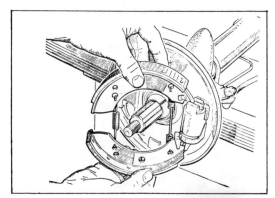

Fig. L:5 Rear brake shoe removal

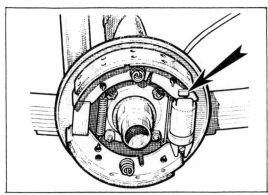

Fig. L:6 Rear brake shoe and spring assembly

1. Union nut
2. Attachment nut

Fig. L:7 Dismantling flexible hose

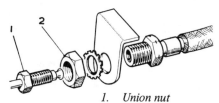

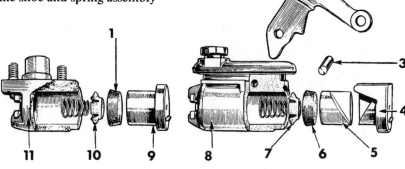

1. Piston cup	5. Piston (hydraulic)	9. Piston and dust cover
2. Handbrake lever	6. Piston cup	10. Cup filler
3. Pivot pin	7. Cup filler	11. Front wheel cylinder
4. Piston and dust cover	8. Rear wheel cylinder	

Fig. L:8 Front and rear wheel cylinder components

Brakes

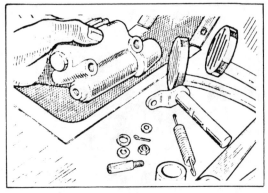

Fig. L:9 Withdrawing the master cylinder from the car

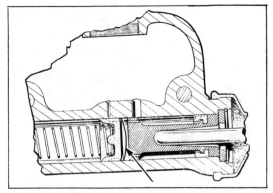

Fig. L:10 Master cylinder dished washer assembly

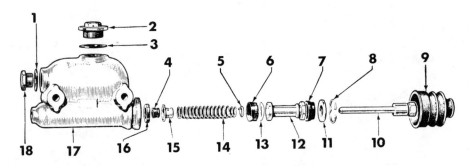

1.	Washer	10.	Push-rod assembly
2.	Filler plug	11.	Piston stop
3.	Gasket	12.	Piston
4.	Valve cup	13.	Dished washer
5.	Spring seat	14.	Piston return spring
6.	Master cup	15.	Valve body
7.	Secondary cup	16.	Valve washer
8.	Circlip	17.	Master cylinder
9.	Rubber boot	18.	Drain plug

Fig. L:11 Exploded view of the master cylinder

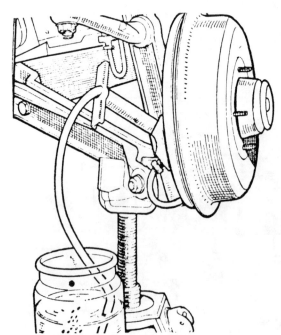

Fig. L:12 Bleeding the brakes

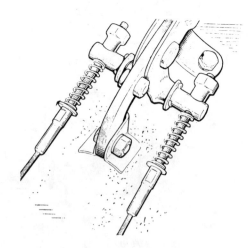

Fig. L:13 Handbrake cable adjustment points

Brakes

end of the cable to the handbrake lever at the brake backplate. Release the cable from the abutment bracket at the backplate and remove it from the car.

Install the new cable in the reverse order of removing the old one. Nip the corners of the sector flange to hold the cable in position. Also ensure that the guide channel, sector pivot and operating lever clevis pin are adequately lubricated with grease.

Finally, adjust the handbrake cable as detailed in the Routine Maintenance section previously.

Technical Data

EARLY MODELS

Type . . . . Hydraulic 7 in dia. (17.8 cm)
Type of linings . . . . MR 11
Lining size:
    Front/Rear . . . . 6.54 in x 1.22 in x 0.198 in
    (16.6 cm x 31.0 mm x 5.0 mm)

LATER MODELS

Front
Drum diameter . . . . 8 in (20.3 cm)
Swept area . . . . .73.9 sq in (477 cm^2)
Lining material . . . . Ferodo AM8

Rear
Drum diameter . . . . 7 in (17.8 cm)
Swept area . . . . .53.6 sq in (346 cm^2)
Lining material . . . . Ferodo AM8

BRAKES
Trouble Shooter

FAULT	CAUSE	CURE
Excessive brake pedal travel	1. Brakes need adjusting or replacement. 2. Air in system. 3. Leaking or contaminated fluid. 4. Faulty master cylinder.	1. Adjust or renew brake shoes. 2/3. Bleed hydraulic system. 4. Fit new master cylinder.
Brake fade	1. Incorrect pad or lining material. 2. Old or contaminated fluid. 3. Excessive use of brakes or car overloaded.	1. Fit new pads or shoes. 2. Renew brake fluid. 3. Check vehicle load.
Spongy brake pedal	1. Air in hydraulic system. 2. Shoes badly lined or distorted. 3. Faulty hydraulic cylinder.	1. Bleed system. 2. Fit new pads or shoes. 3. Check hydraulic circuit.
Brake pedal too hard	1. Seized wheel cylinder or caliper piston. 2. Glazed friction material.	1. Replace seized component. 2. Fit new shoes/pads.
Brake pedal requires pumping or loss of pedal	1. Brakes wrongly adjusted. 2. Air in hydraulic system. 3. Fluid leak from component or brake pipe. 4. Loss of fluid from master cylinder.	1. Adjust brakes. 2. Bleed system. 3/4. Check hydraulic circuit and replace parts as necessary.
Brakes grab when applied	1. Contaminated friction material. 2. Wrong linings fitted. 3. Scored drums or discs.	1/2. Replace (don't clean) pads or shoes. 3. Fit new drum or disc.
Brake squeal	1. Worn retaining pins (disc). 2. Faulty damping shims or shoe retaining clips. 3. Dust in drum. 4. Loose backplate or caliper.	1. Fit new pins. 2. Fit new shims or clips. 3. Remove dust from drums and shoe. 4. Tighten caliper or backplate.
Brake judder	1. No clearance at master cylinder operating rod. 2. Shoe tension springs either broken or weak. 3. Wheel cylinder or caliper piston seizing. 4. Faulty self-adjusting mechanism. 5. Seized handbrake mechanism.	1. Adjust rod if possible. 2. Replace tension springs. 3. Fit new caliper or cylinder. 4. Check mechanism. 5. Check handbrake operation.

FAULT	CAUSE	CURE
Brake pull to one side only	1. Contaminated friction material on one side (grease, oil or brake fluid). 2. Loose backplate. 3. Seized cylinder. 4. Faulty suspension or steering.	1. Replace shoes/pads all round. 2. Tighten backplate. 3. Replace seized cylinder. 4. Check suspension and steering.
Handbrake ineffective	1. Worn rear shoes or pads. 2. Brakes require adjusting. 3. Faulty handbrake linkage. 4. Cable or rod requires adjustment.	1. Fit new pads/shoes. 2. Adjust brakes. 3. Check linkage and operating mechanism. 4. Adjust cable or rod.
Servo (where fitted) late in operation	1. Blocked filter. 2. Bad vacuum sealing or restricted air inlet.	1. Clean or replace filter. 2. Tighten vacuum hose connections and check hoses.
Loss of servo action when braking heavily	1. Air leak in servo - vacuum low.	1. Either overhaul servo or replace.
Loss of fluid (Servo only)	1. Seal failure. 2. Scored servo bores. 3. Damaged or corroded fluid pipes.	1/2. Replace or overhaul servo. 3. Inspect and fit new pipes.

Brakes

General Electrics

FUSES . . . .[1]

Two 35 amp fuses are fitted to a fuse block situated on the left-hand wing valance (Fig. M:1) immediately to one side of the voltage regulator. The first of the two fuses - marked A1 and A2 - protects the lighting and horn circuits. It works irrespective of the ignition being on or off.

The second fuse - marked A3 and A4 - protects components such as the fuel gauge, flasher unit, windscreen wiper motor and stop lights, which only operate with the ignition switched on.

Later vehicles are fitted with an additional fuse, with a 10 amp blow rating, in the pilot and tail light circuit. This fuse is held in a cylindrical tube alongside the wiring loom beneath the regulator.

To replace this 10 amp fuse, hold one end of the tube, push in, twist, and pull off the other end. The fuse is then accessible.

A blown fuse is indicated by the failure of all the units protected by it and is confirmed by examination of the fuse (Fig. M:2). Before renewing a blown fuse, inspect the wiring of all the units that have failed for evidence of a short circuit or any other fault that may have caused the fuse to blow. This is essential, otherwise the new fuse is liable to blow on fitting.

HEADLAMP ASSEMBLIES . . . .[2]

Various types of headlamp assembly were fitted to the Minor 1000. Earlier models had reflector units with provision for headlamp and sidelamp pilot bulbs. Later models were fitted with separate headlamps and sidelamps. Later still, sealed beam units were used. The sidelamp bulb in those cases is also housed under a separate lens. Fig. M:3 shows the various bulb holders and fixings.

The headlamp bulb or sealed beam unit can be easily replaced as follows:

Remove the screw securing the headlamp rim (Fig. M:4) and detach the rim from the headlamp unit.

Remove the three headlamp rim retaining screws and detach the rim. The headlamp unit can then be turned and withdrawn (Fig. M:5). With the sealed beam type unit, merely withdraw the three pin connector from the back of the unit and remove the lamp unit.

With the bulb type unit, withdraw the connector from the rear of the lamp unit. Disengage the spring clip from the reflector lugs and withdraw the bulb from the rear of the reflector. Fit the new bulb, ensuring that the pip on the bulb flange engages the slot in the reflector. Refit the spring clip ensuring that the coils in the clip are resting on the base of the bulb and that the legs of the clip are fully engaged under the reflector lugs.

In either case, reconnect the three-pin connector and refit the lamp unit in the reverse order of removing.

Where the side lamp is incorporated in the headlamp, the bulb holder may be incorporated in the headlamp three-pin connector or may be a separate push-fit holder which locates in an aperture in the headlamp reflector. In either case, replacement of the bulb is a straight forward procedure after removing the headlamp unit as detailed above.

Headlamp Alignment (Fig. M:6)

1. Inflate the tyres, if necessary, to the recommended pressures.
2. Find a level road where the car can be parked 25 feet (7.6 m) from a blank wall.
3. Drive the car as close to the wall as possible and mark a cross directly in front of each headlamp centre (Fig. M: 6).
4. Drive the car straight back until it is 25 feet away from the marks on the wall.
5. Have two people sit on the car's back seat, to simulate a normal load.
6. Remove the chrome bezel from both headlamps by first removing the single screw from the base of each (Fig. M:4).
7. Cover one headlamp while adjusting the other and switch them on, dipped.
8. The beam should now be below and slightly to the

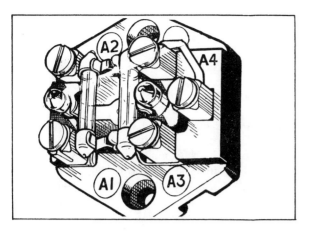

Fig. M:1 Fuse box with cover removed

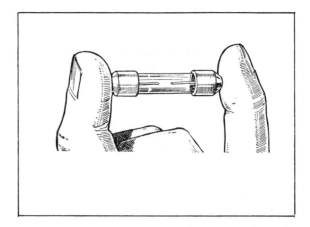

Fig. M:2 The appearance of a burnt-out fuse

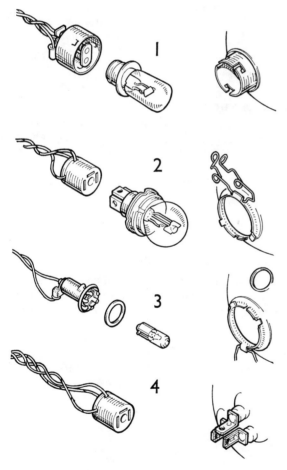

1. Cap type holder
2. Spring clip type
3. Headlamp pilot lamp
4. Sealed beam unit

Fig. M:3 Bulb holders and fixings

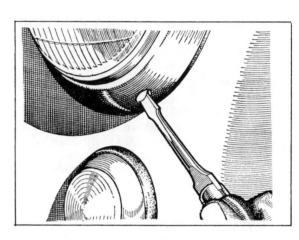

Fig. M:4 Removing the chrome rim from the headlamp assembly

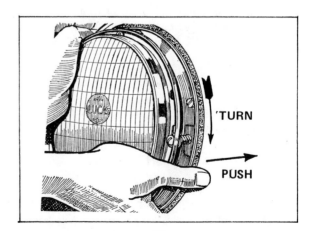

TURN

PUSH

Fig. M:5 Removing the headlamp unit from the wing

left of the cross. Adjust three screws to align each lamp. Horizontal adjustment is effected by adjusting the screws on either side of the lamp and vertical adjustment with the screw on top of the headlamp.

NOTE: The lights should be adjusted in this way only in emergencies. Light setting equipment at garages is far more accurate and should be used in preference.

FRONT SIDELAMPS . . . . [3]

The front sidelamps fitted to Minor 1000 vehicles are either included in the headlamp reflectors or in a separate lens underneath.

Bulb Replacement (Fig. M:7)

Where the lamp is in the headlamp reflector, remove and replace the bulb as described in the HEADLAMP ASSEMBLIES section of this chapter, previously.

Where the bulb is in a lens under the headlamp unit, prise the lens cover from the rubber surround (Fig. M:7), and replace the bayonet type bulb - see Technical Data for correct rating. In some cases, the sidelamp bulb lens also includes the front indicator bulb (Fig. M:8).

INDICATOR LAMPS . . . . [4]

Bulb Replacement (Figs. M:7 & M:8)

The front indicator lamps on saloon models are either under separate lenses, or included in the lens which houses the sidelamp. In both cases bulb replacement is simply a question of prising the lens from its rubber surround, changing the defective bulb and replacing the lens cover.

REAR LIGHT BULBS . . . . [5]

Bulb Replacement

The arrangement of Minor 1000 rear lights changes slightly, according to the age of the vehicle and whether or not it is a saloon or a traveller.

Older saloons and all travellers are fitted with individual brake/rear lamps and indicator lamps (Fig. M:9). In these cases, bulb replacement is the same as described previously in the INDICATOR LAMPS section of this chapter.

Later saloon cars have the indicator and brake/rear lamps housed under one lens (Fig. M:10). Replacement of either bulb is a question of removing the two screws which secure the lens to the body, replacing the defective bulb and refitting the lens.

NUMBER PLATE LIGHT . . . . [6]

Bulb Replacement (Fig. M:11)

The number-plate is illuminated by a separate lamp with two miniature bayonet-fitting bulbs. The cover is removed by unscrewing the single attachment screw, which enables it to be withdrawn, giving easy access to the two

bulbs. Later models are only fitted with one bulb, but the procedure is exactly the same.

INTERIOR LIGHT . . . . [7]

Bulb Replacement

The interior light is located on the roof and is controlled by a switch on the forward edge of the lamp.

Access to the bulb for replacement is achieved by removing the two screws in the plastic lamp cover and removing the cover. The bulb can then be changed.

PANEL/WARNING LAMPS . . . . [8]

Bulb Replacement

The panel and warning light bulbs are fitted to the speedometer. To gain access, remove the speedometer by undoing the cross-head screws on either side of the instrument and pulling it out. The defective bulb can then be pulled out of the back of the instrument and replaced.

FLASHER UNIT . . . . [9]

Replacement

The flasher unit is mounted with a single screw under the instrument panel, adjacent to the steering column. To remove it, mark the three wires attached to it for correct reassembly, remove them, disconnect the flasher unit and replace it. Finally, refit the wires and reattach the flasher unit.

STOP LAMP SWITCH . . . . [10]

Replacement (Fig. M:12)

The stop lamp switch is located on top of the hydraulic brake pipe union which distributes fluid from the master cylinder to the rest of the system. It is mounted at the front of the car on a chassis crossmember.

To change the switch, mark the two wires attached to the top of the switch for correct reassembly, remove them, unscrew the switch, replace it and refit the wires.

FUEL GAUGE . . . . [11]

Description

The bi-metal resistance equipment for the fuel gauge consists of an indicator head and transmitter unit connected to a voltage stabiliser. The indicator head operates on a thermal principle, using a bi-metallic strip surrounded by a head winding, and the transmitter unit is of a resistance type. The system by which the equipment functions is voltage-sensitive, and the voltage stabiliser is necessary to ensure a constant supply of a predetermined voltage to the equipment.

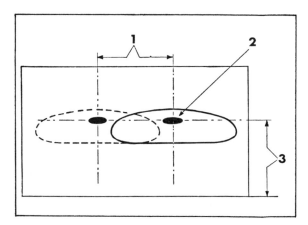

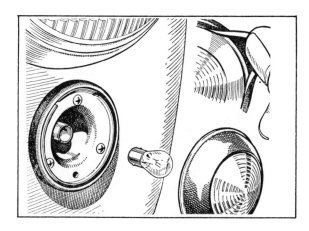

1. *Distance between centres* 3. *Height of centre of lamps*
   of headlamps   *from the ground*
2. *Concentrated area of light*

Fig. M:6 Diagram for correct headlamp alignment

**Fig. M:7 Removing front sidelamp or
indicator bulb**

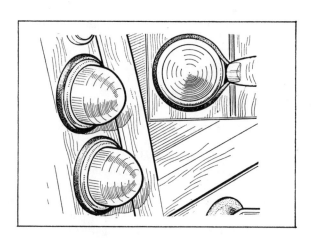

**Fig. M:8 Combined sidelamp and indicator bulb
assembly**

**Fig. M:9 Rear lighting equipment on Traveller
models**

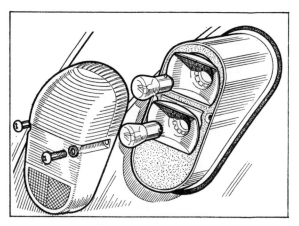

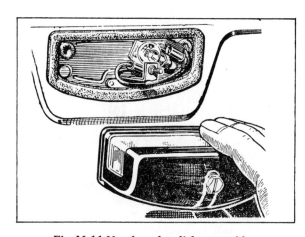

Fig. M:10 Rear lamp assembly on later saloon cars

Fig. M:11 Number plate light assembly

Checking

If the gauge is inoperative, the first thing to check is the voltage stabiliser. To gain access, remove the two cross-head screws - one on either side of the speedometer - and pull the speedometer away from the dashboard. Remove the knurled nut holding the speedometer drive cable to the back of the speedometer head, mark all the attached wires for correct reassembly and remove them. Remove the voltage stabiliser from the back of the speedometer. See Fig. M:13.

Check the voltage through the stabiliser with a voltmeter between the output terminal 'I' and a good earth. With the battery connected and the ignition switched on, the reading should be 10 volts. If it is not, fit a new stabiliser.

If the gauge is still inoperative, disconnect the wires from behind the fuel gauge indicator and check for continuity between the terminals.

Next step is to check the wiring between the component units. Check for bad earths, short-circuits to earth and wiring security.

If after all these checks, the fuel gauge still refuses to operate, take the car to an auto electrician.

SPEEDOMETER . . . . [12]
Removal (Fig. M:13)

1. Locate the small hole on the inner wall of the glovebox.
2. Pass a cross-head screwdriver into the hole and remove the cross-head screw. Remove the cross-head screw from the other side of the instrument.
3. Pull the instrument a small way from the dashboard.
4. Undo the knurled nut which secures the speedometer cable to the speedometer head and push the cable out of the way.
5. Pull out all the warning lamps and panel light bulb from the back of the instrument, carefully noting the colours of each wire for correct reassembly.
6. Remove the speedometer.

Installation

Installation is a straightforward reverse of the removal procedure, but make sure the speedometer inner cable locates properly in the speedometer head before replacing the outer cable.

Cable Replacement (Fig. M:14)

1. Remove the speedometer cable knurled nut as already described.
2. Draw the inner cable out of the outer cable. If the cable is broken some way down, the outer cable will also have to be unscrewed at the gearbox.
3. A pair of Mole grips will help to loosen the nut on the side of the gearbox. Remove the inner cable.
4. If only the inner cable is being renewed, refit the outer cable to the gearbox. Feed the inner cable in from the top, making sure it locates properly at the gearbox end, and replace the cable to the speedometer head.
5. If the outer cable is being removed as well, undo both ends of the outer cable and remove the whole assembly by pulling it into the car through the bulkhead.
6. Route the new outer cable through the bulkhead and fit the inner cable.

INDICATOR SWITCH . . . . [13]
Replacement

1. Remove the steering wheel as described in the Steering Chapter.
2. Disconnect the horn and direction indicator wires at the snap connectors beneath the fascia and draw them through the grommeted hole in the fascia. Reference to the appropriate wiring diagram at the end of this section may make wire identification easier.
3. Remove the column support bracket clamp below the fascia to release the wires.
4. Remove the three chromed screws from the switch plastic cover. Pull the cover upwards off the switch over the end of the steering column.
5. Extract the two screws securing the switch clamp to the column outer tube and remove the switch assembly.
6. Reassembly is a reversal of the removal procedure. Make sure that the switch is.located on the column outer tube so that the cancelling mechanism works correctly.
7. Position the plastic cover so that it does not foul the switch operating lever.

IGNITION SWITCH . . . . [14]

Some of the latest Minor 1000 cars were fitted with a steering lock ignition switch. Its operation and method of removal is fully described in the Steering chapter. Before the steering lock type ignition switch, Minor 1000s were fitted with the rotary barrel-type lock, fitted to the fascia panel. The first turn of the key in a clockwise direction switches on the ignition. Further rotation of the key in the same direction, against a slight resistance, switches the current to a solenoid located near the battery and operates the starter motor.

Replacement

1. Disconnect the battery earth lead.
2. Disconnect the clip surrounding the switch body behind the fascia.
3. Disconnect the cables from the switch terminals, making sure they are marked for correct reassembly.
4. Withdraw the switch from the fascia.
5. Fit the new switch by reversing the removal procedure.

HORN . . . . [15]

All horns are adjusted to give their best performance before leaving the factory and will give a long period of service without any attention; no subsequent adjustment is normally required.

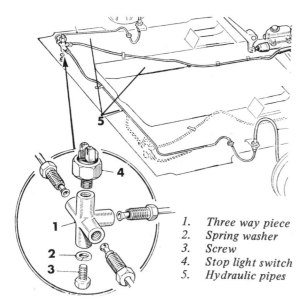

1. Three way piece
2. Spring washer
3. Screw
4. Stop light switch
5. Hydraulic pipes

Fig. M:12 Position of stop lamp switch

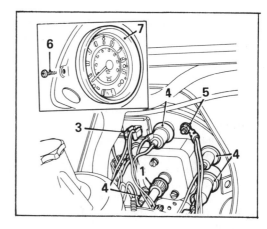

1. Speedo cable
2. Fuel gauge leads
3. Voltage stabiliser leads
4. Bulb holders
5. Earth lead
6. Speedo securing screws
7. Speedometer

Fig. M:13 Centrally mounted speedometer installation

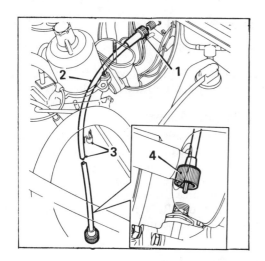

1. Speedo connection
2. Speedo cable
3. Retaining clip
4. Drive pinion connection

Fig. M:14 Speedometer cable replacement

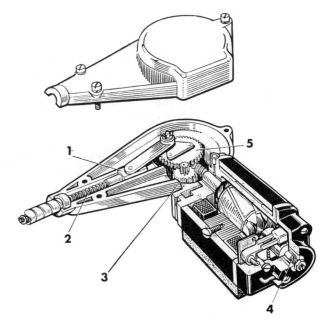

1. Crosshead
2. Flexible cable rack
3. Intermediate gear
4. Thrust screw and ball
5. Final gear

Fig. M:16 Windscreen wiper motor and gearbox with lid removed

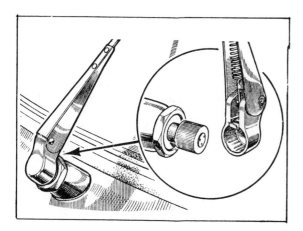

Fig. M:15 Replacing the windscreen wiper arm

©BLUK

If a horn fails or becomes uncertain in its action it does not follow that the horn has broken down. First ascertain that the trouble is not due to a loose or broken connection in the wiring of the horn. The trouble may be due to a blown fuse or discharged battery. If the fuse has blown examine the wiring for the fault and replace with the spare fuse provided.

It is also possible that the performance of a horn may be upset by the fixing bolts working loose, or by some component near the horn being loose. If, after carrying, out the above examination, the trouble is not rectified the horn may need adjustment, but this should not be necessary until the horns have been in service for a long period.

Adjustment does not alter the pitch of the note: it merely takes up wear of moving parts. When adjusting the horns short-circuit the fuse, otherwise it is liable to blow. Again, if the horns do not sound on adjustment release the push instantly.

Adjustment

Remove the fixing screw from the top of the horn and take off the cover. Detach the cover securing bracket by springing it out of location.

Slacken the locknut on the fixed contact and rotate the adjusting nut until the contacts are just separated (indicated by the horn failing to sound). Turn the adjusting nut half a turn in the opposite direction and secure it in this position by tightening the locknut.

WINDSCREEN WIPERS. . . . . [16]

The windscreen wiper motor fitted to all Minor 1000 models is mounted under the bonnet on the left-hand wing valance (Fig. M:16). It has a self returning mechanism built in.

The windscreen wiper arms and blades are retained on the splined drive spindles with spring clips.

Arm Replacement (Fig. M:15)

1. Lift the arm and blade away from the windscreen.
2. Depress the spring retaining clip (Fig. M:15) and remove the arm from the splines.
3. Refitting the assembly is a reverse of the removal procedure.

Blade Replacement

1. Lift the arm and blade assembly away from the windscreen.
2. Depress the clip which locates the blade to the top of the arm and remove the blade.
3. Fitting the new blade is a question of sliding it on to the arm until it locks into position.

Motor Removal

Detach the cable rack from the motor as detailed above. Disconnect the motor cables. Remove the three nuts, spring washers, and rubber distance pieces securing the motor to the bracket and remove the motor.

Cable Rack Removal

Unscrew the pipe union nut; remove the gearbox cover.

Remove the split pin and washer from the crank pin and final gear wheel; lift off the connecting link.

Parking Position Adjustment

Remove the windshield wiper arms as already described. Slacken the three cover securing screws and rotate the automatic parking switch until the two rivet heads are at one o'clock to the drive cable and towards the outlet for it; retighten the three cover screws. Switch on the motor and then switch off. Refit the wiper arms to the drive spindles in the parked position.

Technical Data

ELECTRICS

System . . . . 12 volt, positive

BATTERY

Type. . . . . .Lucas BT7A (BTZ7A Export)
Lucas N9 (NZ9 Export)
Lucas D9 (DZ9 Export) - later models

Capacity (type D9): 20-hour rate . . . . 40 amp.-hr

BULBS

Headlamps . . . . 40/45 watts
Sidelamps . . . . .4 watts
Stop/tail . . . . 21/5 watts
Direction indicators (front and rear) . . . . .21 watts
Rear number plate lamp . . . . .5 watts
Interior lights . . . . .5 watts

ELECTRICAL

Trouble Shooter

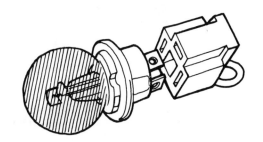

FAULT	CAUSE	CURE
STARTER		
Starter doesn't turn (lights dim)	1. Battery flat or worn. 2. Bad connection in battery circuit	1. Charge or fit new battery. 2. Check all feed and earth connections.
Starter doesn't turn (lights stay bright)	1. Faulty ignition switch 2. Broken starter circuit	1. Check switch. 2. Check starter circuit.
Solenoid switch chatters	1. Flat battery	1. Charge or replace battery.
Starter just spins	1. Bendix gear sticking	1. Remove starter and clean or replace Bendix gear.
CHARGING CIRCUIT		
Low or no charge rate	1. Broken or slipping drive belt 2. Poor connections on or faulty alternator	1. Fit new belt. 2. Check and replace alternator.
LIGHTING CIRCUIT		
No lights (or very dim)	1. Flat or faulty battery, bad battery connections	1. Check battery and connection.
Side and rear lights inoperative although stoplights and flashers work	1. Fuse blown	1. Fit correct value fuse.
One lamp fails	1. Blown bulb 2. Poor bulb contact 3. Bad earth connection. 4. Broken feed	1. Fit new bulb. 2/3. Check connections. 4. Check feed.
Flasher warning bulb stays on or flashers twice as fast	1. Faulty bulb or connection on front or rear of offending side	1. Fit new bulb, make good connection.
Lights dim when idling or at low speed	1. Loose drive belt 2. Flat battery 3. Faulty charging circuit	1. Tighten belt. 2/3. Check charge output and battery.
One dim light	1. Blackened bulb 2. Bad earth 3. Tarnished reflector	1/3. Fit new bulb or sealed-beam. 2. Check earth connections.
WINDSCREEN WIPERS		
Wipers do not work	1. Blown fuse 2. Poor connection 3. Faulty switch 4. Faulty motor	1. Fit fuse. 2. Check connections. 3. Check switch. 4. Remove and examine motor.
Motor operates slowly	1. Excessive resistance in circuit or wiper drive 2. Worn brushes	1. Check wiper circuit. 2. Remove motor and check brushes.

Keys to Wiring Diagrams

Colour key for wiring diagrams on pages 119 to 127.

1. Blue	17. Green	33. Brown	49. Purple
2. Blue with Red	18. Green with Red	34. Brown with Red	50. Purple with Red
3. Blue with Yellow	19. Green with Yellow	35. Brown with Yellow	51. Purple with Yellow
4. Blue with White	20. Green with Blue	36. Brown with Blue	52. Purple with Blue
5. Blue with Green	21. Green with White	37. Brown with White	53. Purple with White
6. Blue with Purple	22. Green with Purple	38. Brown with Green	54. Purple with Green
7. Blue with Brown	23. Green with Brown	39. Brown with Purple	55. Purple with Brown
8. Blue with Black	24. Green with Black	40. Brown with Black	56. Purple with Black
9. White	25. Yellow	41. Red	57. Black
10. White with Red	26. Yellow with Red	42. Red with Yellow	58. Black with Red
11. White with Yellow	27. Yellow with Blue	43. Red with Blue	59. Black with Yellow
12. White with Blue	28. Yellow with White	44. Red with White	60. Black with Blue
13. White with Green	29. Yellow with Green	45. Red with Green	61. Black with White
14. White with Purple	30. Yellow with Purple	46. Red with Purple	62. Black with Green
15. White with Brown	31. Yellow with Brown	47. Red with Brown	63. Black with Purple
16. White with Black	32. Yellow with Black	48. Red with Black	64. Black with Brown
			65. Dark Green
			66. Light Green

Key for wiring diagrams on pages 128 and 129.

1. Alternator - 11AC (Dynamo)	31. R.H. headlamp main beam
2. Ignition warning light	32. Line fuse - 10 amp
3. Fuse unit	33. Panel light switch
4. Fuse pump	34. Panel light
5. Ignition and starter switch	35. Panel light
6. Stop lamp switch	36. Flasher switch
7. R.H. stop lamp	37. L.H. rear flasher
8. L.H. stop lamp	38. L.H. front flasher
9. Ignition coil	39. L.H. headlamp main beam
10. Distributor	40. R.H. headlamp dip beam
11. Control unit - 4TR (control box)	41. L.H. headlamp dip beam
12. Interior light and switch - when fitted	42. Dipper switch
13. Courtesy light switch - when fitted	43. Flasher unit
14. Courtesy light switch - when fitted	44. Flasher warning light
15. Instrument voltage stabilizer	45. L.H. pilot lamp
16. Fuel gauge	46. R.H. pilot lamp
17. Fuel tank unit	47. R.H. tail lamp
18. Heater switch - when fitted	48. Number-plate lamp
19. Heater - when fitted	50. Number-plate lamp
20. 12-volt battery	51. Windscreen wiper switch and motor - earthed to control box terminal 'E'
21. Starter solenoid switch	52. Snap connectors
22. Starter motor	53. Terminal blocks or junction box
23. Horn	54. Earth connections made via cable
24. Horn-push	55. Earth connections made via fixing bolts
25. Oil filter warning light and switch (when fitted)	56. Relay - 6RA
26. Oil pressure warning light and switch	57. Warning light unit - 3AW
27. R.H. front flasher	58. Ammeter - when fitted
28. R.H. rear flasher	
29. Lighting switch	
30. Main beam warning light	

CABLE COLOUR CODE

B.	Black	P.	Purple	Y.	Yellow
U.	Blue	R.	Red	D.	Dark
N.	Brown	W.	White	L.	Light
G.	Green			M.	Medium

When a cable has two colour code letters the first denotes the main colour and the second denotes the tracer colour.

Wiring Diagram

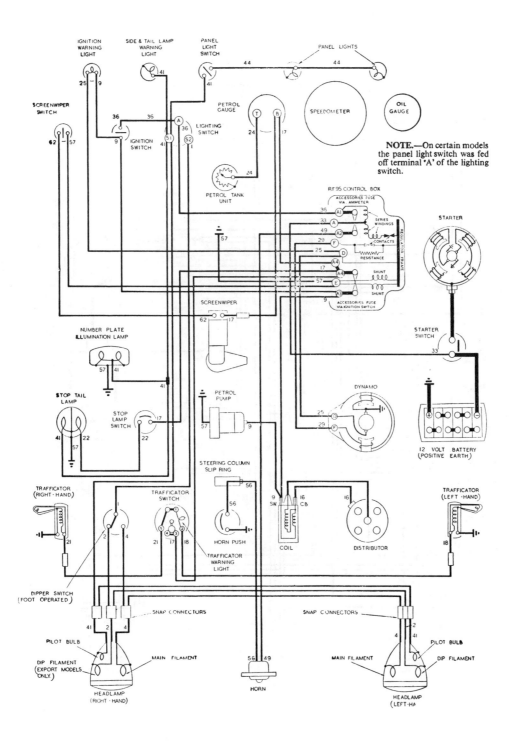

NOTE.—On certain models the panel light switch was fed off terminal 'A' of the lighting switch.

All models with combined head and pilot lamps

©BLUK

Wiring Diagram

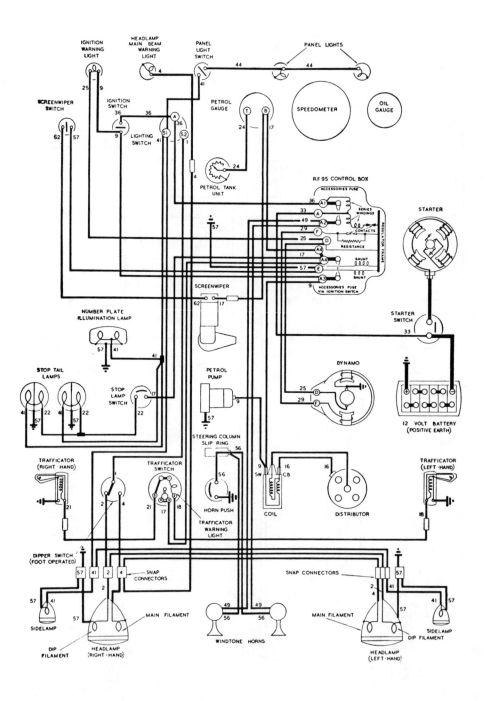

U.S.A. models

Wiring Diagram

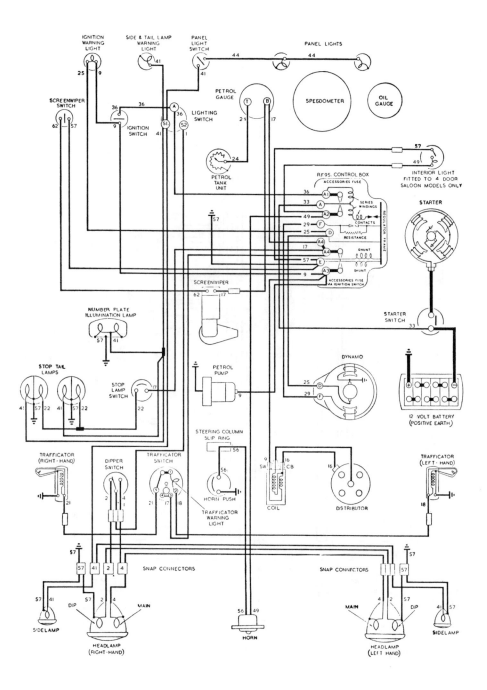

All models with separate head and pilot lamps - except U.S.A. models

© BLUK

Wiring Diagram

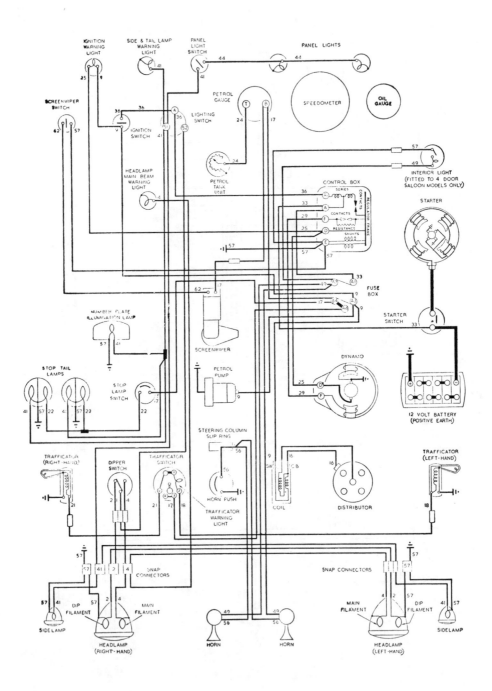

U.S.A. models only, with separate control boxes and fuse boxes

Wiring Diagram

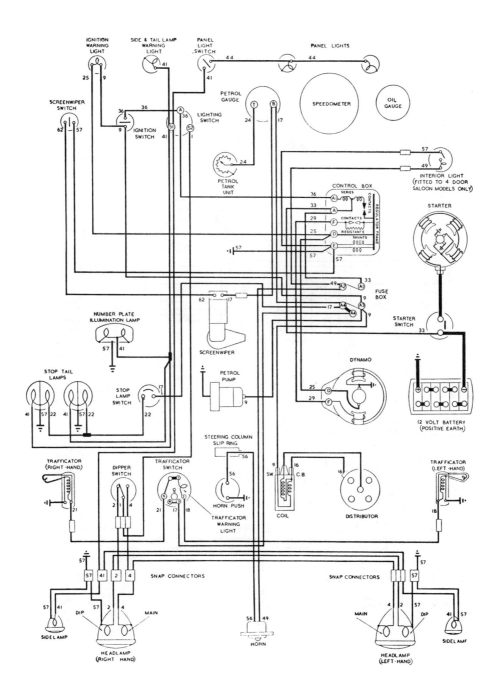

Models with separate control boxes and fuse boxes

©BLUK

Wiring Diagram

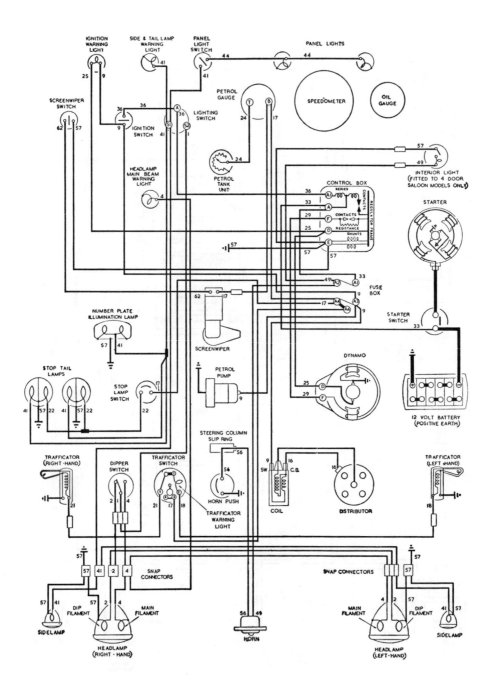

Models with separate control boxes and fuse boxes and head lamp main beam warning light

Wiring Diagram

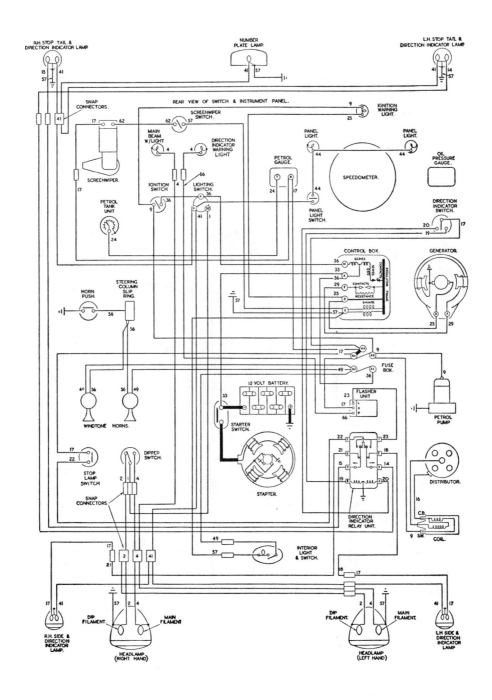

Models fitted with flashing direction indicator equipment

Wiring Diagram

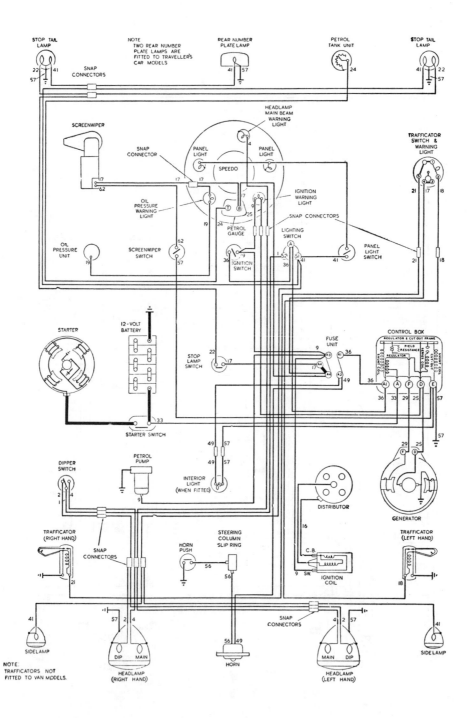

Home and export (Right-hand drive modes with central instrument dials)

Wiring Diagram

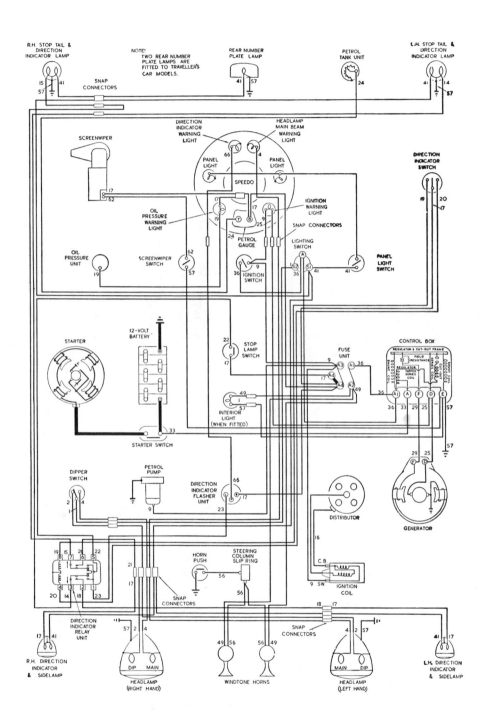

Export (Left-hand drive models with central instrument dial and flashing indicators)

© BLUK

Wiring Diagram

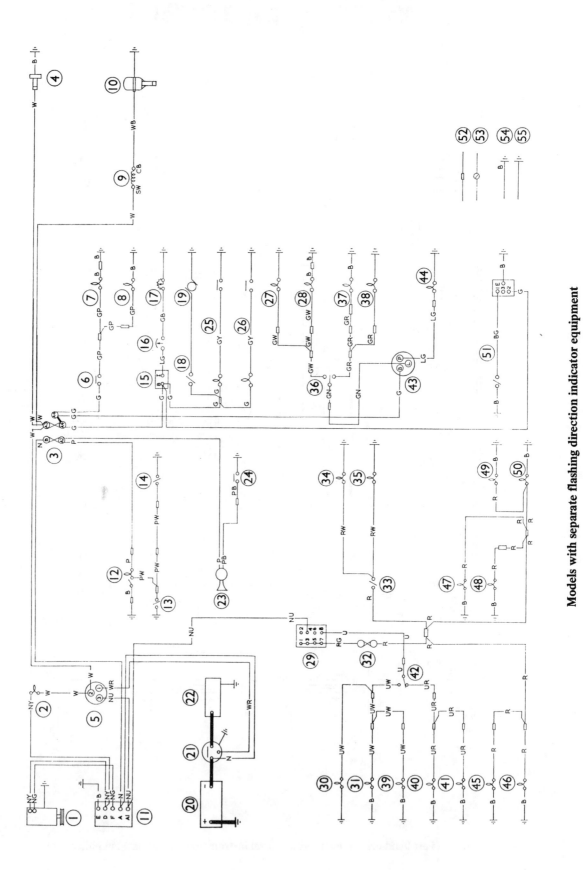

Models with separate flashing direction indicator equipment

Wiring Diagram

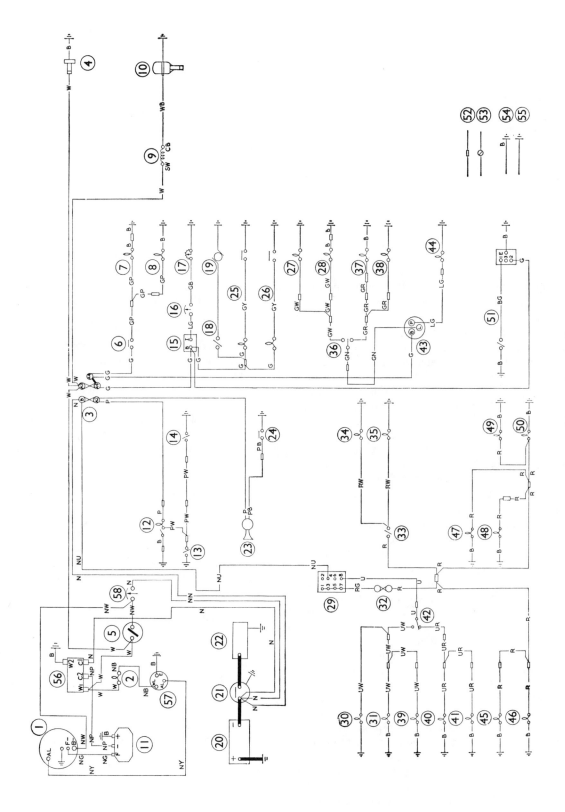

Models filled with the Lucas 11 AC alternator

©BLUK

Body Fittings

CORROSION . . . . [1]

We all recognise rust when it starts to appear around certain parts of our car's anatomy. Then, before we are aware, it's too late and metal has been replaced by a very poor substitute. The result is costly, can be dangerous and will not win the car any beauty awards!

The only way to beat rust is to prevent it in the first place or at the very least slow it down. To do this, first of all we must realise how rust is formed.

Think of a piece of metal with a bead of water sitting on top. The metal below the water is starved of air and is called anodic. The metal outside this area is known as cathodic. An electrolytic action is formed between these two conditions and it is this process that causes corrosion. There are acceleration factors involved such as dirt, grit or salt. These can be contained in the water and will increase the conductivity. So basically rust is formed by an electro-chemical reaction. Bear in mind that rain needn't necessarily be the water factor involved in the process - condensation plays its role too.

Obviously it doesn't take much logic to understand how rust can be prevented in the first place. The metal work of the car has to be protected from moisture and air. This protection is partly taken care of by the car manufacturer when the car is put together - paint on the outside and special inhibitors used on the inside. However, the rust protection is only as good as the application of these materials and one spot missed means that rust will accelerate all the more in this particular spot.

The importance of regular washing and touching up paintwork play their part in rust protection. For example, regular hosing down of the underneath of the car can help prevent any build up of mud forming in certain areas. Mud can act like a damp sponge during wet weather so that you have a constant moisture problem even during dry spells. You'll find that common rust problems on particular models usually originate from mud-traps.

You can always go one step further and improve on the manufacturers rust protection by tackling your own rustproofing. This involves applying light viscosity water-displacing material inside all the box sections and/or applying underbody sealant.

There are various kits on the market designed specifically for the keen DIY motorist and even if you don't treat all the box sections it is worthwhile devoting some time to protecting the rust prone areas of your particular car.

An important part of protection is treating the car with an underbody sealant. Here preparation is of the utmost importance because if the sealant doesn't attach firmly to the car body then the air gap between seal and metal can help accelerate corrosion rather than prevent it.

First of all the car will have to be thoroughly cleaned underneath. A high pressure hose is obviously helpful in removing dirt but better still is to have the car steam cleaned first. Applying an underbody sealant is a dirty job and you should be well prepared with old clothes, gloves and a hat. If you are venturing underneath the car and it has to be jacked up then make certain that it is well supported on axle stands.

After thoroughly cleaning the underside you should go over stubborn dirt or caked mud with a good fine wire brush. The important thing is that the surface to be treated is absolutely clear of any foreign matter. For good application of underbody sealant use a cheap paint brush. It is important that the sealant used will remain flexible and will not chip or flake at a later date. Obviously care will have to be taken not to cover moving parts such as the drive shaft, handbrake linkages, etc. If necessary, mask these areas first.

The first part of this section on corrosion concentrates on the matter of protection. Which is fine before corrosion takes place. But what happens if corrosion has already taken a hold?

It can be a costly business when corrosion dictates the vehicle being taken off the road through an MoT failure. As already explained in 'Pass the MoT' page at the beginning of this Repair Manual, an MoT tester will check for damage or corrosion in or on a vehicle that is likely to render it unsafe.

With the Minor 1000 the tester will pay special attention to the rear suspension mounting points, side sills, and the floor. Also he'll check the seat belt mounting areas, if belts are fitted.

Having checked and identified the important areas, the MoT tester will check the extent or level of suspect corrosion. He should do this by pressing hard against the area and testing the amount of 'give' which results. Often he will also tap the component lightly (it should not be

Fig. N:1 Components of the body

1. Door assembly - RH
2. Door assembly - LH
3. Trunk lid assembly
4. Trunk panel assembly
5. Panel assembly lower rear squab support
33. RH panel rear quarter inner
34. LH panel rear quarter inner
35. RH panel rear wheel arch
36. LH panel rear wheel arch
37. Shackle plate and towing eye
39. Jack plates
40. Boxing plate RH front wheel arch to body side

42. Bracket trunk opening to floor
43. Support member assembly trunk floor
45. Reinforcement back light
46. Panel assembly fascia
47. Top portion fascia panel assembly
48. Lower portion - fascia panel assembly
49. Reinforcement RH roof side inner
50. Panel assembly RH shut pillar - upper
51. RH panel quarter-light top facing
52. RH panel door opening top facing
54. Panel assembly LH shut pillar - upper
57. RH panel rear quarter

59. Panel assembly roof and windscreen opening
60. Panel windscreen opening
61. RH panel body side front
62. LH panel body side front
63. Extension assembly RH hinge pillar
65. RH finisher drip moulding
70. Panel assembly upper rear squab support
74. RH wing rear
75. Bonnet assembly
76. Cross-member assembly - bonnet
99. RH wing front
100. LH wing front
109. Connecting piece rear wheel arch RH

necessary to subject the area to heavy blows), listening for differences in sound which will result from unaffected metal compared with corroded metal.

The DIY owner should bear in mind that any damage caused by corrosion or crash damage should be repaired correctly. For example, any repair to a load bearing part of the car's structure such as plating or welding should be such that it is clear that the strength of the repair is approximately the same as that of the original component. It is important to remember that repairs to load bearing members or sections by riveting or use of glass fibre are not acceptable to the tester. However, these methods can be used for other parts of the car.

ADJUSTMENTS . . . . [2]

Bonnet Lock

The spring-loaded striker pin may be adjusted for length after slackening the locknut which secures it to the bracket beneath the bonnet lid.

When the pin is correctly positioned the bonnet lid will lock in the fully closed position and also open sufficiently to allow the safety hook to be depressed when the bonnet catch is released by the control ring beneath the instrument panel.

Front Seats (Fig. N:2)

Each front seat pivots about the forward support and may be raised to allow passengers to reach the rear seats. On later models the squab of the seat is also hinged. The position of the driving seat may be adjusted forwards or backwards when the spring-loaded lever that extends beyond the front of the seat is depressed.

If the normal range of adjustment is not capable of providing comfort for drivers of exceptional stature the seat can be repositioned by moving the seat hinge bracket into the required position on the floor of the car.

Doors and Trunk Lid (Figs. N:3 and N:4)

When closed and correctly adjusted, the doors and trunk lid will be a tight fit on the rubber surround. Should a door require adjustment, slacken the two Phillips screws securing the lock striker plate to the door pillar and move the plate in the required direction. Firmly tighten the screws and check the door. If the door will not secure in the fully closed position check the adjustment of the socket plate, which is secured to the door pillar below the striker plate.

Ventilating Windows (Fig. N:5)

Provision is made for regulating the frictional resistance of the hinges of the door ventilating windows should they show signs of closing of their own accord under wind pressure.

The insertion of a screwdriver in the larger of the screws in the lower window frame permits the resistance of the hinge to be adjusted to the required extent. Some models are fitted with slotted screws and some with Phillips screws.

WINDOW REGULATORS . . . . [3]

Removal

Remove the window regulator handle and the interior door handle. Carefully prise the trim panel from the door, to which it is attached by a series of spring fasteners.

Wind the window to the fully closed position and remove the four bolts and spring washers securing the winder to the door.

Disengage the quadrant arm from the glass lift channel and pass it between the guide channel and door panel.

Withdraw the winder assembly from the bottom of the door.

Installation

Installation is a reverse of the removal procedure.

TRIM PANEL . . . . [4]

Removal

The trim panel is secured to the inside of the door with spring clips. However, before it can be removed, remove the window regulator handle and inside door handle. Both of these are held in place with a crosshead screw. Remove the handles and lever the trim panel gently off the door.

Installation

Installation is a straightforward reverse of the removal procedure, but make sure the spring clips are guided into their correct holes before pushing the panel home.

DOOR GLASS . . . . [5]

Removal (Fig. N:6)

Remove the window regulator handle and interior door handle as described previously. Carefully prise off the door trim panel.

Remove the rubber grommets from the edge of the door and extract the three bolts securing the door glass channel.

Unscrew the two bolts from the under side of the ventilator panel and the bolt and nut securing the lower end of the glass channel to the door.

Wind the window glass up until the quadrant arm can be disengaged from the lift channel and the whole assembly lifted from the door.

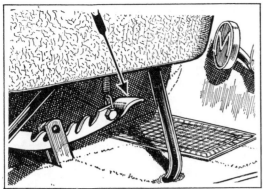

Fig. N:2 Front seat adjustment point

Fig. N:3 Door striker plate, showing its adjustment

Fig. N:4 Later type door adjustment points

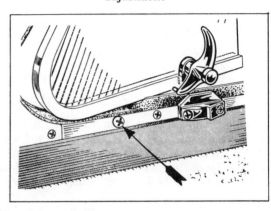

Fig. N:5 Adjusting screw for ventilating window

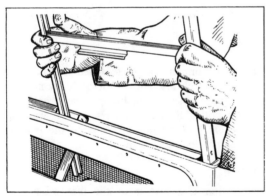

Fig. N:6 Removing the door glass assembly

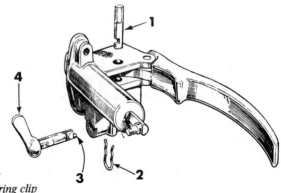

1. Locking bolt
2. Retaining spring clip
3. Eccentric pin
4. Locking lever

Fig. N:7 Modified door lock fitted to two door and Traveller models

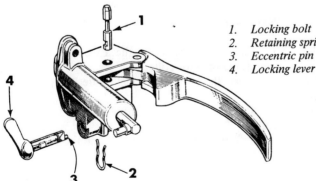

Fig. N:8 Door lock fitted to older models and four door saloon

Installation

Place the glass in the frame assembly and engage the lower ends of the guide channel with the door. With the glass at the top of the channel, engage the winder quadrant arm with the lift channel below the glass.

Lower the glass with the winder and assist the frame assembly to follow into position.

Place the sealing rubber in position beneath the ventilator frame.

DOOR LOCK ASSEMBLY . . . . [6]

Remove the door glass channel assembly as detailed in the previous section.

Traveller and Two Door

Withdraw the split pin, spring, and flat washer securing the remote control link to the lock plunger.

Remove the three Phillips screws securing the handle and lock, and withdraw the assembly from the door (Fig. N:7).

Before removing the lock from the door fitted with an interior safety catch extract the spring clip and withdraw the door locking lever. Immediately the lock assembly has been withdrawn replace the locking lever and retaining clip to prevent loss of the lock bolt, which is free to fall out if the lock is inverted.

On later models the lock bolt is retained in position by a pin and thus remains in the body of the lock unless the pin is withdrawn.

To replace the lock bolt withdraw the locking lever and spindle and replace the lock bolt in its housing from the top with its slotted end downwards and facing the inside of the lock. Insert the locking lever with the handle upwards so that its eccentric pin engages the bolt slot. Insert the retaining spring clip.

On models fitted with escutcheons to the door handle opening, the escutcheon is removed by releasing the Spire tension locknut retaining it in position. When replacing an escutcheon, hook the front end in the door panel cutout, feeding the peg at the other end through the hole in the handle depression, and fix it in position with the Spire locknut.

Four Door

Remove the screw securing the escutcheon to the guide plate; remove the escutcheon from the handle.

Unscrew the three screws securing the guide plate and handle to the edge of the door; withdraw the handle. The upper screw is shorter than the other two.

Unscrew the four screws securing the remote control to the door panel and the two screws securing the lock.

Support the lock (Fig. N:8) and push the remote control into the door. Lower the lock and withdraw the lock and remote control assembly through the hole in the door panel.

Installation

Installation, in both cases, is a reverse of the removal procedure.

TRAVELLER WOODWORK . . . . [7]

The ash woodwork on Traveller models should be inspected at regular intervals. A regular coat of varnish will go a long way to increasing its life.

Signs of wood worm or rot should be treated in much the same way as damaged body panels by using filler and sanding.

BONNET AND BOOT LID . . . . [8]

Removal

1. Drill a hole 1/8 in (3 mm) in diameter through the hinge and inner skin of the bonnet to facilitate replacement. Take great care not to allow drill to penetrate violently and dent the outer panel as it strikes its underside.
2. Remove the screws holding the support arm in position, and the bolts attaching the bonnet to the hinge while an assistant at each side supports bonnet panel. To avoid risk of paint damage, place thick padding on front wings under the rear corners of bonnet as the panels are heavy and unwieldy.

Installation

Installation is a reversal of the removal procedure, but refitting the bolts only loosely at first. Place a drill in both previously drilled holes to ensure correct alignment and then tighten the bolts.

BUMPERS. . . . . [9]

Removal

The front bumpers can be removed after undoing the two brackets which are held to the body frame by nuts, bolts, and spring washers. The bumper bar is held to each bracket by bolts, distance washers, spring washers and nuts. The rear bumpers are attached to the rear of the bodyframe in an identical fashion.

Installation

Installation is a reverse of the removal procedure.

RADIATOR GRILLE. . . . . [10]

Removal

1. Carefully prise away the chrome trim which surrounds the radiator grille.
2. Open the bonnet and make sure it is properly secured.
3. Remove the screws from around the edge of the grille.
4. Lift the grille away from inside the engine compartment.

Installation

Installation is a reversal of the removal procedure.

Accessories

AERIAL . . . . [1]

Installation (Fig. O:1)

1. Mark out a suitable position for the aerial hole on the nearside wing as shown in Fig. O:1 and drill a 7/8 in (22 mm) hole.
2. Scrape around the underside of the hole to reveal bright metal in order to ensure a good earth connection. Failure to do this may result in aerial-borne interference being transmitted to the radio.
3. Drill a similar sized hole in the wing valance, behind the aerial. It might be found easier to drill the second hole from inside the car.
4. Mount the aerial to the wing as detailed in the fitting instructions supplied with it, or as shown in Fig. O:2.
5. Route the aerial lead through the hole in the valance and into the car. Seal the valance hole with a grommet. Route the lead to the passenger side footwell.

RADIO/SPEAKER . . . . [2]

Radio Fitting (Figs. O:3 and O:4)

First ensure the radio is suitable for the car. Minors were built with a positive earthed electrical system. Since the early 60's, most cars have had a negative earthed system. Radios can only be fitted to the system for which they have been designed. Since there are more negative earthed cars around than positive earthed, finding a suitable radio may prove a little difficult. Whatever, it is IMPERATIVE that the radio is suitable for positive earthed electrical systems.
1. Buy some perforated radio mounting brackets and some nuts and bolts small enough to pass through the holes.
2. Disconnect the battery.
3. Bend two pieces of the perforated strip across the top of the radio so that the holes in the strip line up with the mounting holes on the sides of the radio.

4. Attach the strips to the radio temporarily with the bolts which will be supplied with the radio. Use a pencil to mark around the edge of the brackets on the underside of the parcel shelf.
5. Drill four holes in the parcel shelf, remove the brackets from the radio and bolt them to the parcel shelf.
6. Bolt the radio to the bracket, and plug in the aerial.
7. Connect the red lead from the radio to the terminal behind the ignition switch, carrying the feed wire, (see Wiring Diagrams).
8. Temporarily connect the speaker and reconnect the battery.
9. Turn the radio on and turn it to a weak station - about 200 metres on the medium waveband.
10. Find the aerial trimming screw - as detailed with the radio fitting instructions - and adjust until the clearest reception is obtained (Fig. O:4). It should not be necessary to rotate the screw more than half a turn in either direction. Disconnect the speaker.
NOTE: These instructions are designed to be used as a rough guide. Because of the different sorts of radio it is possible to fit, it would obviously be better to follow the manufacturer's fitting instructions if included.

Speaker Installation (Fig. O:5)

1. Make a speaker grille out of hardboard or thick cardboard - unless one is supplied with the radio fitting kit - to fit on the front parcel shelf as shown in Fig. O:5.
2. Using the grille as a template, drill two 1/8 in (3.175 mm) diameter holes through the trim panel and metal of the front inner side bulkhead. Then drill a 1/8 in (3.175 mm) diameter hole through the trim and front bulkhead.
3. Remove the grille from the parcel shelf and attach the speaker to the back of it with four self-tapping screws and spring washers.
4. Attach the speaker wires and reposition the grille.
5. Fit self tapping screws to hold the grille in position and route the speaker wires to the back of the radio.

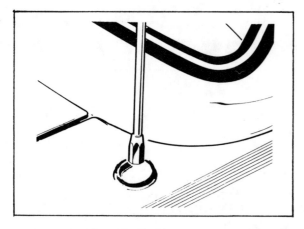

Fig. O:1 Drill a hole and fit aerial in a suitable position

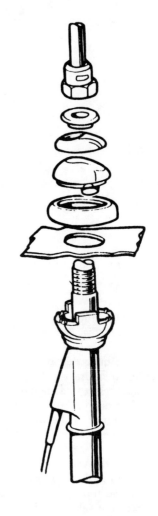

Fig. O:2 Typical aerial fitting assemble the components in the correct order

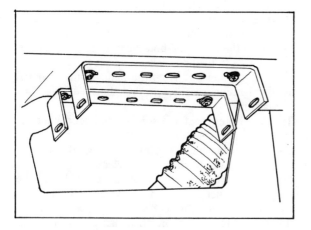

Fig. O:3 Fit the perforated brackets to the parcel shelf

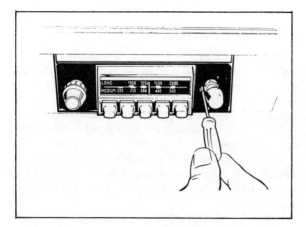

Fig. O:4 Typical radio fine trimming adjustment

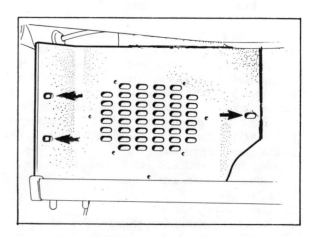

Fig. O:5 Fitting front speaker grille to parcel shelf

©BLUK

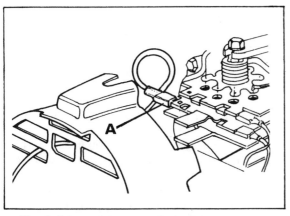

Fig. O:6 Connecting a 1 mfd capacitor to terminal 'A' on alternator models

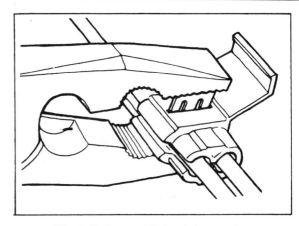

Fig. O:7 Connecting extra wire with special connector

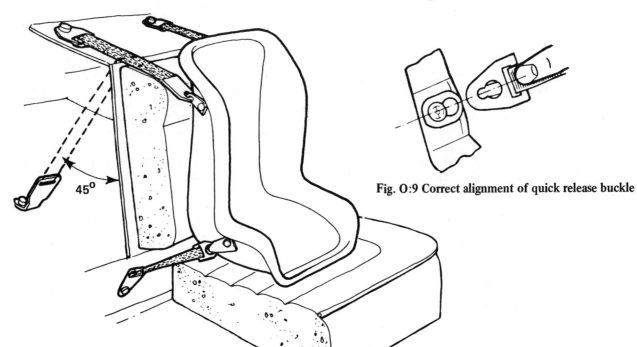

Fig. O:9 Correct alignment of quick release buckle

Fig. O:8 How the body seat should be located on saloon and traveller models

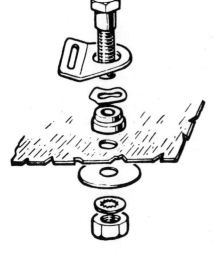

Fig. O:10 The correct way to assemble the KL seat anchorage fitting

Fig. O:11 Action of sound waves through Sound Barrier Mat

© BLUK

SUPPRESSION . . . . [3]

It is possible that no suppression will be necessary, so try the set first without any; this is especially likely should good earth connections have been made at the aerial fitting and should the control unit be earthed well.

To suppress a dynamo, connect a 1 mfd capacitor to the output terminal. Attach the capacitor under a dynamo fixing bolt and connect the lead to the larger of the dynamo terminals.

To suppress an alternator, disconnect the battery supply on vehicle, then pull off the two plug connections on the alternator back plate. Then withdraw the two moulded cover securing screws and remove cover.

Route fly lead of capacitor through slot in moulded cover and ensuring that associated wiring is not disturbed, connect lead to the spare 3/16 in terminal blade attached to the main battery lead termination on alternator (Figs. O:6 and O:7).

Refit the moulded cover and reconnect the plug-in connections to alternator. Secure the capacitor mounting clip under alternator rear fixing bolt. Reconnect battery supply.

Other parts that may need attention are the instrument voltage stabiliser where a 1 or 3 mfd capacitor should be connected to the 'B' terminal and attached to an adjacent screw. The wiper motor is suppressed by connecting a capacitor between the earth lead under wiper gearbox screw and a motor fixing bolt.

SEAT BELTS . . . . [4]

Only the very last Minor 1000's were fitted with seat belts as standard. For some years before, the cars were all fitted with anchorage points so that seat belts could be fitted quite easily if desired.

However, on earlier models, there was no provision for seat belts at all. This doesn't mean they can't be fitted, but it is a difficult job.

Quite an assortment of tools is needed for putting the anchorage points in the correct positions. Because of this, the job would be better left to a Leyland dealer.

BABY SEAT . . . . [5]

Only by fitting a safety seat or harness, secured firmly to the structure of the car, can a child have a good chance of coming through even a mild collision without injury. Furthermore, with the child safely in place in the back of the car, a driver can concentrate on driving without being distracted, while the child can enjoy the ride in safety and comfort.

There are many different baby seats and cot restraints on the market and it is essential for the child's safety that whichever one is fitted meets the relevant safety stan-

dards. KL Jeenay Safety Systems are BSI approved and are generally accepted as being among the best on the market.

Baby or child seats are normally suitable for children aged from 6/9 months to children aged 5 years. KL Jeenay safety seats or harness can, if necessary, be fitted 2 or 3 abreast, doubling up anchor plates at anchorage points where necessary.

The Minor 1000 range does not have in-built anchorage points but fitting instructions are supplied with these seats and harnesses and they should be followed exactly. The following points should always be borne in mind:
1.   Remove the seat cushion (bottom part). If anchorage points have to be drilled then it should be stressed that only fixed parts of the steel structure should be used. The size of the holes should be 0.44 in (11.5 mm). Always check the position of petrol tank, brake fluid pipes, electrical wiring, spare wheel and other obstructions before drilling.
2.   When fitting anchorage points refer to Fig. O:10 for correct order of assembly. This is important.
3.   Fit the four restraint strap assemblies to the anchorage points using short straps for the bottom of the seat and obviously the long straps for the top (Fig. O:8).
4.   Adjust seat straps to keep the safety seat as high as possible.
5.   Attach lower straps to seat and adjust webbing to suit, without overtightening.
6.   To remove the seat press into car squab and remove lower lugs first.
7.   Adjust the harness straps to fit as tightly as comfortable. The lap straps should rest low over the bony part of the hip. Always ensure that the crotch strap is used and the quick release buckle correctly fastened (Fig. O:9).

SOUNDPROOFING . . . . [6]

In any car a certain amount of noise is transmitted to the passenger compartment; not only is this annoying but, especially in excess, it makes long journeys extremely tiring. It follows that any reduction in noise level is desirable for more enjoyable and safer motoring.

The noise in a car has various sources; wind blowing round badly fitting doors and windows, mechanical noise from engine and transmission, exhaust noise, noise from tyres on road and noise from vibrating body panels. By proper application of the material most suitable for each type of noise, it is invariably possible to make a very considerable reduction in noise level. Sound Service (Oxford) Ltd, of West End, Witney, Oxon. are leading suppliers of sound insulating materials and their Autosound kits for individual models, contain all that is needed for the effective insulation of the car.

Before the Autosound kit can be fitted, the front and rear seats should be removed as well as all the carpets and floor mats.

With the floor/bulkhead area clear, check for any holes and seal them with the mastic sealing strip supplied in the Autosound kit. This should also be applied to all rubber grommets where cables and pipes pass through the bulkhead and to the area at the base of the steering column. The object is to obtain an air-tight seal between the engine and passenger compartments.

All the components of the kit are pre-cut to shape and numbered and the next step should be to lay them out and identify them. Rigid bitumen damper pads are included and these should be stuck in each footwell and in other areas of the floor where vibration is apparent. These can be found by gently tapping with a rubber hammer; if they emit a thumping sound, they should be treated. Each damper pad is self-adhesive on one side allowing it to be stuck in place and it acts as a stiffener. As the panel vibrates, the pad is alternately stretched and compressed and thus acts to slow down the vibration, reducing the noise level.

The next job is to fit pre-cut pieces of Sound Barrier Mat to the bulkhead, gearbox hump and transmission tunnel. These are made from a grey foam material with a stiff rubber like facing on one side. The material is glued in place on the panels, using the adhesive supplied in the kit, the foam being placed against the steel panel. In practice, this allows the sound waves to pass through the panel into the foam where some of the energy of the vibrating air particles is dissipated as they pass through its tiny passages, and then bounce back from the stiff outer layer. In this way, much of the sound is trapped between the two layers and gradually loses its energy as it bounces to and fro (Fig. O:11).

For the underbonnet area, the Autosound kit includes a large pad of Neoprene coated felt which is glued under the bonnet with the smooth surface outermost. Like the Sound Barrier Mat, the felt has tiny passages between its fibres that help dissipate energy of the vibrating air particles. This material cuts down multiple reflections of sound within the engine compartment, preventing the build up of noise.

The remaining material in the kit is made from a heavy composite material called Acousticell. This is made from a mixture of foam and waste fibre material blended together to form a heavy mat. It provides damping of the vibrations from the floor panels in two ways: by friction when the fibrous parts move against each other and by the vibrating air particles passing through the tiny passages in the foam.

One further item provided is a roll of Weatherseal tape for sealing doors, etc. Rather than placing this round the entire opening, it is often more effective simply to place it where the air is actually leaking through the seal, and to find this is a simple matter. It is necessary to drive the car with a passenger who should have a section of normal garden hose. By holding one end of the hose to his ear and the other to the door seal, he can determine exactly where the seal is deficient. By marking the extremities of the leak with chalk or some similar means, it is a simple matter to cut the Weatherseal tape to size and install it exactly where needed.

The final job is to replace the carpets and seats and to check the operation of all instruments and lights, etc., in case any wires have been displaced during the operation.

REAR SCREEN HEATER . . . . [7]

One of the latest accessories available to the do-it-yourself market is the full width rear screen heater from Lucas (part number 60067047). This heater has been specifically designed to fit any car, including your Minor 1000, and can be installed with very little effort.

Preparation

1. Before attempting to fit the heater, it is advisable to prepare the wiring (see Fig. O:12). This allows the heater to be switched on, helps with the removal of the white backing sheet and final adhesion of the element.
2. If the ignition switch is already heavily loaded with extras — fog and spot lamps for example — a relay will have to be fitted (see Fig. O:13).
3. If the heater is too big for the rear screen, one of its elements can be completely removed. This should be done whilst positioning the heater as described in the Installation procedure.

Installation

1. Fit the switch in a convenient position under the instrument panel. Disconnect the battery and wire circuit as shown in Fig. O:12, or Fig. O:13 if a relay is being fitted. *NOTE: Two electrical connections are required at the screen — one each side — either at the top or at the bottom. Where cables are routed through or behind the parcel shelf, connections should be made at the bottom. Where cables have to be routed through the headlining, connections should be made at the top.*
2. Place the heater against the outside of the rear screen and tape it in position (see Fig. O:14). Check position of the heater from the driver's seat by looking through the rear view mirror. If the position is satisfactory, mark around the edges. Make sure there is sufficient space for the two side bars to be fitted — essential for electrical contact.
3. The inside surface of the rear screen must be thoroughly cleaned and dried. A proprietry silver cleaner — Duraglit is ideal — should be rubbed all over the screen. The polish should then be cleaned off with methylated spirits.
4. Ensure that the screen is absolutely free from condensation by using a hair dryer to warm it up. If condensation forms when a hand is held close to the screen, it is too cold.
5. Place the heater assembly on a clean table with the protective lined sheet uppermost. Carefully remove the protective sheet, but not the backing sheet, cut it down the

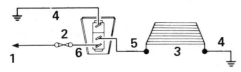

1. 12v (via ignition switch)
2. 35 amp fuse
3. Heater
4. Black wire
5. White wire
6. Green wire

Fig. O:12 Heater circuit without relay

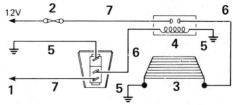

1. 12v (via ignition switch)
2. 35 amp fuse
3. Heater
4. Relay
5. Black wire
6. White wire
7. Green wire

Fig. O:13 Heater circuit with relay.

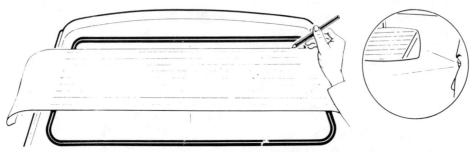

Fig. O:14 Putting the heater in position on the outside of the rear screen

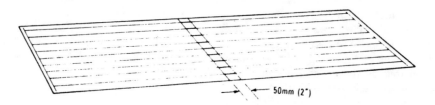

50mm (2")

Fig. O:15 Heater assembly after cutting and repositioning the protective sheet

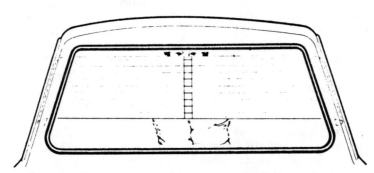

Fig. O:16 Positioning heater on inside of rear screen

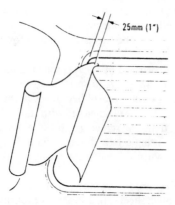

25mm (1")

Fig. O:17 Pulling protective sheet away from heater assembly

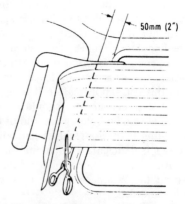

50mm (2")

Fig. O:18 Cutting away excess heater elements and protective sheet

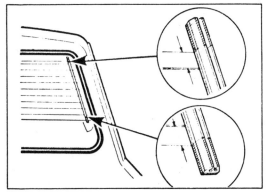

Fig. O:19 Correct positioning of heater channel

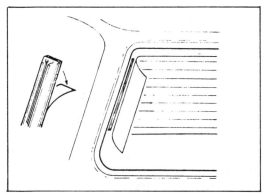

Fig. O:20 Removal of channel adhesive backing strip

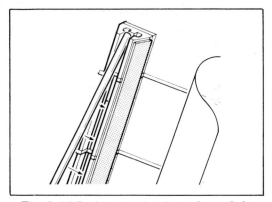

Fig. O:22 Fixing adhesive strip to channel

Fig. O:21 Positioning elements on side of channel

Fig. O:23 Elements pressed into channel slot

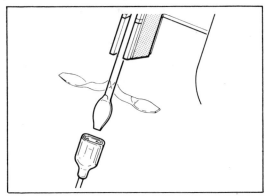

Fig. O:24 Fitting connector to bus-bar

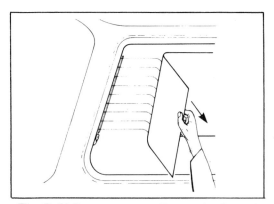

Fig. O:25 Pushing bus-bar into channel slot

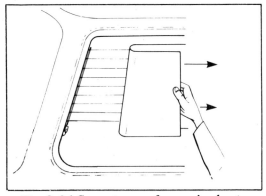

Fig. O:26 Correct way of removing heater backing sheet

Fig. O:27 Incorrect way of removing heater backing sheet

middle and reapply it to the heater leaving a 2 in. (50 cm.) gap down the middle (see Fig. O:15).

6. After making sure the rear screen is dry and warm, position the heater on the screen, using alignment marks. The exposed section should be right in the centre of the screen. (see Fig. O:16).

7. Working from the centre outwards, slowly peel back one half of the cut lined sheet — pressing and smoothing the heater on to the screen at the same time — until 1 in. (25 mm.) from the outside edge of the screen.

8. Keep pulling the protective sheet until the elements are about 2 in. (50 mm.) beyond the edge of the screen. Cut away the surplus (see Fig. O:17 or O:18) and then do exactly the same for the other side.

9. Take one of the channels from the fitting kit and place it on the outside edge of the screen. Using a knife or scissors, cut it so it is 0.25 in. (6 mm.) above and below the top and bottom elements. (see Fig. O:19).

10. Peel the backing paper from the channel (Fig. O:20) and fit it to the inside of the screen, following the curvature of the glass. The word Lucas is printed on both channels and must be installed to face the right way up.

11. Attach the elements to the side of the channel, cut the adhesive channel securing strip to the correct size and fit as shown in Figs. O:21 & O:23.

12. Press the element ends, after peeling away a few inches of the backing sheet, into the channel slot. Take great care not to twist or break them (see Fig. O:23).

13. Cut the bus-bar to the same length as the channel. Make sure the bar with the connector end is adjacent to cable terminals (see Fig. O:24) and push it into the slot (see Fig. O:25). Cut off any surplus element and then repeat paragraphs 8 - 13 for the second side.

14. Connect the white and black leads to the heater terminals, reconnect the battery and switch on the heater. Leave it on for ten minutes — 20 minutes in cold damp weather — until the screen is warm. Smooth down any air bubbles by running a thumb along the backing sheet over the heater elements to ensure good adhesion. Now peel off the backing sheet by pulling horizontally from left to right. Do not rush (see Fig. O:27) — a slow even pull is best (see Fig. O:26).

NOTE: Do not wash or wipe the screen for at least two days, so that the adhesive can have a chance to dry properly. Adhesion will be improved considerably if the heater is used as frequently as possible for the first few days.

WING MIRRORS . . . . [8]

Installation

1. Mark out the hole location in a suitable position on the front wing panel, then cover the mark with clear adhesive tape to prevent damage to the paintwork as the hole is drilled.

2. Use a centre punch to make a slight indentation in the panel to locate the drill.

3. Drill an 11/16 in. dia. (17.46 mm.) hole. Most domestic electric drills will not take a drill larger than about ½ in. (13 mm.), and if this is the case, then drill as larger hole as possible and then carefully file out the hole to the correct diameter. Remove the tape around the hole.

4. Remove the nut and washers from the wing mirror stem, then position the wing mirror in the hole with the rubber washer on top of the wing.

5. Fit the nut and washers, then, holding the mirror in the required position, tighten the securing nut.

6. Slacken the nut securing the mirror to the stem and then adjust the mirror to the required angle. Tighten the securing nut.

Tightening Torques

ENGINE

Cylinder head nuts. . . . . 40 lb ft (5.5 kg m)
Main bearing cap bolts . . . . 65 lb ft (10.0 kg m)
Connecting rod big end bolts . . . . 36 lb ft (5.0 kg m)
Rocker cover . . . . 4 lb ft (0.55 kg m)
Rocker bracket nuts. . . . . 25 lb ft (3.5 kg m)
Manifold to cylinder head . . . . 15 lb ft (2.0 kg m)
Cylinder block side covers . . . . 2 lb ft (0.28 kg m)
    Second type - deep pressed cover . . . . 4 lb ft (0.55 kg m)
Timing cover
    ¼ in UNF bolts . . . . 6 lb ft (0.8 kg m)
    5/16 in UNF bolts . . . . 14 lb ft (1.9 kg m)
Crankshaft pulley nut. . . . . 75 lb ft (10.5 kg m)
Water pump . . . . 16 lb ft (2.2 kg m)
Water outlet elbow . . . . 8 lb ft (1.1 kg m)
Oil filter . . . . 16 lb ft (2.2 kg m)
Oil pump. . . . . 9 lb ft (1.2 kg m)
Sump drain plug . . . . .18 (max) lb ft (2.5(max) kg m)
Flywheel housing bolts & nuts . . . . 18 lb ft (2.5 kg m)
Flywheel bolts . . . . 40 lb ft (5.5 kg m)

CLUTCH & TRANSMISSION

Clutch spring housing to pressure
    plate bolts . . . . 16 lb ft (2.2 kg m)

FRONT SUSPENSION

Swivel hub ball pin nuts
    (top & bottom ball joints). . . . . 40 lb ft (5.5 kg m)
Swivel hub ball pin retainer . . . . 70 lb ft (9.6 kg m)
Suspension arm pivot pin nuts . . . . 40 lb ft (5.5 kg m)
Tie-rod nut. . . . . 35 lb ft (4.8 kg m)
Road wheel nuts . . . . 42 lb ft (5.8 kg m)

REAR SUSPENSION

Rear spring U-bolt nuts. . . . . .12.5 lb ft (1.7 kg m)

STEERING

Track rod end ball pin nut. . . . . 25 lb ft (3.5 kg m)
Steering wheel nut. . . . . 35 lb ft (4.8 kg m)
Steering column clamp bolt. . . . . 9 lb ft (1.2 kg m)

BRAKES

Bleed screw
Front brakes . . . . 8 lb ft (1.0 kg m)
Rear brakes . . . . 5 lb ft (0.7 kg m)

ELECTRICAL EQUIPMENT

Generator pulley nut . . . . 15 lb ft (2.0 kg m)
Generator mounting bolts. . . . . 18 lb ft (2.5 kg m)
Generator mounting bracket . . . . 22 lb ft (3.0 kg m)
11 AC alternator - pulley nut. . . . . 30 lb ft (4.0 kg m)
Starter motor mounting bolts . . . . 25 lb ft (3.5 kg m)

Index